Palgrave Critical University Studies

Series Editor
John Smyth
University of Huddersfield
Huddersfield, UK

Aims of the Palgrave Critical University Studies Series

Universities everywhere are experiencing unprecedented changes and most of the changes being inflicted upon universities are being imposed by political and policy elites without any debate or discussion, and little understanding of what is being lost, jettisoned, damaged or destroyed. The over-arching intent of this series is to foster, encourage, and publish scholarship relating to academia that is troubled by the direction of these reforms occurring around the world. The series provides a much-needed forum for the intensive and extensive discussion of the consequences of ill-conceived and inappropriate university reforms and will do this with particular emphasis on those perspectives and groups whose views have hitherto been ignored, disparaged or silenced. The series explores these changes across a number of domains including: the deleterious effects on academic work, the impact on student learning, the distortion of academic leadership and institutional politics, and the perversion of institutional politics. Above all, the series encourages critically informed debate, where this is being expunged or closed down in universities.

More information about this series at
http://www.palgrave.com/gp/series/14707

Louise J. Lawrence

Refiguring Universities in an Age of Neoliberalism

Creating Compassionate Campuses

Louise J. Lawrence
Department of Theology and Religion
University of Exeter
Devon, UK

ISSN 2662-7329   ISSN 2662-7337 (electronic)
Palgrave Critical University Studies
ISBN 978-3-030-73370-4   ISBN 978-3-030-73371-1   (eBook)
https://doi.org/10.1007/978-3-030-73371-1

This Palgrave Macmillan imprint is published by the registered company Springer Nature Switzerland AG.
The registered company address is: Gewerbestrasse 11, 6330 Cham, Switzerland

Acknowledgements

This book has been in the making (albeit largely unconsciously) throughout the last seven years of my term as Director of Education in Theology and Religion and Liberal Arts programmes at the University of Exeter (2013–2020). It was certainly not a book I intended to write whilst on research leave in 2020 (I was meant to be in Namibia doing fieldwork and working collaboratively with colleagues there on a project on religion, culture, and disability), but as Covid-19 hit the world, plans changed and our kitchen table suddenly became the immediate focus of life, home-schooling, research, and writing. In the face of much uncertainty (what one colleague aptly termed 'discombobulation'), compassion and kindness within individuals and institutions suddenly seemed more critically important than ever.

Many debts have been incurred over the duration of the project. I am grateful to Rebecca Wyde and Palgrave Macmillan for their warm support of this book from proposal to production. Particular members of the senior management team at the University of Exeter deserve especial mention. Professor Timothy Quine, Deputy Vice-Chancellor of Education, has supported the institutional championing of compassion and generously offered opportunities for me, both internally and externally to the university, to develop ideas associated with it. Also, Professor Janice Kaye, The Provost, who has led and spearheaded cultural change within our institution and tirelessly pursues an active and ongoing commitment to making our campuses more equitable, and safe, for all. I am also grateful to the College of Humanities for granting me research leave to write (albeit not the planned book, but a book nonetheless) and to Professor Jo

Gill, Pro-Vice Chancellor of the college, for commenting on sections of the book and all her ongoing support.

Particular colleagues in the Department of Theology and Religion also deserve especial mention. Professor Susannah Cornwall, Professor Morwenna Ludlow, and Professor Francesca Stavrakopoulou read and commented on the draft manuscript and offered invaluable feedback. I am grateful to them all, not just for this, but also for their kindness, commitment to justice, and warm collegiality. It is a privilege to work with them. Professor David Horrell too has, as always, offered incisive comments on the draft, and copious 'Covid-comfort-coffees' throughout. Since the early days when he acted as my PhD supervisor, to now working as colleagues, I have always been able to count on him as a trusty source of wisdom, encouragement, and 'care-full' reassurance. I doubt he knows how much I appreciate and value our friendship and everything he has done for me over the years. But I do.

Last, but most importantly, thanks to my family. To my Mum and Dad for their unshakable love, affection, and support for us all. Whatever challenge we face, or set ourselves, I know we can count on them both 'to the moon and back'. They embraced new and novel lockdown rhythms with gusto and humour (daily Joe Wicks' PE classes, facetime story times, and 'virtual' childcare) and kept us all positive and cake-filled! You truly are 'The Best Nanny and Papa in the Whole Wide World' and loved beyond measure. Thanks also to my treasured boys: Dan and Andrew. You have both witnessed and endured the production of this book more intimately than most. I could not have wished for two better people to be locked down with or allies in the quest to complete not only this manuscript, but also conquer home-school fractions, decimals, and homophones! Thank you all for your love, laughter, care, and caring. Every single day I am so thankful to be part of all your lives, and every single day you teach me more about compassion than anyone.

CONTENTS

CHAPTER 1

Introduction

The UK higher education sector in which I work seems increasingly marred by structural discontent, social disorder, and psychological vulnerability. 74 UK universities were recently involved in a sustained period of industrial action disputing salary inequalities, pensions, insecure contracts, and unwieldy workloads.[1] Distressing (and persistent) cases of sexist, racist, and xenophobic incidents on university campuses—including latterly anti-Asian slurs related to the Covid-19 outbreak[2]—can mark these environments as unsafe, toxic, and dangerous for those marked as 'other' to a presumed normative identity. The university sector is also seeing unprecedented surges in anxiety and depression: many students struggle to manage on a daily basis, or withdraw entirely from their courses, due to mental ill health; the numbers of students who experience suicidal ideation, and/or go on to act on this, are alarmingly high.[3] Such scenarios are regrettably, for many on university campuses, the forbidding current realities.

Many cite the ascendancy of neoliberalism—'a varied collection of ideas, practices, policies, and discursive representations … united by three broad beliefs: the benevolence of the free market, minimal state intervention and regulation of the economy, and the individual as a rational economic actor'[4]—as a political, ideological, and discursive force in higher education, as in part accountable for this state of affairs. Carol Mutch and Jennifer Tatebe accordingly posit 'universities as instruments of neoliberalism', 'academics as managed subjects', and 'students as consumers'.[5]

© The Author(s), under exclusive license to Springer Nature
Switzerland AG 2021
L. J. Lawrence, *Refiguring Universities in an Age of Neoliberalism*,
Palgrave Critical University Studies,
https://doi.org/10.1007/978-3-030-73371-1_1

1

Within such constructions there has been an associated tendency to accentuate education as 'product' (a means to employment) as opposed to formative 'process'[6]:

> Rather than promoting their potential to be uniquely-positioned spaces to foster empathetic, civically engaged, critically thinking, and globally minded change-makers, colleges and universities [too often] function as certifiers. They sustain the 'information-services-credentialing complex' by marketing to social fears about gaining and maintain[ing] traction in the economy.[7]

Henry Giroux, from a US context, talks about the 'corrosive effects of corporate culture' which produces 'self-interested individuals' who are content to 'either ignore or cancel out social injustices in the existing social order by overriding the democratic impulses and practices of civil society through an emphasis on the unbridled workings of market relations'.[8] Martha Nussbaum similarly in her rousing tract, *Not for Profit: Why Democracy Needs the Humanities*[9]—which calls out those neoliberal dynamics within universities which lead to the perilous neglect of the arts, humanities, and social sciences—laments the compulsion for voracious economic gain, and the narrow (and mechanistic) identity models of 'productive citizens' manufactured and marked by self-interest and disregard for others:

> Thirsty for national profit, nations, and their systems of education, are heedlessly discarding skills that are needed to keep democracies alive. If this trend continues, nations all over the world will soon be producing generations of useful machines, rather than complete citizens who can think for themselves, criticize tradition, and understand the significance of another person's sufferings and achievements. The future of the world's democracies hangs in the balance.[10]

Others see neoliberal forces as complicit in the marketisation of education,[11] the global rise of far-right politics leaking into university campuses,[12] and mental ill health experienced therein.[13]

This book will give clear instances and specific examples where universities can be perceived as serving neoliberal purposes, but it will also suggest that university campuses are contested spaces, where neoliberal demands frequently and uncomfortably co-exist alongside other more affiliative values. Moreover, it is often these affiliative values which are under particular strain from a neoliberal frame and therefore need specific defence and support as a primary objective and viable and meaningful operative mode for higher education institutions. Accordingly I will ask how can the sector reclaim the 'university', as the Latin etymological origins of this word indicates—*universus* ('whole, entire')—as a collective, inclusive, safe, and healthy community of 'persons associated into one body, a society, company, community, [or] guild'?[14] I will also probe what moral principles and competencies would need to be championed and instilled in university cultures to build inclusive citizenship, positive associations with others, and models of other-regard for campus communities to flourish. 'Compassion' will be posited as such a value, and bodies of emergent work on compassion from diverse disciplinary perspectives will be drawn upon here in reflecting on institutional, cultural, pedagogical, and lived experiences within universities. Compassion, a term derived from the Latin '*compati*', meaning to 'suffer with', is understood in transdisciplinary terms 'as the *noticing* of distress and/or disadvantage to self or others, and a commitment to *take action* to reduce it'.[15] Compassion is an 'other-regarding' response and prompt to action that bridges the interpersonal, intercultural, and international. It stands in many ways counter to neoliberal dynamics which focus on marketisation and competitive individualism. It is also a value which is too scarcely taught, experienced, or advocated as a principal purpose in higher education contexts. Kathryn Waddington calls out this 'Compassion Gap' within the sector where instrumental views of education in economic terms identify students as 'consumers rather than learners with power'.[16] She invites reparative compassionate academic reflection and practice through a threefold lens: (a) using narrative methodologies and critical appreciative inquiry to 'reveal, and rectify, failures of compassion', (b) encouraging brave whistle-blowing with regard to 'dysfunctional organisational systems and processes', and (c) promoting leadership development to 'include the application of skills of compassion in organisational settings'.[17] These lenses will be important and recurring stimuli for reflection throughout the ensuing chapters of this book.

Illustrations and case studies herein will be drawn primarily from my own research fields and location: (i) theology, religion, and biblical studies, and (ii) disability studies. These fields can aid in tracing cultural, spiritual, embodied, and material archaeologies of compassion. Beyond nested illustrations, these disciplines too, I maintain, offer useful resources to critically think with in relation to compassion and neoliberal university dynamics, discourses, relationships, and values. Compassion has been posited as a trait common to many religions,[18] particularly popularised within

Karen Armstrong's work on the Charter of Compassion (see Chap. 3).[19] This Charter's rallying call is

> to make compassion a clear, luminous and dynamic force in our polarized world. Rooted in principled determination to transcend selfishness, compassion can break down political, dogmatic, ideological and religious boundaries. Born of our deep interdependence, compassion is essential to human relationships and to a fulfilled humanity. It is the path to enlightenment, and indispensable to the creation of a just economy and peaceful global community.[20]

Beyond a focus on compassion, Timothy Peters maintains that neoliberalism itself functions in some ways as a quasi-'religion': 'one which intensifies liberal individualism and involves a faith in the market redefining all social interactions in terms of contract'.[21] And therefore 'part of the solution may be a theological[ly reflective] one' in imagining alternative values and forms of inclusion, participation, community, authority, sociality, and corporate-ness to those centred on 'neoliberal state', 'corporation', or the 'contracting individual'.[22] Disability studies too resists neoliberal focus on hyper-productivity, individual meritocracy, and a valuing of individual bodies through capitalist economic lenses. Akemi Nishida, among others, has shown not only how neoliberalism feeds ableism and sanism (prejudice and discrimination against those bodies and minds perceived as 'non-normative') but also how the social model of disability, and disability advocacy, offers alternative models to a biomedical model which views individual minds and bodies as problematic and in need of cure, to rather celebrate diversity, justice, and 'democratic ways of living'[23] within organisations and learning communities. In this sense, disability studies is potentially incredibly useful in identifying and framing ways in which types of 'othering' occurs (in relation to 'other' non-normative—'dis-abled' bodies—often marked along intersectional lines of gender, race, mental ill health, etc.) in neoliberal institutions. The European, and more broadly Western, academy traces its origins to an Enlightenment scientific paradigm which constructed the disembodied (and often white, male, able, and sane) scholar as a 'rational subject positive outside of time and space'.[24] This has inevitably mitigated against an embodied regard for the other in both practice and certain cultural discourses within the academy.

I will also critically reflect on illustrations and incidents from within the particular institution in which I am employed—the University of Exeter—a

Russell Group, research-intensive university, in the South West of England.[25] The University of Exeter has in particular advocated compassion and intercultural competence and sought to develop (among other initiatives) compassionate anti-racist pedagogies and compassionate approaches to mental ill health, within its institutional culture. In this sense, it offers an illuminating case study for this book. Much of my work here is drawn from my experience in institutional educational leadership, and therefore accents and focuses on student voices, lived experiences, and practical interventions within programmes. As Covid-19 erupted, certain themes in this project have been sharpened and given greater urgency as I wrote the manuscript. Reflection on an emerging re-imagination of values based on collaboration and connectivity within the pandemic, as opposed to individual competition, offers a unique opportunity to re-imagine and re-figure higher education along more compassionate lines. This book's aims can therefore be summarised as threefold:

(a) To trace selected cultural constructions of compassion within my own field of biblical studies. Employments of compassion within Western discourses can often be traced in some way to classical and biblical texts, including in the current Covid-19 era which has variously cited compassion as a primary objective in different spheres.

(b) To offer through the examples of disciplinary case studies in theology, religion, and biblical studies, and disability studies, the valuing of compassion as a primary objective in affiliative communities posits this as both challenge and alternative to neoliberal dynamics and discourses.

(c) To trace and evaluate, through the University of Exeter institutional case study, the beginnings of a move to embed compassion within a whole institutional approach. Also the practical interventions, challenges, and transformations that have been (and continue to be) demanded as a result. Whilst there has been a lot of literature generated in different disciplinary domains on compassion, seldom are these transdisciplinary insights critically synthesised in relation to diverse aspects of a single institution's life (from curricula to sexual misconduct).

OVERVIEW OF BOOK

Chapter 2, 'A Prolegomenon to Refiguring the Neoliberal University: Reading with Early Christian Traditions of Compassion in the Throes of a Pandemic', will seek to trace the emergence of so-called catastrophe compassion (affiliative responses within and after crisis situations). Tracing selected cultural histories of compassion within biblical traditions (in particular 'the view from the ditch' in the parabolic 'Good Samaritan' tradition) and their 'afterlives' and receptions (including in the midst of Covid-19), this chapter will argue that the present moment provides an opportunity, like never before, for neoliberal imaginaries to be transformed.

Chapter 3, 'Envisioning Compassionate Campuses: Critically Probing Organisational Values and Mission Statements', will posit compassion as a value which has been at the fore-front of instruction for affiliative community development in many spiritual and religious traditions, professional care bodies, and justice systems throughout history.[26] Most crucially, the tutelage and conventions of compassion in such traditions often deliberately develop mutual regard for those beyond the known or agreeable (unmarked) 'us'.[27] Visions of modern secular universities as sites of formation for 'intellectual virtue, in sustaining vibrant communities of inquiry, and in serving the public good'[28] and for the development of 'moral compassion' will be central. Compassion-centred institutional examples outside higher education, including Armstrong's ambitious development of a 'Charter of Compassion', a principle she sees as lying at the heart of many religious, ethical, and justice-driven traditions, and Britain's National Health Service (NHS), will be employed as examples to 'think with'.[29] This chapter will then trace higher education institutions across North America and the UK, who have variously signed up to or sought to implement the charter or moralised compassion, within their organisational cultures.

Chapter 4, 'Compassionate Curricula? Northern and Southern Epistemologies and Cognitive [In-]Justice', will employ southern, feminist, and postcolonial perspectives to trace the outcomes of global knowledge economies patterned by colonial histories and north-south inequalities. Focusing on biblical studies and disability studies, here southern perspectives will be seen as important stimulants for destabilising and limiting the dominant and dominating 'global north' patterns of knowing.[30] Such perspectives are critical sites for cultivating compassionate and intercultural competent modes of learning. Attuned to the politics of citation with regard to geography, gender, race, ability, and epistemological diversity, we must honestly ask 'Whose methodologies and worldviews do we privilege?' 'Who are we reading?' 'Who is excluded?' 'Why and how can we address this?'[31]

Chapter 5, 'Compassionate Campus Climates: Confronting Privilege and Prejudice with Compassionate Citizenship', will focus on the handling, fallout, and institutional reforms emerging from highly publicised racist incidents on campus at Exeter.[32] It explores the prejudices arising from both 'whiteness' and 'laddish masculinities' and interventions based on compassion and other-regard which have been integrated institutionally to seek to prevent prejudice, bigotry, and hate speech/crime.[33]

Chapter 6, 'Compassion and Kindness: Refiguring Discourses of Student Mental Health and Wellbeing', traces an institutional response to the *Universities UK Stepchange: Mental Health in Higher Education Framework*[34] particularly regarding (a) neoliberal discourses surrounding student mental (ill) health and wellbeing within the institution and (b) whole campus ethos and interventions, with compassion, care, and kindness in particular promoted. Informed by critical disability studies, this chapter will outline associated models of slow scholarship—subverting neoliberal transcripts of time, performance, and hyper-productivity—which are known causes of distress.

Chapter 7, '[Mis]Directed Compassion? Power, Sexual Violence, and Misconduct in the Neoliberal Academy', will take a number of high-profile cases in biblical studies, religion, and theology relating to sexual violence and staff sexual misconduct. It will petition for a 'detoxifying' of the curriculum whereby individual convicted scholars' ideas, despite their individual renown or celebrity, are not preserved or perpetuated at the expense of their victims. It will also explore compassionate reforms in the Church of England in this area, to think about ways in which restorative practice, focusing not just on individuals involved nor single case management but rather more thoroughgoing processes of collective and cultural change within institutions, can be achieved.

In short, this book is an invitation to critically reflect on selected aspects of the neoliberal identity, discourses, and practices of the higher education sector, and propose compassion (focusing attention on those frequently rendered 'other' by dominant transcripts) as a viable alternative and meaningful operational mode and purpose for universities. Whilst 'suffering' might well be an inevitable part of all organisational lives,[35] surely higher education should never be a perpetrator, but rather always an incubator of preventative forces against such suffering. In William Kahn's terms, university campuses must re-conceive of themselves as 'care-giving institutions'[36] in which human beings in all their diversity can feel safe, flourish, and succeed. Leaders of compassionate campuses would not fear stepping outside the dominant neoliberal transcripts, or venturing beyond the routinely accepted, to rediscover, imagine, or co-design inclusive models of citizenship, that have at their centre values which generate kindness, respect, and genuine openness to collaborate and connect with others, and serve the public good.

NOTES

1. 'UCU announces 14 strike days at 74 UK universities in February and March' *University and College Union* (3rd February 2020). Available online at: https://www.ucu.org.uk/article/10621/UCU-announces-14-strike-days-at-74-UK-universities-in-February-and-March
2. In Exeter 'A 19-year-old university student was punched, kicked and spat at while being told, "go back to your own country – you must have coronavirus"'. See Paul Greaves, 'Exeter is Better Than This' *DevonLive* (6th March 2020). Available online at: https://www.devonlive.com/news/devon-news/exeter-better-this-racist-coronavirus-3923885.   Sussex University too noted: 'The Students' Union has been made aware of students experiencing racism, hate crime and discrimination both on campus and in town, in light of the recent coronavirus outbreak in Brighton.' See 'Statement: Hate Crime and Corona Virus' *Sussex Student* (11th February 2020). Available online at: https://www.sussexstudent.com/news/article/ussu/Students-Union-statement-regarding-hate-crime-and-coronavirus/
3. 'In the 12 months ending July 2017, the rate of suicide for university students in England and Wales was 4.7 deaths per 100,000 students, which equates to 95 suicides or about one death every four days.' Samira Shackle, '"The way universities are run is making us ill": inside the student mental health crisis' *The Guardian* (27th September 2019). Available online at: https://www.theguardian.com/society/2019/sep/27/anxiety-mental-breakdowns-depression-uk-students
4. Daniel B. Saunders, 'Neoliberal Ideology and Public Higher Education in the United States' (8th January 2002). Available online at: http://www.jceps.com/wp-content/uploads/PDFs/08-1-02.pdf
5. Carol Mutch & Jennifer Tatebe, 'From collusion to collective compassion: putting heart back into the neoliberal university', *Pastoral Care in Education* 35:3 (2017), 221–234. Available online at: https://doi.org/1 0.1080/02643944.2017.1363814

6. William Carpenter, 'Finding Compassion in Higher Education: A Provocation' *Bringing Theory to Practice* (Winter 2018), no pages. Available online at: https://www.bttop.org/news-events/feature-finding-compassion-higher-education-provocation
7. Carpenter, 'Finding', no pages.
8. Henry Giroux, 'Neoliberalism, Corporate Culture, and the Promise of Higher Education: The University as a Democratic Public Sphere' *Harvard Educational Review* Vol. 72, No. 4 (2002), 425–464. Available online at: https://doi.org/10.17763/haer.72.4.0515nr62324n71p1, 425.
9. Martha Nussbaum, *Not for Profit: Why Democracy Needs the Humanities* (Princeton: Princeton University Press, 2010).
10. Nussbaum, *Not for*, 2.
11. Roger Brown, Chris Pratt and Trevor Curnow, 'The abject failure of marketization in higher education' *The Guardian* (5th April 2019). Available online at: https://www.theguardian.com/education/2019/apr/05/the-abject-failure-of-marketisation-in-higher-education
12. 'Right-wing populism has been on the rise in recent years, intensifying following the 2008 global financial crisis. 2016 marked a key moment in the right populist turn, with both Brexit and the US Presidential election constituting formal political legitimacy for right-wing populist leaders and movements. Despite widespread opposition following the election of Donald Trump—itself often taking populist forms—a range of right-wing populist forces continue to push forward. In both Europe and North America, anti-immigrant and anti-Islamic rhetoric and violence has escalated. Populist figures are giving voice to and emboldening longstanding racist and xenophobic currents in western societies. Other variants of authoritarian right-wing populism are also growing. Recep Tayyip Erdoğan's government in Turkey has now dismissed over 7,000 academics and in some cases jailed scholars.' See Steven Tufts and Mark Thomas, 'The University in the Populist Age' *Academic Matters – OCUFA's Journal of Higher Education* (2017), no pages. Available online at: https://academicmatters.ca/the-university-in-the-populist-age/. See also Mike Finn, *British Universities in the Brexit Moment: Political, Economic and Cultural Implications* (Bingley: Emerald Publishing, 2018).
13. Ruth Kain, 'How Neoliberalism is Damaging your Mental Health' *The Conversation* (30th January 2018). Available online at: http://theconversation.com/how-neoliberalism-is-damaging-your-mental-health-90565
14. 'University', https://en.wiktionary.org/wiki/university
15. NHS Professor of Clinical Psychology, Paul Gilbert OBE (and founder of the Compassionate Mind Foundation that focuses on the empirical study of compassion) takes the current (multi-disciplinary line) that compassion is a 'sensitivity to the suffering of self or others and a commitment to

reduce or prevent that'. Paul Gilbert, *The Compassionate Mind* (London: Constable & Robinson Ltd., 2010), 2. Also Paul Gilbert (ed), *Compassion: Concepts, Research and Applications* (London ; New York: Routledge, 2017); J. L. Goetz, D. Keltner, E. Simon-Thomas, 'Compassion: An evolutionary analysis and empirical review' *Psychological Bulletin*, 136 (3) (2010), 351–374; Clara Strauss et al., 'What is compassion and how can we measure it? A review of definitions and measures' *Clinical Psychology Review* Volume 47 (2016), 15–27. In teaching, learning and assessment in higher education (HE) specifically, Theo Gilbert has applied this and the theoretical base behind it, so that compassion can be assessed within filmed HE student group work. For pedagogically practical purposes, he resets the above definition of compassion specifically for student group work as: 'the noticing of distress and/or disadvantage to self or others, and a commitment to take action to reduce or prevent it'. See Theo Gilbert, 'When Looking Is Allowed: What Compassionate Group Work Looks Like in a UK University' in P. Gibbs (ed), *The Pedagogy of Compassion at the Heart of Higher Education* (Switzerland: Springer, 2017), 189–202.

16. Kathryn Waddington, 'The Compassion Gap in UK Universities' *International Practice Development Journal* 6 (1), (2016). Available online at: doi:https://doi.org/10.19043/ipdj.61.010

17. Waddington, 'The Compassion'. See also Kathryn Waddington, 'Understanding and Creating Compassionate Institutional Cultures and Practices' in P. Gibbs, J. Jameson, and A. Elwick (eds), *Values of the University in a Time of Uncertainty* (Switzerland: Springer, 2019), 241–260; Kathryn Waddington, 'Developing Compassionate Academic Leadership: The Practice of Kindness' *Journal of Perspectives in Applied Academic Practice*. 6 (3), (2018), 87–89; Kathryn Waddington, 'Creating conditions for compassion' in P. Gibbs (ed.) *The Pedagogy of Compassion at the Heart of Higher Education* (Switzerland: Springer. 2017), 49–70.

18. Amanita Nihongi Balslev and Dirk Evers (eds), *Compassion in the World's Religions: Envisioning Human Solidarity* (New Brunswick: Transaction Publishers, 2010).

19. Karen Armstrong is a former Roman Catholic nun. She is well known for her popular books on comparative religion. See, for example, *The Battle for God: Fundamentalism in Judaism, Christianity and Islam* (New York: Alfred Knopf, 2000); *The Great Transformation: The Beginning of Our Religious Traditions* (London: Atlantic Books, 2006); *The Lost Art of Scripture* (London: Bodley Head, 2019). She was the winner of the 2008 TED prize, in which she posited the founding of a 'Charter of Compassion' as her major idea.

20. Karen Armstrong, *Twelve Steps to a Compassionate Life* (London: The Bodley Head, 2011), 5.

21. Timothy D. Peters, 'Corporations, Sovereignty and the Religion of Neoliberalism' *Law and Critique* 29 (2018), 271–292, 271. Moreover, selected religious discourses have been seen to have been absorbed in certain ways by neoliberal universities. Luke Winslow, for example, traces echoes between evaluation of staff's ability to garner external grant funding, and 'discursive structures of prosperity theology', a theological stance particularly found in American Evangelicalism, (controversially) centred on 'competitive-egotism', equating health and wealth as blessings for elect or religiously loyal and 'measure of personal worth', and so on. Luke Winslow, 'Rich, Blessed, and Tenured: A Homological Exploration of Grant Writing, Prosperity Theology, and Neoliberalism', *Western Journal of Communication* 79 (2015), 257–282. Available online at: https://www.tandfonline.com/doi/abs/10.1080/10570314.2015.1035748

22. Peters, 'Corporations', 271–275.

23. Nishida, Akemi, 'Neoliberal Academia and a critique from Disability Studies' in Pamela Block, Devva Kasnitz, Akemi Nishida, Nick Pollard, *Occupying Disability: Critical Approaches to Community, Justice, and Decolonizing Disability* (Switzerland: Springer, 2016), 145–157, 145.

24. Elisabeth Schüssler Fiorenza, *Democratizing Biblical Studies: Toward an Emancipatory Educational Space* (Louisville: Westminster John Knox, 2009), 92. See also Louise J. Lawrence, *Bible and Bedlam: Madness, Sanism and New Testament Interpretation* (London: Bloomsbury, 2018), 17–44.

25. The University of Exeter. https://www.exeter.ac.uk/

26. 'In the US, compassion is enshrined in the American Medical Association's (AMA) Principles of Medical Ethics, with Item 1 stating that "A physician shall be dedicated to providing competent medical services with compassion and respect for human dignity" (AMA, 1981). In the UK, compassion is one of the six core values in the NHS constitution (Department of Health; DoH, 2013), and calls for a greater focus on compassion have been driven in part by high profile exposés of serious failings in compassionate care at some hospitals and care homes. The international "Compassion in Education" foundation (CoED, 2014) offers a range of services to educational professionals in order to promote compassion in the education system. It has also been argued that compassion should lie at the core of the ethical framework guiding our justice systems' (Norko, 2005). Clara Strauss et al. 'What is compassion and how can we measure it? A review of definitions and measures' *Clinical Psychology Review* Volume 47 (2016), 15–27.

27. Dalai Lama notes: 'Without an enemy you cannot practice tolerance, and without tolerance you cannot build a sound basis of compassion'. Dalai Lama, cited in Strauss et al 'What is compassion', 16.

28. Mike Higton, *A Theology of Higher Education* (Oxford: Oxford University Press, 2012).

29. Karen Armstrong views compassion 'calling us always to treat all others as we wish to be treated ourselves. Compassion impels us to work tirelessly to alleviate the suffering of our fellow creatures, to dethrone ourselves from the centre of our world and put another there, and to honour the inviolable sanctity of every single human being, treating everybody, without exception, with absolute justice, equity and respect. It is also necessary in both public and private life to refrain consistently and empathically from inflicting pain. To act or speak violently out of spite, chauvinism, or self-interest, to impoverish, exploit or deny basic rights to anybody, and to incite hatred by denigrating others—even our enemies—is a denial of our common humanity.' Karen Armstrong, 'Charter for Compassion' (2008). Available online at: https://charterforcompassion.org/charter. See also Karen Armstrong, *Twelve Steps to a Compassionate Life* (London: Bodley Head, 2011).

30. See Raewyn Connell. 'Using Southern Theory: Decolonizing Social Thought in Theory, Research and Application' *Planning Theory* 12 (2), (2013), 210–223. Also Debbie Epstein and Robert Morrell 'Approaching Southern Theory: Explorations of Gender in South African Education' *Gender and Education* 24 (2012), 469–482.

31. Raewyn Connell optimistically notes: 'The global workforce has more room for manoeuvre than the bald facts of Northern hegemony and Southern extraversion might suggest. Researchers and teachers can respond to regional needs, developed distinctive research centres and agendas, renovate curricula and create links with local communities, while staying within the research-based knowledge formation. It is also possible, though more difficult, for university staff to move outside the dominant knowledge formation, connect with other formations and move towards epistemological pluralism.' Raewyn Connell, *The Good University: What Universities Actually Do and Why it's Time for Radical Change* (London: Zed Books, 2019), 94.

32. https://en.wikipedia.org/wiki/2018_Bracton_Law_Society_Scandal

33. Sefer discussed in Dave Mercer 'Imagined in Policy, Inscribed on Bodies: Defending an Ethic of Compassion in a Political Context Comment on "Why and How Is Compassion Necessary to Provide Good Quality Healthcare?"' *International Journal of Health Policy Management* 4 (10) (2015), 681–683. Available online at: https://doi.org/10.15171/ijhpm.2015.125

34. https://www.universitiesuk.ac.uk/stepchange

35. Jacoba Lillius et al 'The Contours and Consequences of Compassion at Work' *Journal of Organizational Behaviour* 29 (2008), 193–218, 194.
36. William A. Kahn, 'Caring for the Caregivers: Patterns of Organizational Caregiving' *Administrative Science Quarterly* Vol. 38, No. 4 (Dec., 1993), 539–563.

CHAPTER 2

A Prolegomenon to Refiguring the Neoliberal University: Reading with Early Christian Traditions of Compassion in the Throes of a Pandemic

In spring 2020, amidst UK lockdown due to the Covid-19 pandemic,[1] medical students at the University of Exeter opted to graduate early and join colleagues in the National Health Service (NHS) caring for communities across the UK. The Vice-Chancellor commended their compassion, courage, and service to others, and how 'humbled and inspired' he felt 'by their selflessness':

> Now, in the time of our greatest national and global crisis since the Second World War, we see the young people of this country and of our University standing up to be counted and making huge personal sacrifices.[2]

Whilst 'the themes involved [in] plague[s] and people are ancient'[3] (divine wrath and judgement, and/or protection of elect and apocalyptic refiguring of future worlds),[4] the ways in which roles and identities can transform in such situations continue to be enlightening and instructive. Covid-19 will be posited here as a 'prolegomenon' to refiguring the identity and vision of the neoliberal university: in particular, in relation to northern hegemony, discourses of mental ill health, and systems of prejudice and privilege (all themes to be developed in later chapters of this book). The pandemic provides an opportunity to address the vision of the modern UK neoliberal university and promote compassion as the centre of this re-imaging. In this current moment within higher education, delivery and

L. J. Lawrence, *Refiguring Universities in an Age of Neoliberalism*, Palgrave Critical University Studies, https://doi.org/10.1007/978-3-030-73371-1_2

15

practice has had to rapidly change as campuses were forced to close, and face-to-face interactions were restricted in lockdown. Digital modes of operation were swiftly adopted,[5] online assessments were devised, and universities vocalised explicit cognisance of the ways in which institutions (and the human staff and students which comprised them) were being affected not only economically but also mentally, physically, socially, and emotionally by the situation. After the first initial reactive weeks, and as institutions have started to look to their futures, opportunities have emerged to re-define dominant transcripts of education, imagine 'emancipatory post-pandemic pedagog[ies]',[6] and more fundamentally refigure the identity of the neoliberal university:

> [The pandemic has] given us a space to see it and permission to be compassionate. What was hidden and unremarked upon is being noticed as an essential part of our existence, enabling us as a society to keep faith in the future and to believe that we can get through this.[7]

In the Covid-19 moment imposed physical distance due to infection has perhaps ironically brought home for many the critical importance of our human interconnectedness and has variously birthed co-operative responses which subvert the individualised competition of neoliberal contexts. It has also hailed a realisation of the importance of 'compassion' and 'kindness'—the noticing of distress, and 'practical response to the suffering or vulnerability of another'[8]—and their potential to transform existent status quos,[9] including the notable devaluing of affiliative dynamics and solidarities within neoliberal institutions.[10] Kathryn Waddington was among those who, before the pandemic, explicitly urged the UK higher education sector to champion compassion. She counsels universities to assume identities of 'caregiving' (rather than depersonalised market-driven) organisations.[11] European thinkers too have underscored the importance of compassion in challenging instrumental views of education as knowledge transfer for the labour market.[12] Pedro Ortega Ruiz and Ramon Munguez Vallejos accordingly characterise compassion as 'help, commitment, and protest' nested in the 'recognition of responsibility we feel towards human beings'.[13] Accordingly, they see compassion-based education 'imparted by means of strategies leading to social behaviours, respect for the other, personal responsibility'[14] and crucially a recognition of one's place (and commitment to active change) within systems which oppress, marginalise, or cause suffering. Such perspectives undoubtedly warrant increased attention in the current times.

This chapter will first introduce plagues and pandemics and their role in mobilising significant change, including underscoring the importance of compassion (and associated kindness and care), within social contexts. So-called catastrophe compassion (other-regarding dynamics born out of crisis events) will be outlined. Second, discussion here will seek to document selected cultural histories of compassion in biblical traditions and early Christianity (the areas in which I primarily work) which have and continue to exert influence in broader Western culture.[15] It will be seen that these purposively develop affiliative and collective dimensions of communal identity and can provide, in the pandemic panorama, a counterpoint to individualising neoliberal paradigms, which many see as increasingly 'moral[ly] bankrupt'.[16] Paul Gibbs' recent edited collection, *The Pedagogy of Compassion at the Heart of Higher Education*, petitions for 'the need for the cultivation of compassion from a multicultural higher education perspective',[17] and contributors to his volume accordingly offer wisdom from various Islamic and Eastern traditions in this regard. Alongside perspectives such as these, traversing higher education's road to the future, cultural traditions of compassion can aid in critically reflecting on 'a capitalist world order based on greed, aggression, and power' and crucially show this vision 'does not necessarily need to be our common fate'.[18] Christopher Marshall likewise claims that awareness of the spiritual archaeologies of compassion is critical. For, in his view, reflection on pedagogy or institutional mechanisms in isolation can risk 'disguis[ing] efforts to control and subjugate citizens in the name of implementing compassion'.[19]

All (sacred and secular) traditions (including humanities perspectives, and the spiritual/biblical archaeologies of compassion outlined here) can be useful to 'think with' in refiguring the neoliberal university, for as Jing Lin and Rebecca Oxford submit:

> It [higher education] should see itself not only as a venue for knowledge production and transfer, but also as a means for building greater human beings who embody multiple forms of wisdom.[20]

They go further in stating it is not sufficient to depend solely on 'rational, scientific, individualistic and materialistic frameworks for higher education'. For 'humans are not only intellectual beings but we are all (at least potentially) emotional, moral, social and spiritual beings.'[21] The importance of bodily experiences, stories, and cultural histories in this sense are critical starting points in re-imagining and re-figuring higher education. For stories, both of our own and others, constitute 'much more than abstract rules or philosophical principles'.[22] They crucially plot individual and collective character, and have the potential to challenge and change our imaginaries surrounding organisational values, identities, visions, purposes, cultures, communications, and practices, as the ensuing chapters of this book will attempt to show.

PLAGUES, PANDEMICS, AND THE AFFILIATIVE DYNAMICS OF COMPASSION

Citing the second-century Greek historian Polybius' insight that 'the world is interconnected', William Foege, with some legitimacy, declares that 'plagues bend history'.[23] Deriving from the Latin term *plaga*, denoting a 'blow' or 'wound',[24] the etymology of plagues 'privilege the world of the sufferer, rather than the healer [or] interpreter. A plague is what one has been assaulted with.'[25] Plagues and pandemics have the sharply contrasting potential not only to cause division, rupture, xenophobic abuse, and stigmatisation, but also to engender mutuality, affective bonds, and remarkable deeds of benevolence and other-regard.[26] Mika Aaltola in a study of the politics of pandemics notes, however, that within the academy it has too often been the more negative (shadow) dynamics— 'disengagement with the suffering [of a] distant other', 'containment rather than compassion'[27]—which have dominated reflection in this area. Plagues and pandemics have primarily been cast as breeding individualised self-preservation and a suspicion of the 'other'—'"I" extends to "we" and both stand in opposition to "them" and "a foreign element" through a sense of contagion.'[28] Moreover, existing or normative social structures within societies are assumed to likely apportion blame on those who sit most uneasily within their dominant (and dominating) social-identity models:

> Cultural values and social location have always provided the materials for self-serving constructions of epidemiological risk. The poor, the alien, the sinner have all served as convenient objects for such stigmatizing speculations.[29]

Aaltola's work powerfully sets out that compassion provides an alternative imaginary to pandemic fear and its associated 'disease-filled hate', distrust, and deviance-labelling.[30] Disease has affective consequences which can reshape and re-imagine social bonds in more affiliative ways:

> The object world of disease contains the emotions of comfort, compassion, and containment as well as fears of exclusion isolation and aloneness. These emotions are tightly connected with the reconstitution of one's sense of the underlying fabric of social interaction. Through a disease one becomes aware of the complexities of individuality, family, society, economy, medicine and politics in ways that are hard to express in terms of a model of abstractness.[31]

Jamil Zaki too in what he terms 'catastrophe compassion' traces historical records to illustrate how pro-social behaviours and collective feelings are often vital and fundamental in crisis situations and the plotting of futures thereafter:[32]

> Catastrophe compassion is widespread and consistent; it follows earthquakes, war, terrorist attacks, hurricanes, and tsunamis, and – now – a pandemic. As COVID-19 spreads, communities around the world have created 'mutual aid spreadsheets' to help vulnerable neighbours, and billions of people have engaged in physical distancing to protect public health – perhaps the most populous act of cooperation in history. Consistent with its prosocial nature, one recent study found that people expressed greater intent to follow distancing when it was framed as a way to help others rather than as a means to protect themselves.[33]

Zaki proposes that adversity and 'altruism born of suffering' can allow individuals to identify with strangers and have confidence in their own usefulness in noticing and alleviating the suffering of others (being compassionate).[34] Zaki also addresses how such affiliative sentiments can pervade the imagination of post-crisis futures. First, he states that survivors can 'remain visible to each other and salient to the identity of the survivors' by participating in peer support systems where experiences are shared; second, remembrance and cultural rituals can 'bond individuals and generations'; and third, new models of identity 'driven by "otherishness" rather than by "selfishness" during crucially important moments' can be purposefully embodied, championed, and promoted:

One way to honor and extend this positive behaviour is to not be surprised by it any longer, but instead to realize that prosociality is common, and thus to expect – and demand – it from others and from ourselves.[35]

Such transformations, however, also depend on critical analysis of traditions of compassion which are all inevitably conditioned by the circumstances, situations, and purposes within which, and for which, they are engaged. At a UK government Covid-19 press conference in March 2020, the Chancellor of the Exchequer, Rishi Sunak, for example, declared:

> Now, more than any time in our recent history, we will be judged by our capacity for compassion. Our ability to come through this won't just be down to what government or business can do, but by the individual acts of kindness we show one another.[36]

Sunak was not the first politician to employ (or be perceived to be acting with) compassion within political rhetoric amid this, or other social, political, or economic upheavals. Nicola Sturgeon praised volunteers in the pandemic for 'demonstrating the kindness, compassion, and love ... fundamental to any decent society'.[37] Jacinda Adern reacting to the Christchurch shootings was lauded for her 'steel, compassion and absolute clarity' in swiftly identifying Muslims 'as us' and championing 'diversity, kindness [and] compassion' as central values.[38] Angela Merkel became known as 'mitfühlend Mutter' or 'barmherzige Mutter' (compassionate mother) because of her stance on immigration (interestingly, this designation appears to have come from the Syrian refugees themselves, but she does seem to have used the language of compassion herself).[39] Barack Obama too called for compassion during his campaign for immigration reform, citing Deuteronomy 10:19 he urged people to 'love the stranger ... for you were strangers in the land of Egypt'[40] presumably to engender a sense of connection, relationship, and affinity across divides. George W. Bush's strategic use of compassion (in the context of compassionate conservatism) and in relation to both domestic and international issues (including the so-called war on terror) during his presidency is also notable. Confidently Bush declared 'compassion [a]s one of the values that builds communities of character, because every community of character must be a community of service'.[41]

All the above are 'cultural productions' of the concept, dependant on 'specific contexts and social agents, themselves caught in power dynamics and overlapping histories'.[42] How compassion is formed within these various examples is of course fluid, contextual, and socially constructed. There is not one concrete or definitive definition to which all employments of the concept accede. Some have accordingly named it a 'portmanteau concept', which is assumed to contain 'many desirable if underdetermined meanings and being confined to very little that is specific'.[43] Lauren Berlant has been a particularly vocal opponent to a wholesale and uncritical acceptance of compassion as a benevolent, and in Martha Nussbaum's terms, 'basic social emotion'.[44] Many employments are potent political gestures: commenting on Bush's use of compassion, for example, one commentator noted that 'compassion turned interventionist polices into a kind of civilising mission; it also sugar-coated social privilege, disguising it as a moral virtue'.[45] Arrestingly too Berlant writes: 'compassion is a term denoting privilege: the sufferer is over there. You, the compassionate one, have a resource that would alleviate someone else's suffering.'[46] Others have questioned the imposition of compassion without appropriate consent by the 'other':

> The potentially spontaneous, unbidden, even uninvited arousal of compassion in another, joined with its potential for breaching norms and bounds of individual sovereignty and autonomy, might sometimes be gratuitous, invasive and paternalistic.[47]

Such perspectives demand one to critically immerse oneself in specific contexts, stories, and employments of the cultural histories of compassion (including those emerging in a pandemic panorama) to see how it has been variously employed to mould, manipulate, change, transform, or build identities. To this task, in the context of my own discipline of theology, religion, and biblical studies, I now turn.

Cultural Histories of Compassion: Probing Biblical and Early Christian Traditions

June Jones and Stephen Pattison in their study of 'Compassion as a Philosophical and Theological Concept' trace the ancient origins of compassion from Aristotle and Judaeo-Christian traditions which they believe, though often unacknowledged, continues to inform many contemporary constructions of the concept.[48] They note that whilst compassion is often envisaged between persons, it can also extend to different groups, species, and spaces.[49] As such, they define compassion as having at its heart:

> Some undetermined but deeply felt kind of intimate, action-guiding and attitude-shaping relational concern [which] transcends personal boundaries and notions of individualistic isolation.[50]

Jones and Pattison are clear that within biblical traditions, compassion cannot be understood as mere 'passive sympathy'. On the contrary, it performs dynamic social, personal, and political roles, for these dimensions 'were not separable in biblical times'.[51] It also frequently activates not just other-regard but also righteous rage and protest.[52] Biblical traditions, born in collective environments, underscore solidarity and community, rather than individualism and competition, as central for survival. As such, the Hebrew term often rendered as compassion **רחם** ('riham', from 'rehem') is related to the mother or womb, deliberately invoking kin relationships across divides.[53] God is accordingly imaged as a compassionate mother (Isaiah 49:15), and an Egyptian princess is characterised as acting with compassion to the crying Hebrew babe she finds abandoned in the bulrushes (Exodus 2:6).[54] Recurring pronouncements within both legal and prophetic traditions note the importance of compassion towards the socially marginalised—the widow, orphan, and alien—and God's people are impelled to act as their divine covenant partner: being 'full of compassion' (Exodus 34:6). In Judaeo-Hellenistic traditions, too, the force of compassion to form kinship bonds with those in pain and create new affiliations is central. The Book of Tobit, for example, concurrently produces compassion through the language of genealogy and lineage as one which is to be shown towards those in diaspora (Tobit 1:1). In Françoise Mirguet's terms too:

> It [compassion] embodies many requirements of the Mosaic Law, and within humankind, as it represents a common human potential. To feel pity is to feel one's concomitant belonging to both Jewish people and to humanity. . . . The emotion becomes a vehicle to expand the love command to "all human beings".[55]

In the New Testament also compassion is shown through 'agape love', which is often understood as the 'self-giving love of neighbour and of self in the Christian community'.[56] Jesus is frequently seen to act from compassion—σπλαγχνίζομαι—a term which denotes 'movement within inward parts'.[57] The inference of this somatic imagery is being urged to action through bodily felt fury at injustice. Thus, Jesus, in response to the leper's 'plagued' ostracised body, 'rage[s] with compassion' (Mark 1:41).[58] Annette Merz goes as far as to claim that the synoptic gospels can be regarded as 'manuals of compassion'.[59] Jesus is characterised as dedicated to healing corporeal wounds and ending torment and travail caused by disease, social/political/economic/religious oppression, and destitute need.[60] Merz notes that biblical traditions on compassion in this respect are distinct from many other existent traditions of the concept in antiquity:

> The fact that the God of Israel is merciful, concerned about the people, full of compassion with their suffering … is a notion alien to classical antiquity … in Greek tragedies the gods present themselves as merciless spectators of human suffering.[61]

She discusses David Konstan's landmark work, *Pity Transformed*, which claims that according to Aristotle mercy can only be felt by those 'who are [of] a similar nature to the suffering person'. Konstan also submits that pity in classical thought is elicited for those whose suffering is undeserved, but Merz claims the Judaeo-Christian traditions went much further in eliciting outreach to the unknown, the uncommon, the foreigner, or stranger.[62] Others too note that Aristotelian pity is markedly different from early Christian compassion. Edith Hall's work on Greek Tragedy notes that tragedy was designed to move the audience emotionally to pity and fear, but nevertheless only as passive observers—they are never moved to action.[63] Analysis of the historical Jesus and early Christian preaching, however, suggests that it was aimed at moving audience to action, including by evoking pity. Marcus Borg thus characterises Jesus' teaching as a stimulus to a politics of compassion: a 'radical socio-political' agenda.[64] Susan Wessel too in her book *Passion and Compassion in Early Christianity* similarly submits that early Christians (often in contrast to their Roman contemporaries) were admonished to embody compassion in model ways and counselled against potential for falsification or corruption of its authentic nature. She notes that these early Christian histories continue to influence early modern and contemporary philosophical and ethical reflections on compassion's 'intrinsic worth'[65] and no doubt provide at least some of the genealogy for how this concept is still regularly employed in various social and political contexts today. Noteworthy also is the fact that the vehicles of many biblical traditions on compassion are stories as opposed to edicts and/or exhortations.[66] Christopher Marshall too notes that:

> Stories are uniquely efficacious in social and moral formation much more so than abstract rules or philosophical principles. This makes the stories we choose to tell and retell are critically important for how we understand our collective identity and hone our values. Western civilisation has been decisively shaped by narratives drawn from two main sources – classical antiquity and the Bible.[67]

Julianna Claassens accordingly lists biblical texts as useful devices for engendering what Martha Nussbaum identifies as 'participatory imagination[s]':

> In this encounter between text and context the individual is bound to look anew not only at the narrative world created in the text but also at the world the reader finds themselves in.[68]

Here, one particular tradition purposefully entitled—'The View from the Ditch'—will be used to open up and imagine further dimensions of compassion and as Claassens would advise, at the same time, their reception and refiguring in various points in reception history including the present pandemic. It is submitted that this tradition can prompt 'catastrophe compassion' and function as a useful prolegomenon to think with, in creating alternative imaginaries to the current neoliberal episteme.

The View from the Ditch

The narrative of 'The View from the Ditch' (the so-called Parable of the Good Samaritan [Luke 10:25–29]) is often cited as an archetypal story of compassion: other-regard and action on behalf of one who is not only other to one's own kin but also an enemy.[69] In the present moment in response to Covid-19, activist and aid agencies have utilised this narrative anew to support public health interventions in Africa, India, Nepal, Bangladesh, and Korea.[70] Contextual Bible studies on the tradition invite their readers to reflect on: 'Who in this story did not show concern for human life? How did they show this lack of concern? Who in this story showed that human life has great value? How was this shown?'[71] And as a consequence of interpretation, in light of the pandemic, the studies urge readers to action:

> One of the ways you can love and protect your neighbour [at this time] is by keeping physical space from each other. You should not meet in groups, except with those living together in the same house.[72]

In a rather different vein, however, this narrative also featured as a centre point of Margaret Thatcher's theo-political rhetoric in late twentieth-century Britain.[73] In her retelling, the Good Samaritan was not only embodying compassionate action but (like a good neoliberal) had the means and money to do so:

> By implication, a government prepared to restrain public expenditure and reduce taxation is handing moral responsibility for the provision of welfare back to individuals. With a reduced tax burden, the government can be seen as empowering people to put their money where their morals are, which they may exhibit by giving to charity and making provision, through private insurance and savings schemes, for schooling, future health needs, and retirement.[74]

Thatcher, reading the parable from her conservative seat of power, did not, it seem, able to take into account 'vistas from the ditch'. Her employment of this so-called compassion tale harmfully clashes with the marginal, powerless, fledging early Christian community which first documented it and which, though often imitating imperialising discourses within its communications, was also ever aware of its origins in a founder unjustly executed by such power. Tim Anstiss, Jonathan Passmore, and Paul Gilbert similarly cite a classic psychological experiment—'The Good Samaritan Study'[75]—in the 1970s which purposefully engineered students' sense of haste and hurry en route to prepare a session on this parable: '90 per cent of students' in the experiment 'ignore[d] a man slumped in an alleyway' and as such researchers concluded: 'a competing motive ([individualised] desire for achievement or threat of task failure) reduced compassionate responding'.[76]

Reflecting on the parable's construction of compassion in relation to globalisation, Maureen O'Connell powerfully notes that 'massive human suffering, the phenomenon of globalisation and radical social and economic inequality dictate the proverbial journey to Jericho for many'.[77] She sees the pointedly different receptions of the text and its formulations of compassion as interrupting and reinterpreting its tradition history. She also notes that in situations of crisis there have been 'more victims than travellers' and that 'the road to Jericho [is itself often] paved with their labor and social deprivation'.[78] She also affirms that the distinction between 'innocent travellers' and 'guilty robbers' are ever harder to discern. As such, she demands new approaches to compassion in which:

> Suffering with persons languishing in the ditch requires self-critical and collective consciousness on the part of the Samaritans. It demands an individual and collective willingness to listen and to be transformed by the narratives of the victims in the ditch along with the freedom to accept accountability for the conditions which caused their victimisation.[79]

In this vein compassion on the road to Jericho must test and challenge all as they sojourn. Moreover, traversing this road involves less focus on philanthropic activity and far more energy on transforming structures which perpetuate injustice. Just as in responses to plagues and pandemics, such a vision of the 'ditches en route to Jericho' plots a highway as one needing renovation through 'catastrophe compassion'. Such re-imaginations:

> Create upheavals and interruptions in the world [which] causes us to stop, to open our eyes, and to listen so that we might have more accurate and effective vision of what might be and some knowledge of how to move forward to that new destination.[80]

Within my own discipline of biblical studies, the embodied lives of researchers in the academy have already been brought more sharply into view and could usefully be considered through a lens of 'catastrophe compassion'. Editors, for example, note how article submissions by women have plunged significantly during the pandemic.[81] One editor (at home, educating and attending to two small children—'as I write, they run wild') suspects this could reflect 'pandemic-era domestic labor [scaffolded by "heteropatriarchal culture"] ... [which] is not being divided equitably'.[82] Along with race and class injustices, she urges the academy to scrutinise demographics (and leadership) and, through the lens of the pandemic, challenge those spaces which persist in reproducing neoliberal values and privileges. She evocatively asks:

How can we press harder than ever during this pandemic against the insidi-
ous actions of those who care more about the virtues of competition and the
capital of productivity than the pursuit of equity in our guild and the quality
of our scholarship? . . . Let us work together intentionally to prevent what
could otherwise be an irreparable disciplinary regression. The inequities that
this pandemic is intensifying could lead to a moral crisis for our discipline.
The choices we make will necessarily be political and historical, but they
need not be at the dictate of prescribed social roles or economics.[83]

Research too in theology, religion, and biblical studies, emerging in the
wake of Covid-19, attests to more direct attention to structural injustices
perpetuated by neoliberal discourses, in the spirit of 'catastrophe compassion' dynamics. The biblical story of Noah and the Flood (Genesis 6–9) in
the context of a life-threatening pandemic has been interpreted as a powerful invitation to ecological repentance.[84] Psalms 8, 104, and the Book of
Job which underscore the interconnection and creatureliness of all living
things have been employed to mitigate against anthropocentricity and
impel contemporary readers in the pandemic to recognise 'the "hard lim-
its" in our treatment of animals', injustices in industrial food production,
and ill treatment of other creatures.[85] The inequitable effects that Covid-19
is suspected to have on Black, Asian, and Minority Ethnic (BAME) communities have been used to challenge silencing of black voices in theology
and reinvigorate the call to position black theological perspectives as central and fundamental to the futures of Christianity.[86] The 'breath' of the
spirit at Pentecost has also been seen as 'a sharp challenge of relevance' in
these times where breath for so many has been shortened or ceased. Also
in instances of institutional racism and abuse in which breath has variously
been 'contained', 'denied', and 'expelled in protest':

Breaths lost, gasps snuffed out, can return as rushing roaring winds bringing
righteous fire that burns for justice. To those that hear the roar, it can give
the power to attend to new words and speak in different ways. In the identification and pitting to death of that in me and in the System, which dies
and kills there is the potential for new life, new ways to live.[87]

Lament and liberation perspectives have been engaged within the pandemic as an 'ecclesiological awakening' to Christian communities too
often indifferent to the voices and experiences of refugees, rape victims,
the marginalised, and/or domestically abused now enduring even more
extreme experiences during enforced isolation.[88] Others have considered

ecclesial life, practice, and ritual (lockdown church) as transformed and transforming: 'digitally promising, physically smaller, more financially precarious and tentative, and potentially more flexible and interesting'.[89] In short, the pandemic panorama is already enabling the sort of Jericho Road revolutions within the academy in theology, religion, and biblical studies disciplines, of which O'Connell speaks. In the words of Karen O'Donnell, 'theology from the place where it hurts'—the ditches en route to Jericho—is located in a ruptured yet enriching topography: 'familiar touch points and landmarks have slipped from view', yet like the aftermath of many allied plague and pandemic events throughout history, we stand on ground ripe for 'creative, imaginative and life-giving innovation'.[90]

O'Connell herself pinpoints locations of urgent change within institutions marked by 'disengaged empathy' too bound up with neoliberal programmes of individualism, autonomy, production, materialism, and 'propertied abundance'. Such institutions too often cultivate what she, with notable contempt, dismisses as 'compassion by proxy'.[91] Alternative imaginaries for higher education institutions would emphasise 'relationality', 'self-reflective responsibility', and 'non-material aspects of human flourishing'. For in her view:

> These neighbour-orientated values enable compassionate persons to identify more accurately and resist more effectively the structural causes of other's distress, many of which are sustained by the egocentric values we just examined.[92]

Others note that Western educational models must be re-imagined to foster solidarity with others who suffer. This includes raising consciousness within American and Northern European white academics and students, of their privilege to lesser and greater degrees, and to encourage them to be agents, not just spectators, in addressing these inequalities.[93] Such moves will not be based on simplistic or sentimental notions of morality (good versus evil) but rather critical discourses which 'radicalize solidarity'.[94] Marguerite Dennis likewise urges higher education institutions to re-enter a post-pandemic era 'not in isolation but collaboration'[95] both of people, knowledge economies (challenging global north and south cognitive injustices), curricula, and values.

Whilst increasing 'professionalization' within the academy may obscure for many leaders and educators within higher education institutions their role in such projects—'as faculty become professionals and experts over an increasingly narrow and sometimes esoteric body of knowledge and tech-niques, they become increasingly reticent to acknowledge or assume any authority to contribute to the moral formation of students'[96]—neverthe-less, if higher education is going to contribute to the public good, address global challenges, and promote an 'ethics of care', as opposed to 'abstract decision making', then reflection on structures and values are surely some of the most 'morally relevant means of resolving complex problems'.[97] In Jones and Pattison's words:

> Without some clearly articulated understanding of social, interdependent personhood located within a wider frame of values such as community and justice, compassion can be seen to be a ruined [ivory?] tower that has within it little capacity to motivate or inspire.[98]

Compassion also compels institutions and educators to notice and respond to student (mental, emotional, and social) distress, for contra those who see this as beyond the remit of education, it is in reality a fundamental part of the encounter. In Jane Dutton and Monica Worline's words:

> Students will bring their pain to class with them, as reliably as they will bring their curiosity or eagerness to learn. As with their strengths and talents, each student's pain is unique, triggered by differences in their experiences, per-sonalities, backgrounds, and the variety of conditions in their immediate contexts. Whether or not we choose to attune to that suffering is one of the most significant choices we can make about how we enact our roles. Whether or not we acknowledge suffering in our classes has everything to do with whether or not our teaching opens up or closes down compassion.[99]

Higher education's traversing of the ditches en route to Jericho will not be an easy one, but aiming to ensure a safe and just passage is a noble aim, and it is hoped an important legacy to be born from the 'catastrophe com-passion' of this historical moment. University campuses have rehearsed dynamics common in plagues and pandemics: many witnessed an increase in anti-Asian sentiments, and xenophobic, racist, and discriminatory words and actions, in the wake of Covid-19.[100] Many also face hard and stark financial challenges at least in the near future and increased emotional and mental distress among both staff and students. However at the same time, as Manoj Bhusal writes, in many ways these elements should also propel the higher education sector to design an alternate identity born out of 'catastrophe compassion' which stands in marked distinction from the oppressive neoliberal 'corporate capitalism which has served a few and failed the many'.[101] Kristen Renwick Monroe reveals that stories ancient and contemporary of compassion emerging in the wake of historical crises 'suggest[s] ethical acts emerge not so much from choice as much as through our sense of who we are, through our identities'.[102] The present moment pointedly poses the question 'who are we?' to the higher education sector. Embodied rage is a legitimate compassionate response to the suffering of ourselves and others considered 'kind-red' both near and far. We must be suspicious of certain neoliberal dynamics leaking into post-pandemic futures within higher education—'[we] cannot simply watch more Zoom seminars and practice self-care'.[103] As Honor Brabazon justifiably reminds us:

> Critique is essential in times of crisis. It is our job and responsibility, not to accept these directives without questioning their impact on the less privileged among us, on the university community as a whole, and on the project of public research and education in which academics are engaged.[104]

Brabazon underscores that not 'all faculty (and students) are equal': they have 'disproportionate caring responsibilities', there is often prejudice against educators from marginalised groups in teaching evaluations, and the move to a model of blended learning in the pandemic has done nothing to relieve these inequalities. Neoliberalism's construction of the individual also means 'collective advocacy' is often 'delegitimised' and this allows 'social problems to be framed as individual failures'. Productivity and time also become refracted within auditing models of performance, which glorify entrepreneurialism and market 'success', rather than 'collective goals of critical enquiry, deliberation, and the pursuit of knowledge'.[105] It is also true, however, that the present pandemic has also already brought humanitarian and human interconnectedness into sharper view: 'People feel for the fate of humanity [and educational institutions] through the pandemic plays.'[106] Philosophical reflection on plagues and pandemics attest to the ways in which these extreme events often bring questions of values, moralities, and identities into sharper relief.[107] Michael Peters, writing on the philosophy of pandemics, attests to this:

> The philosophy of pandemic is truly a philosophy for all peoples. It reflects not only the human significance of pestilence and plague, or the rise of modern viruses like Covid-19 that show the transition across species, but

also themes of individual/community, self-interest and collective responsibility, the sacrifice of first-contact health workers, and all of those who in the ethic of the other provide a level of care in a neoliberal age less bound by duty or ethos of service and more by market values.[108]

It will shape new horizons and paths.[109] It may also in time be understood to have functioned as a 'prolegomenon' to refiguring the identity and vision of the neoliberal university: the prompt so desperately needed to re-imagine more compassionate forms of higher education. The ensuing chapters of this book will hopefully be one small contribution to this immense yet critically important challenge.

NOTES

1. The World Health Organisation (WHO) declared Covid-19 a pandemic on 11th March 2020. The UK went into lockdown on 23rd March 2020.
2. Sir Steve Smith cited in *Exepose* (12th May 2020). Available online at: https://exepose.com/2020/05/12/medical-students-at-the-university-of-exeter-graduate-early-to-join-nhs-fight-against-COVID-19/
3. Mika Aaltola, *Understanding the Politics of Pandemic Scares: An Introduction to Global Politicosomatics* (Oxford: Routledge, 2012), 2.
4. In biblical texts and receptions, for example, see recurring motifs of divine judgement and wrath (Deut 28 and 32; Amos 4:10; Ezekiel 14:21); protection of the righteous (Exodus 7–12; Ps 91); apocalyptic and the signs of 'end times' (Mat 24; Book of Revelation).
5. Joseph Crawford, Kerryn Butler-Henderson, Jürgen Rudolph, Matthias Glowatz et al., 'COVID-19: 20 Countries' Higher Education Intra-Period Digital Pedagogy Responses' *Journal of Applied Teaching and Learning* 3 (1) (2020), 1–20.
6. Michael P. A. Murphy, 'COVID-19 and emergency eLearning: Consequences of the securitization of higher education for post-pandemic pedagogy' *Contemporary Security Policy* (2020), 1–14. Available online at: https://doi.org/10.1080/13523260.2020.1761749. See also Zoe Hurley, 'Postdigital Feminism and Cultural Visual Regimes: COVID-19 at Women's Only University in the Gulf' *Postdigital Science and Education* (2020). Available online at: https://doi.org/10.1007/s42438-020-00134-3. Also Evelyn Morales Vazquez and John S. Levin, 'The Tyranny of Neoliberalism in the American Academic Profession' *American Association of University Professors* (February 2020). Available online at: https://www.aaup.org/article/tyranny-neoliberalism-american-academic-profession#.Xte1U25FxPY

7. University of Edinburgh, 'Compassion in the time of coronavirus'. Available online at: https://www.ed.ac.uk/COVID-19-response/expert-insights/compassion-in-the-time-of-coronavirus

8. John Forester, "Kindness, Planners' Response to Vulnerability, and an Ethics of Care in the Time of COVID-19', *Planning Theory & Practice* Vol 21 (2020) 1–4. Available online at: https://doi.org/10.108 0/14649357.2020.1757886

9. University of Edinburgh, 'Compassion', no pages.

10. Forester, 'Kindness', 1.

11. Kathryn Waddington, 'Creating Conditions for Compassion in Higher Education' in Paul Gibbs (ed), The *Pedagogy of Compassion at the Heart of Higher Education* (Switzerland: Springer, 2017), 49–70.

12. Pedro Ortega Ruiz and Ramon Minguez Vallejos, 'The Role of Compassion in Moral Education', *Journal of Moral Education* 28:1 (1999), 5–17. Available online at: https://doi.org/10.1080/030572499103278

13. Ruiz and Vallejos, 'The Role', 5–17.

14. Ruiz and Vallejos, 'The Role', 5–17.

15. 'Artists and thinkers from Augustine to Avatar write in its margins, telling their own stories alongside that ancient bundle of tales' Mary Beavis and Michael Gilmour (eds), *Dictionary of the Bible and Western Culture* (Sheffield: Sheffield Phoenix Press, 2012), 213. See also Vishal Mangalwaldi, *The Book that Made Your World: How the Bible Created the Soul of Western Civilization* (Nashville: Thomas Nelson, 2011).

16. Michael D. Beaty and Douglas V. Henry 'Introduction: Retrieving the Tradition, Remembering the End' in Michael D. Beaty and Douglas V. Henry (eds), *The Schooled Heart: Moral Formation in American Higher Education* (Waco: Baylor University Press, 2007), 1–28, 3. This is not, however, to prioritise a biblical or Christian theological account of higher education, quite the contrary, this disciplinary perspective is one among many (albeit one I am most familiar with), but it is no less important given that fact. Mike Higton sums up such a position well when he, reflecting theologically on the higher education sector, writes: 'My proposal is not for a university sector in which a Christian theological account has become the dominant account, but for a university sector formed by a renewed and serious argument about the good of university life—an argument that will include Christian theological voices like mine, and voices from numerous other religious and secular traditions, and in which the very form of the argument will be one of the items debated.' Mike Higton, *A Theology of Higher Education* (Oxford: Oxford University Press, 2012), 7.

17. Paul Gibbs, 'Higher Education: A Compassion Business or Edifying Experience?' in Paul Gibbs (ed), *Pedagogy of Compassion* (Switzerland: Springer, 2017), 1–17, 2.

18. de Lange and Claassens 'Introduction', xiv.
19. Marshall, *Compassionate*, 274.
20. Jing Lin and Rebecca L. Oxford, 'Introduction: Expanding the Roles of Higher Education and Contemplative Pedagogies for Wisdom and Innovation' in Jing Lin, Rebecca L. Oxford and Edward J. Brantmeier (eds), *Re-Envisioning Higher Education: Embodied Pathways to Wisdom and Social Transformation* (Charlotte: Information Age Publishing, 2013), xi–xv, xi.
21. Lin and Oxford, 'Introduction', xi.
22. Christopher D. Marshall, *Compassionate Justice: An Interdisciplinary Dialogue with Two Gospel Parables On Law, Crime, and Restorative Justice* (Cascade Books, 2012), 272.
23. For example, the Black Death, which eradicated nearly 30 million in Europe in the fourteenth century is seen by many as the stimulant to Enlightenment: 'shifting power to increasingly scarce labor resources'. See William Foege 'Plagues: Perceptions of Risk and Social Responses' in Arien Mack (ed), *In Time of Plague: The History and Consequences of Lethal Epidemic Disease* (New York: New York University Press, 1991), 9–20, 9.
24. John Aberth, *Plagues in World History* (Maryland: Rowman & Littlefield Publishers, 2011), 24.
25. Arien Mack, 'Foreword' in Mack (ed), *In Time*, vii–x, vii–viii.
26. Samuel K. Cohn Jr., *Epidemics: Hate and Compassion from the Plague of Athens to AIDS* (Oxford: Oxford University Press, 2018), 2.
27. Aaltola, *Understanding*, 1.
28. Aaltola, *Understanding*, 10.
29. Charles Rosenberg, 'The Definition and Control of Diseases: An Introduction' in Mack (ed), *In Time*, 5–8, 7.
30. Aaltola, *Understanding*, 19. Samuel K. Cohn urges interpreters to 'recognise epidemics' political effects that mobilized citizens to combat governmental neglect in medical and social services … and unjust, abusive and ineffectual controls that stigmatized and persecuted sectors of the population. Yet from the 1990s writing on AIDS began to shift from a view darkly centred on blame to one forged by compassion and political activism.' Cohn, *Epidemics*, 557.
31. Aaltola, *Understanding*, 10.
32. Jamil Zaki, 'Catastrophe Compassion: Understanding and Extending Prosociality Under Crisis' *Trends in Cognitive Sciences* (14th May, 2020), no pages. Available online at: https://doi.org/10.1016/j.tics.2020.05.006. See also Rebecca Solnit, *A Paradise Built in Hell: The Extraordinary Communities That Arise in Disaster* (New York: Penguin/Random House, 2010).

33. Zaki, 'Catastrophe', no pages.
34. Zaki, 'Catastrophe', no pages.
35. Zaki, 'Catastrophe', no pages.
36. Rishi Sunak cited in '"You will not face this alone", Rishi Sunak tells UK workers; unveils wage boost package' *Economic Times* (21st March, 2020). Available online at: https://economictimes.indiatimes.com/news/international/business/you-will-not-face-this-alone-rishi-sunak-tells-uk-workers-unveils-wage-boost-package/articleshow/74746929.cms
37. Angus Cochrane, 'Nicola Sturgeon Praises "kindness, compassion, and love" in Easter Message' *The National Scot* (12th April 2020). Available online at: https://www.thenational.scot/news/18375292.nicola-sturgeon-praises-kindness-compassion-love-easter-message/
38. Suzanne Moore, 'Jacinda Ardern is showing the world what real leadership is: sympathy, love, and integrity' (18th March 2019). Available online at: https://www.theguardian.com/commentisfree/2019/mar/18/jacinda-ardern-is-showing-the-world-what-real-leadership-is-sympathy-love-and-integrity
39. Philip Oltermann, 'Mama Merkel: The 'Compassionate Mother' of Syrian Refugees' *The Guardian* (1st September 2015). Available online at: https://www.theguardian.com/world/shortcuts/2015/sep/01/mama-merkel-the-compassionate-mother-of-syrian-refugees
40. President Obama cited in Michael Gryboski, 'President Obama Cites the Bible in Immigration Speech' *The Christian Post* (21st November, 2014). Available online at: https://www.christianpost.com/news/president-obama-cites-the-bible-in-immigration-speech.html
41. Bush Cited in Richard Holtzman, 'George W. Bush's Rhetoric of Compassionate Conservatism and Its Value as a Tool of Presidential Politics' Bryant University Dissertation, 2010. Available online at: https://digitalcommons.bryant.edu/cgi/viewcontent.cgi?article=1018&context=histss_jou
42. Françoise Mirguet, *An Early History of Compassion: Emotion and Imagination in Hellenistic Judaism* (Cambridge: Cambridge University Press, 2017), 5.
43. June Jones and Stephen Pattison, 'Compassion as a Philosophical and Theological Concept' in Alistair Hewison, Yvonne Sawbridge (eds), *Compassion in Nursing* (London: Palgrave, 2016), 43–56, 44.
44. Nussbaum cited in Mirguet, *An Early*, 21. Many commentators make a distinction between empathy and compassion: 'while compassion may grow out of empathy, it is something quite different. Whereas empathy involves placing oneself metaphorically in the shoes of another ("I feel

your pain") compassion draws on the capacity to be present in the face of suffering and selflessly seek to eliminate it where it occurs.' Peter Kaufman and Janine Schipper, *Teaching with Compassion: An Educator's Oath to Teach from the Heart* (Maryland: Rowman & Littlefield Publishers, 2018), xix.

45. Mirguet, *An Early*, 3.
46. Lauren Berlant, 'Introduction: Compassion (and Witholding)' in Lauren Berlant (ed), *Compassion: The Culture and Politics of an Emotion* (New York: Routledge, 2004), 1–13, 4.
47. Jones and Pattison, 'Compassion', 45. Samuel Wells notes that 'when directed at readers of comparative affluence (in global terms) we are the man at the side of the road. We are the one who is stripped … This is how we begin to reflect on questions of compassion and good deeds and social justice.' Samuel Wells, *A Nazareth Manifesto: Being with God* (New Jersey: Wiley and Sons, 2015), 95.
48. Character and virtue ethics emerging in Aristotelian thought do propose compassion explicitly as a virtue, as these are meant to be 'qualities we take pleasure in'. Nussbaum talks about the differences between compassion and mercy, the former rages against undeserved suffering, the latter is 'appropriate response when faced with deserved suffering'. Jones and Pattison, 'Compassion', 46.
49. They cite 'Compassion in World Farming' advocating for just treatment of animals in food production, as an example in this regard. See Jones and Pattison, 'Compassion', 45.
50. Jones and Pattison, 'Compassion', 45.
51. Jones and Pattison, 'Compassion', 48.
52. Jones and Pattison, 'Compassion', 48.
53. Jones and Pattison, 'Compassion', 46.
54. Kaufmann Kohler, Emil G. Hirsch, 'COMPASSION' in *Online Jewish Encyclopedia*. Available at: http://www.jewishencyclopedia.com/articles/4576-compassion. See also Paul Dowers, 'Pity, Empathy, and the Tragic Spectacle of Human Suffering: Exploring the Emotional Culture of Compassion in Late Ancient Christianity' *Journal of Early Christian Studies* 18 (2010), 1–27. Available online at: https://muse.jhu.edu/article/377440/pdf
55. Mirguet, *An Early*, 48.
56. Jones and Pattison, 'Compassion', 48.
57. https://biblehub.com/greek/4697.htm
58. Jones and Pattison, 'Compassion', 48. See also John Swinton, *Raging with Compassion: Pastoral Responses to the Problem of Evil* (Grand Rapids: William B Eerdmans Publishing Co, 2007).

59. Annette Merz, 'Ways of Teaching Compassion in the Synoptic Gospels' in Frits de Lange and L. Juliana Claassens (eds), *Considering Compassion: Global Ethics, Human Dignity, and the Compassionate God* (Eugene: Wipf and Stock, 2018), 66–86, 66.
60. Merz, 'Ways of', 70.
61. Merz, 'Ways of', 69.
62. Merz, 'Ways of', 69.
63. Edith Hall, *Greek Tragedy: Suffering Under the Sun* (Oxford: Oxford University Press, 2010).
64. Marcus Borg, *Meeting Jesus Again for the First Time* (New York: HarperOne, 2006), 58.
65. Susan Wessel, *Passion and Compassion in Early Christianity* (Cambridge: Cambridge University Press, 2016).
66. Merz, 'Ways of', 83.
67. Marshall, *Compassionate*, 272.
68. Frits de Lange and L. Juliana Claassens 'Introduction' in Lange and Claassens (eds), *Considering*, xiii–xxvii, xxv.
69. Marit Helene Hem and Kristin Heggen (2004) 'Is compassion essential to nursing practice?' *Contemporary Nurse* 17:1–2 (2004), 19–31. Available online at: https://doi.org/10.5172/conu.17.1-2.19
70. 'Lessons from the parable of the good Samaritan weave through a small manual that the Timothy Leadership Training Institute (TLTI) developed in response to the COVID-19 pandemic and has sent to people in dozens of countries around the world. Called "Loving Your Neighbor in the COVID-19 Epidemic".' https://www.crcna.org/news-and-views/good-samaritan-and-COVID-19
71. https://www.crcna.org/news-and-views/good-samaritan-and-COVID-19
72. https://www.crcna.org/news-and-views/good-samaritan-and-COVID-19
73. Nick Spencer, *The Political Samaritan: How Power Hijacked a Parable* (London: Bloomsbury, 2017), 2. See also James Crossley, *Harnessing Chaos: The Bible in English Political Discourse Since 1968* (London: T&T Clark/Bloomsbury, 2014). Also James Crossley 'By What Authority Are You Doing These Things?: A Brief History of the Bible in English Political Discourse from Margaret Thatcher to Jeremy Corbyn' *Biblical Theology Bulletin* 46 (2016), 144–153. Available online at: https://doi.org/10.1177/0146107916655291
74. Alan Lewis, Paul Webley, Adrian Winnett and Craig Mackenzie, 'Morals and Markets: Some Theoretical and Policy Implications of Ethical Investing' in Peter Taylor-Gooby (ed) *Choice and Public Policy* (London: Palgrave Macmillan, 1998), 164–182, 164.

75. J. M. Darley and C. Daniel Batson, 'From Jerusalem to Jericho: A Study of Situational and Dispositional Variables in Helping Behavior' *Journal of Personality and Social Psychology* 27/1 (1973), 100–108.
76. Tim Anstiss, Jonathan Passmore and Paul Gilbert, 'Compassion the Essential Orientation' *The Psychologist* 33 (2020), 38–42. Available online at: https://thepsychologist.bps.org.uk/volume-33/may-2020/compassion-essential-orientation
77. Maureen H. O'Connell, *Compassion: Loving Our Neighbor in an Age of Globalization* (New York: Orbis Books, 2009), online edition, no pages.
78. O'Connell, *Compassion,* no pages.
79. O'Connell, *Compassion,* no pages.
80. O'Connell, *Compassion,* no pages.
81. https://www.aarweb.org/AARMBR/Publications-and-News-/Newsroom-/News-/An-Update-on-Journal-Publishing-and-a-Plea-for-our-Discipline-in-the-Time-of-Pandemic.aspx. I too am a journal editor and can attest to these trends.
82. Andrea Jain, 'Update on Journal Publishing and a Plea for Our Discipline in the Time of a Pandemic' *American Academy of Religion* (2020). Available online at: https://www.aarweb.org/AARMBR/Publications-and-News-/Newsroom-/News-/An-Update-on-Journal-Publishing-and-a-Plea-for-our-Discipline-in-the-Time-of-Pandemic.aspx
83. Jain 'An Update', no pages.
84. Andrew Shepherd, 'COVID-19 an invitation to Ecological repentance?' *Stimulus: The New Zealand Journal of Christian Thought and Practice* Volume 27 Issue 2 (May 2020). Available online at: https://hail.to/laidlaw-college/publication/1tI5uq8/article/DbwFVdI
85. David Clough cited in 'Should Christians eat less meat?' *Church Times* (22nd May 2020). Available online at: https://www.churchtimes.co.uk/articles/2020/22-may/features/features/should-christians-eat-less-meat
86. Robert Beckford, 'Better Must Come: Black Pentecostals, the Pandemic and the Future of Christianity' *Vimeo* (2020). Available online at: https://vimeo.com/414095431
87. Jon Morgan, Facebook Post (31st May 2020). Reflecting on George Floyd's death on the feast of Pentecost.
88. Sanjee Perera 'Waking in Gethsemane' #TheologyinIsolation 12 (10th April 2020). Available online at: https://scmpress.hymnsam.co.uk/blog/theologyinisolation-12-waking-in-gethsemane
89. Rachel Mann, 'Where do we go from here?' (6th May 2020). Available online at: https://therachelmannblogspot.blogspot.com/2020/05/where-do-we-go-from-here-towards.html?spref=tw

90. Karen O'Donnell, 'Theology from the place where it hurts' #TheologyinIsolation 3 (23rd March 2020). Available online at: https://scmpress.hymnsam.co.uk/blog/theologyinisolation-3-karen-odonnell-theology-from-the-place-where-it-hurts

91. O'Connell, *Compassion*, no pages.

92. O'Connell, *Compassion*, no pages.

93. Michalinos Zembylas, 'The "Crisis of Pity" and the Radicalization of Solidarity: Toward Critical Pedagogies of Compassion', *Educational Studies* 49:6 (2013), 504–521. Available online at: https://doi.org/10.1080/00131946.2013.844148

94. Zembylas, 'Crisis', 504.

95. Marguerite Dennis, 'Higher education opportunities after COVID-19' *University World News* (9th May 2020). Available online at: https://www.universityworldnews.com/post.php?story=20200507152524762

96. Beaty and Henry, 'Introduction', 7.

97. Jones and Pattison, 'Compassion', 51.

98. Jones and Pattison, 'Compassion', 52.

99. Jane E. Dutton and Monica C. Worline, 'Educators, It's Time to Put on Your Compassion Hats On' *Harvard Business Publishing* (3rd April, 2020). Available online at: https://hbsp.harvard.edu/inspiring-minds/educators-its-time-to-put-on-your-compassion-hats?itemFindingMethod=Editorial

100. B. Venkat Mani, 'Fighting the Shadow Pandemic' *Inside Higher Ed* (14th May, 2020). Available online at: https://www.insidehighered.com/views/2020/05/14/inclusive-teaching-needed-help-combat-xenophobia-racism-and-discrimination-brought

101. Manoj Bhusal, 'The World After COVID-19: An Opportunity for a New Beginning' *International Journal of Scientific and Research Publications*, Volume 10, Issue 5 (May 2020), 735–741. Available online at: https://tuhat.helsinki.fi/ws/portalfiles/portal/137399898/manoj_bhusal_the_world_after_COVID_19.pdf

102. Kristen Renwick Monroe, *The Hand of Compassion: Portraits of Moral Choice during the Holocaust*, (Princeton: Princeton University Press, 2004), xi.

103. Honor Brabazon 'The academy's neoliberal response to COVID-19: Why faculty should be wary and how we can push back' *Academic Matters OCUFA's Journal of Higher Education* (2020). Available online at: https://academicmatters.ca/neoliberal-response-to-Covid-19/

104. Brabazon, 'The academy's', no pages.

105. Brabazon, 'The academy's', no pages.

106. Mika Aaltola, *Western Spectacle of Governance and the Emergence of Humanitarian World Politics* (London: Palgrave Macmillan, 2009), 163.

107. Alexandra Jones, 'The Pandemic of Kindness: Will We Be More Compassionate After Coronavirus' *Independent* (24th April 2020). Available online at: https://www.independent.co.uk/life-style/coronavirus-response-change-society-acts-of-kindness-politics-homeless-volunteers-a9482531.html

108. Michael A. Peters, 'Love and social distancing in the time of COVID-19: The philosophy and literature of pandemics', *Educational Philosophy and Theory* (April 2020) 1–5, 1. Available online at: https://doi.org/10.108 0/00131857.2020.1750091

109. Bhusal, 'The World', 735.

CHAPTER 3

Envisioning Compassionate Campuses: Critically Probing Organisational Values and Mission Statements

The values and mission statements which organisations profile as core to their collective identities can yield important insights into their self-defined purposes, priorities, and promises.[1] For universities these inevitably influence recruitment, socialisation, culture, and most crucially, 'the kinds of educated humans to be cultivated at a particular institution'.[2] Thematic analysis of the rhetoric of values and vision statements within higher education institutions reveals that these are frequently used to 'create a shared sense of purpose' within an organisation, 'communicate its characteristic values and history to key external constituents', and persuade staff to 'conform to institutional imperatives' and aspirations.[3] They serve a legitimising function, akin to mythology and ritual in religion,[4] in producing and reproducing specific social identities for institutions and the people who work and study within them to embody.[5]

'Values' can be understood as operating philosophies[6]—ethically, morally, and ideologically—but in neoliberal contexts, 'values' are also inevitably gauged as material worth. Both dimensions frequently co-exist (albeit often in tension) within organisations, including higher education:

> Values determine just how the institution conducts its educational business, which in turn determines whether a fair return is produced for everybody connected to that institution, its students, employees, customers,

L. J. Lawrence, *Refiguring Universities in an Age of Neoliberalism*, Palgrave Critical University Studies, https://doi.org/10.1007/978-3-030-73371-1_3

stakeholders, partners, and the greater community. A fair return is generally good business practice.[7]

Carlos Torres and Daniel Schugurensky, in their commentary on the political economy of higher education in the era of neoliberal globalisation, from a Latin American perspective, accordingly attest that:

> In most countries, changes in financial arrangements, coupled with account-ability mechanisms, have forced universities to reconsider their social missions, academic priorities and organizational structures. Concerns about equity, accessibility, autonomy or the contribution of higher education to social transformation, which were prevalent during previous decades, have been overshadowed by concerns about excellence, efficiency, expenditures, and rates of return. The notion that higher education is primarily a citizen's right and a social investment – which has been taken for granted for many decades, is being seriously challenged by a neoliberal agenda that places extreme faith in the market.[8]

Values and mission statements themselves have been viewed suspiciously by some as 'a symbolic avowal of the values of business' by 'the neoliberal "business facing university"' and constructions of value-led discourses 'propound[ing] a managerial institutional narrative'.[9] Whilst this warning is duly acknowledged, it is also true that values and visions have been used constructively by different communities of care and other-regard (religious traditions, professional care bodies, justice advocates, etc.) throughout history, and compassion in particular, for affiliative social development therein.[10] The value of compassion in such traditions often purposefully advances common respect (and equality) for those in conflict, who hurt, suffer injustice, or are perceived as 'other' to an unmarked norm.[11]

This chapter will first trace some of the ways in which compassion as a value and vision has operated (in some cases quasi-theologically) in forging collective moral identities within different communities, organisations, and systems: in particular, Karen Armstrong's 'Charter for Compassion' (2008) and the UK's National Health Service (NHS) which has compassion as one of its core values. It will also raise some of the problems that the promotion of compassion has encountered within these contexts in relation to neoliberal dynamics including 'management practices and outcomes contrary to practical compassion' (dehumanisation, increased inequality, and commodification)[12] and seek to show some of the ways in which organisational culture and compassionate models have, and could, co-exist. Second, I will then review selected examples of values and mission statements from selected universities across the UK and US which have sought to champion compassion. It will be argued that stemming the tide of neoliberal economic 'value' discourses, and instrumental views of education for economic or self-serving advantage, these institutions plot values along compassionate lines as 'an induction into a certain kind of moral community: a reasoning community united by virtuous exchange … and sociality'[13] for the communal and public good. It will also be proposed that those institutions most explicitly striving to envision compassionate campuses are also frequently those not afraid to confront difficult heritages, past injustices, and sufferings of others,[14] with remorse, openness, and trust.[15]

VALUING COMPASSION: THE CHARTER OF COMPASSION AND THE NHS

Belinda du Plooy[16] reflecting on affiliative values in Africa celebrates what she sees as the emerging global value of compassion. Affirmatively she states:

> Arguably for the first time in human history … the emergence of an inclusive existential ethical sensibility that claims to transcend religious and cultural categorizations and is accessible to, and potentially resonates with, a diverse and multifarious mainstream majority. Compassion stands at the centre of this project as a collective commonality and a cohesive driver of contemporary imagination and discourse.[17]

The 'Charter for Compassion' founded in 2009 by TED[18] talk winner, and religious historian Karen Armstrong, is cited by du Plooy in this respect and could in effect be read as a mobilising 'mission statement' for contemporary compassion-centred movements. Based on the Golden Rule[19] which Armstrong submits is common to religious and spiritual traditions—do to others as you would have them to do you—signatories pledge to 'honor the inviolable sanctity of every single human being, treating everybody, without exception, with absolute justice, equity, and respect', to 'refrain consistently and empathically from inflicting pain', and to 'encourage a positive appreciation of cultural and religious diversity'.[20] The Charter (designed in association with leaders and thinkers from diverse spiritual and religious traditions) and drawing on psychological and neuroscientific research stands as a transdisciplinary and multicultural attempt to channel religious (and other) wisdom into a positive influence for concord rather than conflict. The Charter has currently been signed by over 2 million people and organisations across the world (including cities and universities), and has guided energies to respond to UN sustainable development goals through an emphasis on praxis[21]—commitment, engagement, behaviour, and repetition—'placing compassion at the centre of moral and religious thinking, refusing any fundamentalist or violent interpretations of scriptures, [and] providing empowering education that emphasises diversity'.[22] Armstrong has more recently produced a book entitled *Twelve Steps to a Compassionate Life*,[23] which deliberately alludes to the well-known 12-step programmes to combat addiction: for 'egotism' is a dependence for which compassion is a curative practice, to 'retrain our responses and reform mental habits that are kinder, gentler, and less fearful of others'.[24] These steps comprise 'Learn about Compassion'; 'Look at your Own World'; 'Compassion for Yourself'; 'Empathy'; 'Mindfulness'; 'Action'; 'How Little We Know'; 'How Should we Speak to One Another?'; 'Concern for Everybody'; 'Knowledge'; 'Recognition'; and 'Love Your Enemies'.[25] In Armstrong's words:

> I am a religious historian, and it is my study of the spiritualities of the past that has taught me all I know about compassion. I think that in this respect the faith traditions still have a great deal to teach us. But it is important to say that the twelve-step programme does not depend on supernatural or creedal convictions. I am in agreement with HH the Dalai Lama that "whether a person is a religious believer does not matter much. Far more important is that they be a good human being." At their best, all religious, philosophical and ethical traditions are based on a principle of compassion.[26]

The Charter has been cited as a significant example of 'communal self-telling'[27] and social-identity construction. It constructs, as du Plooy notes, a simple, if powerful basis in common humanity, and thus 'marries the humanist concepts of rights and responsibilities under the umbrella of compassionate action'.[28] Some have dismissed the charter as lacking real agency—'a rhetorical device rather than a practical tool to mobilize and facilitate peace-making'[29]—and despite Armstrong's original global vision, others have called out its Western-centricity (majority Western partners, approach, and marketing) and implicit tendencies in replicating social and geopolitical hierarchies. What cannot be denied, however, are concrete changes experienced under the Charter's auspices across the world, including a 'Compassionate Schools Network' in Karachi, Pakistan, created to combat gang violence and violence against women, by building an auxiliary educational curriculum to teach empathy, courage, gratitude, and tolerance through school activities, art, and physical education,[30] also the support and development of Jewish and Palestinian women's collaborative peace initiatives in Kfar Vradim, Northern Israel, and interfaith projects in Ethiopia, Bosnia, and Herzegovina, to name just a few.[31] Significantly, the Charter does not (perhaps due to its trans-organisational appeal) lay out consequences of uncompassionate behaviour—though admittedly constructive values and mission statements rarely do—nor does it seek to address the 'shadow side' of compassion, its oft-times ineffectiveness in challenging unjust structures, or worse still, its employment as a political device for exertive control. Khen Lampert laments how too many neoliberal power wielders have 'exploited the sense of calling compassion arouses in order to mitigate social oppression and mask the immoral, belligerent, and manipulative nature of society's power structures and mechanisms'.[32] Such abuses are of course symptomatic of 'inauthentic compassion' and 'forced submissiveness that is likely to lead to distress'.[33] The Charter nonetheless still stands as an important intervention, in what Less Marsden calls, 'the context of a post-secular international society and faith-based diplomacy, in which religious and interreligious initiatives emerge as serious, rather than peripheral, actors in developing sustainable peace making through bottom-up approaches'.[34]

Professional healthcare organisations have also championed compassion in their self-definitions. The UK's National Health Service (NHS) founded in 1948 with the noble and altruistic mission to provide free health care for everyone at the point of need lists compassion as one of its core values[35]:

Compassion: We respond with humanity and kindness to each person's pain, distress, anxiety or need. We search for the things we can do, however small, to give comfort and relieve suffering. We find time for those we serve and work alongside. We do not wait to be asked, because we care.

The NHS itself has been viewed by some as akin to a 'theological institution'—'a church for rationalists'—in public consciousness. Its moral purpose is firmly 'believed in' and public devotion is made manifest in people collectively dedicating themselves to others.[36] In cases where this ethos has been judged to be betrayed or abused in the NHS, compassion has been referred back to, in order to call out the injustice.[37] Unlike Armstrong's Charter of Compassion which functions in a trans-organisational domain, within individual organisations such as the NHS, a core value like compassion does seem to have the potency to critique as well as construct. The NHS is a 'care-giving' institution which has also had to negotiate its identity and potential 'compassion-deficits' (often perceived not to be inherent within front-line health workers, but rather structural 'government health policy and NHS organisational culture') within a stretched economy.[38] Interestingly, from the viewpoint of managerial and organisational culture, one study of NHS trust managers across London notes that they demonstrated a 'collective commitment to the altruistic ethos of the NHS' but were also aware that their perceived public image as '"trying to make [the institution] ever more efficient, rational and controlled cannot at the same time be caring and people centred"'.[39] The NHS has also had to face burdens, cut backs, and stretched resources, which have led in places to 'compassion fatigue'—'unique stressors affecting people in caregiving professions' (including vicarious trauma and work place stress)—among staff.[40] Likewise, the coercion for the workforce to focus on targets, tasks, and problems is also often perceived to foster dehumanisation. Responses to such pressures have included the development of compassionate leadership in the healthcare sector including the rejection of individualistic models for more democratic, mutual, reciprocal, and distributive models, with attention to both the development of the compassionate tone of communications and all interactions within the system:

> Developing leadership for compassionate care requires acknowledging and making provision for the difficulties and challenges of working in an anxiety-laden context. This means providing appropriate training and well-being programs, sustaining high levels of trust and mutually supportive interpersonal connections, and fostering the sharing of knowledge, skills, and workload across silos. It requires enabling people to experiment without fear of reprisal, to reflect on their work, and to view errors as opportunities for learning and improvement. Tasks and relational care need to be integrated into a coherent unity, creating space for real dialog between patients, clinicians, and managers, so that together they can co-create ways to flourish.[41]

Other important initiatives have included a 'Cultivating Compassion' programme for NHS health professionals and support staff. Using appreciative enquiry to identify good and sustainable practice within the
organisation, the project developed 'compassion awareness training',
'evaluation[s] of compassion lead' roles, and a 'multi-modal compassion
toolkit'. Enablers to instilling compassionate culture within the NHS were
identified as 'effective senior-level support', 'organizational leadership in
cultivating compassion within a healthcare organization', and 'integration
of compassion-promoting resources within existing staff development
initiatives'.[42]

The NHS perhaps more explicitly than most is an 'organization[al] site
of everyday healing and pain'[43] and experiences therein attest that 'organisational ecosystems which detach people from each other, prize economic
or other targets over emotional responses, and separate affective dimensions from rationality'[44] risk impeding compassionate action.[45]
Implementations of the Charter for Compassion, and the NHS core value
of compassion, also reveal the tensions between cherishing of compassionate affiliation and the socioeconomic neoliberal frameworks in which this
value is often compelled to operate. But are all business models and compassionate organisational cultures bound to be mutually exclusive?
Hendrik Opdebeeck and Andre Habisch in their study of Chinese and
Western perspectives on compassion in management[46] point to some of
the ways in which the two have co-existed. Religious and cultural wisdom
and worldviews within each context have, and continue, to influence interpersonal exchange and relationships. They note how classical Chinese wisdom is experiencing a revitalisation in China that is also sustained by the
government. For example, for Taoism the expansion of 'virtue is in mod-
eration, humility and especially in compassion'; in Zen Buddhism relationships are central 'only by giving the right answer in the relation to one
another, can people coexist'; in Confucian thought people are called 'to
"really love humanity" and to "hate inhumanity"'.[47] Accordingly in
Chinese contexts such worldviews have inspired compassion management
which arises from principles of curtailing self-interest and augmenting
reciprocally valuable relations. They note how such values have inspired
entrepreneurs to create job opportunities for the underrepresented, and
so on.[48] Similarly Jewish, Christian, and Islamic spiritual traditions too
value thinking of oneself in solidarity with others, and philosophical perspectives influenced by these also:

call for compassion evolved as a universal imperative strongly influencing even modern times philosophy. Compassion is now grounded in the personal dignity of every human as a creature of God stated as a natural law by renaissance and humanist authors. Even the positive international law of enlightenment ages and later the social and labour laws of industrialization are rooted in that generalized cultural concept of the west.[49]

Opdebeeck and Habisch also introduce the often-forgotten (leave alone celebrated) effects of compassion on local economic development in Europe and the advent of modern corporations. They cite, for example, in the financial sphere, the 'Montes Pietatis', which was instituted by Franciscan monks to provide loans for those in poverty to improve their living conditions:

> The main motivation for their foundation was to offer to poor families a secure, long-term and interest-bearing investment vehicle – thus triggering regional development and fighting against poverty. Therefore, it was the basic notion of compassion with the poor, which triggered economic development on a local level including the foundation of small and medium companies in decentralized areas of many European countries. The modern corporation evolved in the nineteenth century not only as an economic but first and foremost as a social entity.[50]

Similarly, in industrialisation where many workers lived in poor conditions, socially and spiritually motivated entrepreneurs looked to provide housing, education, and civil society establishments to influence the 'political process of crafting social and labour institutions'.[51] As such compassionate businesses became 'a critical civic and political force shaping the modern corporation and for the emergence of an institutional framework to humanize industrialization'.[52] In such examples, business organisations and institutions became ecosystems of compassionate response to human and social needs. Consequently, such organisations,

> perceive these values as being not a burden ... relationship[s] with employees and the social environment ... [were] the desirable consequences of trust generated by compassionate management.

Examples such as these can function as important stimuli in reflection on higher education values. How (if at all) have, and could, allied compassion-centred institutional models operate within the academy?

Universities, Organisational Values, and Cultures

Universities traditionally have been seen to have a tripartite purpose: to conduct research, to deliver education, and to contribute to the public good. However, many see these purposes risking certain distortions within dominant socio-political and economic narratives. A study of different UK universities (including pre-1992 or old universities, collegiate universities, new universities of the 1960s, and large civic technological universities) noted the recurrent link between 'Academic Values' and the 'University as a Corporate Enterprise': 'administration' of the sector, including funding councils' research excellence exercises and other quality assurance measures regarding teaching, instilled a neoliberal ideology of performativity.[53] As such:

> Academics and their institutions become vulnerable like other institutions [to being] valued for utilitarian ends. They lose their exceptional status, and the principle of individual autonomy by which academics have traditionally set such store is challenged.[54]

A study of 72 public university value statements in the US similarly revealed many centring on economic advantage to students, or competitive claims to excellence: '"Becoming a well-known, leading, and respected research university both nationally and internationally" was among the most commonly underlined messages.'[55] In such statements quality and excellence become 'indistinguishable' (and often impersonal) promises across the university sector with individual institutions in effect 'risk[ing] characteristic convergence'.[56] Research on self-presentation of Scottish Universities, too, showed, through textual analysis of value and mission statements, an overall impression of faceless uniformity rather than exceptionality: 'often focused on competitiveness at national and global level' but surprisingly lacking in relation to other areas such as student lived experience, campus culture, moral affiliations, and connectivity.[57] The University of Exeter as a research-intensive, Russell Group UK institution, is also fairly typical in this respect. It denotes its mission as 'mak[ing] the exceptional happen by challenging traditional thinking and defying conventional boundaries' and is explicit in its 'driving ambition ... to be a global 100 research leader and create graduates of distinction within a community of the most talented and creative minds'.[58] It lists its core values as follows:

Ambition: Ambition has driven us to where we are today and will
                help us to sustain a position within the global 100.
Collaboration: We work at our best in active collaboration between stu-
                dents, colleagues, and external partners.
Challenge: We relish challenge and reach for the previously
                unachievable.
Community: We support and inspire each other to be the best that
                we can be.
Impact: Making the exceptional happen requires disruptive think-
                ing, fresh ways of working and solutions with impact.
Rigour: We strive to reach the highest standards of scholarship
                and service.[59]

The narrative of achievement, competition, and institutional self-enhancement comes across quite strongly. Frank Gaffikin and David Perry in their study of research universities as an 'institutional manifestation of neoliberalism in a global era' make instructive reading in this regard[60]: 'Faced with new rivals, [universities] are pressured to be more entrepreneurial and competitive.'[61] Yet whilst measures of social impact of research and public engagement are increasingly monitored within research-driven university cultures, the challenge remains 'how to structurally and practically connect personal development and public benefit with the current focus on marketable skills'.[62] Gaffikin and Perry searchingly ask: Is education predominantly judged on its own terms or for economic gain? Is the public or private sphere prioritised? They also warn against the commodification of knowledge[63] in such economic systems where knowledge is product and used by certain advantaged sectors/groups.[64] In light of all these forces, they petition for 'rival [value] imaginaries' in higher education to the dominant and dominating neoliberal transcripts. For,

> Whatever the *structural* pressures toward a convergent neoliberal and market-driven framework for institutional decision making, there remains political space for the *agency* of staff, students, community, and state to intervene with an alternative agenda.[65]

Striking in this regard are institutional value statements, which are far more explicitly compassionate—'noticing', 'feeling', 'sense-making', and 'acting'—with regard to their own social location and history. In South Africa, Rhodes University's vision statement, for example, 'is to be an outstanding internationally-respected academic institution which proudly affirms its African identity and which is committed to democratic ideals, academic freedom, rigorous scholarship, sound moral values and social responsibility'.[66] Jìmí O. Adésínà in his article on 'The Discursive and Institutional Challenges of Becoming an African University'[67] notes that the 'African' identity of Rhodes was not included in the mission statement until 2012 and that this institutional accent on African identity is an important alternative to generic convergence of institutional statements. As such the mission statement

> help[s] to focus our gaze on those practices and norms ... and the university's sense of Africanity. By the same token, it alerts us to the importance of taking our locale seriously in fulfilling the core mandates of a university, and asking the question: What are the specifics of positioning the university to take advantage of these locales? Knowledge production and dissemination is local and global; specific and generic. The issue is not a pursuit of either or but a dynamic interplay of the two.[68]

Moreover, it was compassionate action (in response to suffering and noticing of distress) that first stimulated Rhodes University's 'epistemic shift' in values. The institution bravely confronted the challenge of shifting from colonial institution to national institution, considerate of, and dynamically engaging with, its contested heritage and location. Adésínà tells how the institution, in response to staff complaints, acknowledged that Rhodes' 12th September 'Founders' Day' celebration had more to do with the 'hoisting of the settler imperial flag in what became Rhodesia than with anything that happened in Grahamstown in 1904 or after'.[69] The rapid reaction of the Vice-Chancellor, Senate, and Council to the protest and the ensuing transformation of the Founders' Day is an eloquent testimony to the power of institutional compassion and will.[70] What is more, it was the fore-fronting of this postcolonial experience, and reflecting on the injustices of past histories which envision Rhodes as a compassionate campus: at once 'a centre of excellence in knowledge production and dissemination' but also one responsive in 'critical self-interrogation' of its own identity and history.[71]

Positive models of organisational life are also instructive here with regard to developing a moral (and compassionate) imaginary. The emphasis on 'collaboration' and 'community' within the University of Exeter's core values perhaps holds promise in this area: especially if 'support[ing] and inspir[ing] each other to be the best that we can be'[72] is measured not just economically, but also morally. Behavioural scientists note how people, 'humanity', and 'aliveness' are often lost in instructional values and statements,[73] and observe a certain reticence by organisations to narrate self-identities and aims through emotionally expressive communications.[74] Yet, human feelings and values have significant impact on organisational operations. Team practices which emotionally review tasks and systems, and collectively respond and co-ordinate policies and practices in human-centred ways, are surely important parts of developing emotionally literate communities.

Tess Maginess and Alison Mackenzie, in their study of 'Achieving Moralised Compassion in Higher Education',[75] also offer workable suggestions about how moral values based on compassion might transform and inform life and interactions in universities: most specifically, forefronting moral compassion in 'relations and institutions' with 'institutional and global value'.[76] Leaders, educators, researchers, students, and administrators need to embody and practise moralised compassion, which in their view should 'extend not only to those whom we know and love, or who look and sound like us, but also, non-contingently, to people distant from us in terms of class, race, religion, ethnicity, custom or sexual orientation'.[77] Moreover, the aim of instilling moral compassion should be to

> help develop non-contingent evaluative judgments on the grounds that merit our compassion. Moralised compassion is an altruistic emotion that arouses desire for the good of the other person and whose wellbeing we take to be an important part of one's own flourishing.[78]

'Interculturality', the imagination which allows one to see the world from another perspective, is given as an example of emergent moralised compassion:

> It offers an understanding of the size or scale of the painful conflict of competing identities, it acknowledges that a fracture of identity, private and public, is blameless in that every person should be afforded the respect to strive for the life that many of us enjoy. And, contingently, that we acknowledge that many of us were, to borrow from the Northern Irish poet, John Hewitt … 'once alien here'. This allows us to imagine similar possibilities.[79]

Intercultural competence, too (the skill in responding appropriately to persons from diverse cultures, beliefs, and needs), strikes a similar chord.[80] In reference to knowledge, institutions have also sought in their values to counter commodification of knowledge through adopting a much broader understanding of this to incorporate global and local forms of effective and co-operative citizenship: 'valuing indigenous and experiential learning through which we might learn to develop our humanity'.[81] Others see action and in-service learning as a priority in envisioning compassion institutionally[82] where positive effects can spread 'emotional contagion'[83] within learning environments and which allow emotional dynamics of compassion in learning to be developed, by taking students out of their 'comfort zones'. This is especially effective in developing moralised compassion to those perceived as 'other'.[84] To give just one example from my own experience, I have sought to challenge ableism and sanism (prejudice and oppression of those with perceived non-normative bodies or minds) through my teaching to sensitise students to the limitations of a deficit model of disability (x can't do y because they are disabled) and rather encourage students to try and capture voices of experience (what disability studies calls the 'minority model') to try and think about how different people experience the world. Awareness-raising class visits to the Bridge Collective ('a democratic community where people who have experiences, beliefs, and feelings that have sometimes been labelled as mental illness are welcomed and can talk about these experiences freely, safely and without judgement')[85] and the Sense Café[86] (for a session on d/Deaf-blind awareness) provide students with more accurate knowledge of conditions. Merging content-based knowledge with well-defined fieldwork visits is particularly well-suited to play key roles in transforming student viewpoints towards disability and inclusion. Student 'Grand Challenges' (often cited in reference to the institutional values of collaboration and community) at the University of Exeter is another good example of an opportunity to develop moralised compassion within learning: students work together (and in collaboration with external bodies) to design innovative solutions to real-world challenges and problems including the climate emergency, social loneliness, mental ill health, and food insecurity.[87]

Other universities in the global north have also tried to respond to this sort of moralised compassion and fore-fronted it within their core values and mission statements. In the UK, the University of Worcester was the first UK University to sign the Charter of Compassion. Its vision is accordingly stated as 'promot[ing] ethical and responsible behaviour, encouraging an understanding of the values of sustainability, inclusion and mutual respect' and equipping graduates 'to make a direct contribution towards the wellbeing and development of others'.[88] Its values are 'professionalism, inclusiveness, integrity and community' which are located 'at the heart of everything we do'.[89] Worcester campus has introduced 'The Hive', the first combined university and public library (including a children's library and a local heritage and community information hub), itself 'symbolic of this inclusive commitment to opportunity'[90] and 'transformative social impact'.[91] The University of Derby, likewise, has recently forefronted compassion and care as a core institutional value, building on its institutional expertise in relation to wellbeing and mental health in this area to posit its campus as a 'caring, aspirational environment'.[92] The University of Westminster, too, the first 'polytechnic' in the UK, founded in the nineteenth century to educate the 'working classes' of London, has as its vision statement: 'We strive to help students from different backgrounds fulfil their potential' and has also prized compassion as a core institutional value:

> Compassionate: We are thoughtful and sensitive, supportive and encouraging, making time to talk, especially when the pressure is on. As a University community we are inclusive and united, careful to consider what enables each and every one of us to play our part.[93]

In the US, compassion has also been envisioned institutionally by some universities. The University of Stanford most prominently has set up 'The Stanford Compassionate University Project'.[94] This initiative launched in 2013 has seen principles around compassionate action and attention— Justice, Equity, Peace, Respect, and Empathy—prioritised in all aspects of campus culture and inaugurated the Charter of Compassion for all citizens of the campus in a bid to positively transform the campus ethos. The University of Virginia, too, a large public university, has also sought to institute a compassionate culture. Juliet Trail and Tim Cunningham have documented this institutional transformation[95] through pan university initiatives (compassion ambassadors and mentors, contemplative pedagogies, and curricular programming), which were instituted in a bid to shift the social, ethical, and philosophical strategies of the entire university over time.

Others have legitimately highlighted the complexities and challenges of implementing and championing the value of compassion in organisational settings. In his study of compassion as a virtue within social policy, for example, James Gregory questions whether virtues can really be promoted and exercised by institutions, but rather only individuals.[96] This may be true, but it also underlines the oft-forgotten fact that higher education institutions (and other collective bodies) are the sum of interconnected individuals. What institutions can do is provide the infrastructure and scaffolding which allows and encourages people to be able to enact affiliative values in their day-to-day business. Others have questioned the bounds of 'organisational compassion' when balanced against 'performance needs':

> Can unequal responses create envy or resentment? How long can compassionate efforts be sustained without burnout or compassion fatigue? Are there cultural differences that must be understood in a pluralistic work force?[97]

All these are of course legitimate concerns and questions. Perhaps, the current global health emergency (the worldwide Covid-19 outbreak) which is imposing social isolation for the greater good of society[98] will generate some noteworthy answers to these questions. In this extraordinary context, it has perhaps become more obvious to many that higher education institutions (as all organisations) are constituted by embodied human beings with affective and emotional dimensions. The material life and conditions which have characterised daily life within universities across the world have abruptly and substantially changed. There seems a palpable realisation (lacking for many over the last few years) of the needs, fragilities, and emotions of human beings. Certainly within my own institution, where we are day to day learning to communicate, teach, research, and 'be' a university in a substantially different mode of operation, there is a sense in which the organisational 'tone' has shifted. Whilst changed modes of operation have been facilitated largely by technology, the situation has also without doubt stimulated more thoughtful, compassionate, and socially responsible values to be profiled, and compassionate communications to be produced and encountered. Leaders are sending frequent (and largely atypical) messages which acknowledge the lengths staff are going through at this time, and the various responsibilities and challenges which they, and their bodies, have personally to family and human networks both within and beyond the university. Managers are signing off messages urging our campus community to show compassion and kindness to each other and colleagues are urging each other to look after themselves, keep well, and keep safe. Such dynamics are perhaps more inevitable in times of crisis or trauma, but one would hope that the universities and institutions will emerge from this experience indelibly changed, and emboldened to act in more morally compassionate ways. How ironic that a viral epidemic may be the start of a 'compassion contagion'. Our modes of being in this emerging crisis may just become the sort of 'alternative imaginary' to the impersonal neoliberal script that university campuses, and their self-identified values, mission statements, and cultures, have needed for such a long time.

NOTES

1. A. E. Austin, 'Faculty cultures, faculty values' *New Directions for Institutional Research* 68 (1990), 61–74. See also G. Ozdem, 'An analysis of the mission and vision statements on the strategic plans of higher education institutions' *Educational Sciences: Theory and Practice, 11*(2011), 1887–1894; E. G. Rozycki, 'Mission and vision in education' *Educational Horizons* 82 (2004) 94–98; S. L. Moore, J. B. Ellsworth, & R. Kaufman, 'Visions and missions: Are they useful? A quick assessment' *Performance Improvement* 50 (2011), 15–24.
2. Robert Abelman, David Atkin, Amy Dalessandro, Sharon Snyder-Suhy, and Patricie Janstova, 'The Trickle-Down Effect of Institutional Vision: Vision Statements and Academic Advising' *NACADA Journal* 27 (2007), 4–21.
3. C. C. Morphew and M. Hartley, 'Mission statements: A thematic analysis of rhetoric across institutional type' *The Journal of Higher Education*, 77 (2006), 456–471, 457.
4. Morphew and Hartley, 'Mission', 458.
5. One particular theological example of this is Jesuit education, a Catholic faith position which values social justice as an expression of compassionate values and action. See discussion in Erin Callister and Thomas Plante, 'Does Faith That Does Justice Education Improve Compassion?' in Thomas Plante (ed), *The Psychology of Compassion and Cruelty, Understanding the Emotional, Spiritual, and Religious Influences* (Santa Barbara: Praeger, 2015), 109–124, 112.
6. William B. Calder, 'Achieving an Institution's Values, Vision, and Mission' *College Quarterly* 17 (2014). Available online at: https://www.jisc.ac.uk/full-guide/vision-mission-and-values
7. Calder, 'Achieving', no pages.

8. Carlos A. Torres and Daniel Schugurensky, 'The political economy of higher education in the era of neoliberal globalization: Latin America in comparative perspective' *Higher Education* 43 (2002), 429–455.
9. H. Sauntson and L. Morrish, 'Vision, values and international excellence: the 'products' that university mission statements sell to students' in M. Molesworth, R. Scullion, and E. Nixon (eds.) *The Marketisation of Higher Education and the Student as Consumer (London and New York,* Routledge: 2010), 73–85.
10. 'In the US, compassion is enshrined in the American Medical Association's (AMA) Principles of Medical Ethics, with Item 1 stating that "A physician shall be dedicated to providing competent medical services with compassion and respect for human dignity" (AMA, 1981). In the UK, compassion is one of the six core values in the NHS constitution (Department of Health; DoH, 2013), and calls for a greater focus on compassion have been driven in part by high profile exposés of serious failings in compassionate care at some hospitals and care homes. The international "Compassion in Education" foundation (CoED, 2014) offers a range of services to educational professionals in order to promote compassion in the education system. It has also been argued that compassion should lie at the core of the ethical framework guiding our justice systems' (Norko, 2005). Clara Strauss et al 'What is compassion and how can we measure it? A review of definitions and measures' *Clinical Psychology Review* Volume 47 (2016), 15–27, 18.
11. The Dalai Lama notes: 'Without an enemy you cannot practice tolerance, and without tolerance you cannot build a sound basis of compassion.' Dalai Lama, cited in Clara Strauss et al 'What is compassion', 18.
12. Marjolein Lips-Wiersma and Venkataraman Nilakant 'Practical Compassion: Toward a Critical Spiritual Foundation for Corporate Responsibility' in Jerry Biberman and Len Tischler (eds), *Spirituality in Business: Theory, Practice and Future Directions* (New York: Palgrave Macmillan, 2008), 51–72.
13. Mike Higton, *A Theology of Higher Education* (Oxford: Oxford University Press, 2012), 8.
14. John R. Thelin, *A History of American Higher Education* (John Hopkins University Press, 2001), 3.
15. Luuk van Leeuwen, Kees Winkel, Hans Dijkstra, *Vision, Mission, Compassion: Why People Matter in Organisations* (van Gorcum, 2007), 5.
16. Belinda du Plooy says this in the context of her study of 'Ubuntu' that is 'usually associated with the phrase "umuntu ngumuntu ngabantu", which translates as "I am a person through other persons" ... ubuntu is "the art of being human". Ubuntu has, however, also been criticized for inducing denial of past atrocities . . . another criticism focuses on the ways in which it has been appropriated, for all too familiar nationalist purposes, through

moralizing discourses of nation-building and citizenship, which glorifies an invented tradition and imagined past and results in cultural conformism, implied exclusions and the stifling of dissent.' Belinda du Plooy 'Ubuntu and the recent phenomenon of the Charter for Compassion' *South African Review of Sociology* 45 (2014), 83–100, 85. Available online at: DOI: https://doi.org/10.1080/21528586.2014.887916

17. du Plooy, 'Ubuntu', 85.
18. Technology, Entertainment and Design. The apparent irony of starting a project of compassion, with reference to a large cash sum TED prize, was not lost on the reviewer: 'It is accordingly a bold move on her part to start her book in this way (although it brings to mind Lord Longford quizzing a bookshop about why it was not displaying his book on humility more prominently)' 'Stephen Bates learns to be a better person with the help of Karen Armstrong' *The Guardian* (12th Feb 2011). Available online at: https://www.theguardian.com/books/2011/feb/12/twelve-steps compassionate-life-karen-armstrong
19. Lee Marsden notes, 'Many faith traditions each have versions of The Golden Rule, beginning with the sayings of Confucius who described shu or "consideration" as his key teaching, holding all others together. Shu also refers to "likening to oneself," the principle of empathy, as is essential to peacemaking (Armstrong 2011, 6). Confucius urged his followers to: "Never do to others what you would not like them to do to you" (Analects 15: 23). Within the Christian tradition, Jesus commanded his disciples to "Do to others as you would have them do to you" (Matthew 7:12). Muhammad similarly insisted that we should: "Wish for others what you wish for yourself" (Hadith 13, Nawawi). In the Jewish tradition Rabbi Hillel was asked by a gentile to explain the Torah while he stood on one foot, his reply invoked the Golden Rule: "What is hateful to you, do not do to your fellow: this is the whole Torah; the rest is the explanation; go and learn" (Talmud, Shabbat 31a). The Buddha advised people to: "Treat not others in ways, you yourself would find hurtful" (Udana-Varga 5:18). Hindus are also advised: "Do not do to others what would cause pain if done to you" (Mahabharata 5: 1517).' Lee Marsden, 'The Golden Rule: Interfaith Peacemaking and the Charter for Compassion' *The Review of Faith & International Affairs*, 16 (2018), 61–75, 66–67. Available online at: DOI: https://doi.org/10.1080/15570274.2018.1509286. du Plooy notes, 'As a historian of religions Armstrong holds a decidedly anti-dogmatic and pluralistic view. She believes that all religious traditions have a unique contribution to make to our understanding and practice of compassion, but she very strongly argues against any dogmatic attachments— she asks that we "value spirituality more than theology".' du Plooy 'Ubuntu', 89.

20. https://charterforcompassion.org/. See also Gonsalves Maria Goretti, 'The Confluence of Creeds' *ACADEMICIA: An International Multidisciplinary Research Journal* 8 (2018), 41–45.
21. Marsden, 'Golden Rule', 8.
22. Compassion Charter cited and discussed in du Plooy, 'Ubuntu', 85.
23. Armstrong, *12 Steps*, cited in du Plooy.
24. Armstrong, *12 Steps*, 21, cited in du Plooy.
25. Armstrong, *12 Steps*. Each 'step' heads 1 of the 12 chapters of the book.
26. Armstrong, *12 Steps*, 19–20.
27. du Plooy, 'Ubuntu', 88.
28. du Plooy, 'Ubuntu', 88.
29. Marsden, 'Golden Rule', 61.
30. Marsden, 'Golden Rule', 69.
31. Marsden, 'Golden Rule', 69.
32. Khen Lampert, *Traditions of Compassion: From Religious Duty to Social Activism* (London: Palgrave Macmillan, 2005) vii. See also Simpson, Clegg and Freeder's critique of the assumption that 'compassion in organisational contexts is motivated only by a noble intent. The paper draws on a study of organisational responses to the flood that devastated the City of Brisbane Australia on the morning of 11 January 2011. We use a framework of "circuits of power" to provide a triple focus on interpersonal, organisational and societal uses of power together with a model of coercive, instrumental and normative organisational power. We present our findings in a framework constructed by overlapping these frameworks. The unique contribution of this paper is to provide a conceptualisation of organisational compassion enmeshed with various modes of power exercised in and by organisations.' See A.V. Simpson, S.R. Clegg & D. Freeder 'Compassion, Power and Organization' (2013) Available online at: https://opus.lib.uts.edu.au/bitstream/10453/27945/4/Organization_and_Compassion_8.4.pdf
33. Paquita C de Zulueta, 'Developing compassionate leadership in health care: an integrative review' *Journal of Healthcare Leadership* 8 (2016) 1–10.
34. Marsden, 'Golden Rule', 72.
35. Other NHS values are 'Respect and dignity; Commitment to quality of care; Improving lives; Working together for patients; Everyone counts.' See https://eput.nhs.uk/about-us/nhs-constitution/nhs-core-values/. Faruk Merali notes how 'Over the last two decades NHS managers have been given the responsibility for the implementation of the various NHS reforms which have been aimed at making the NHS more efficient, effective, accountable and business like. [He explores] the extent to which the managers in this role as change agents believe that they hold core values that are in line with the altruistic service ethos of the NHS and as a result

the extent to which they believe they are seen to be performing and behaving in a socially responsible manner.' Faruk Merali 'NHS managers' commitment to a socially responsible role: the NHS managers' views of their core values and their public image' *Social Responsibility Journal* (2005) Available online at: https://pdfs.semanticscholar.org/ed54/f65a1c377fcdb503e054a6ed081cca346849.pdf

36. Julia Neuberger, 'The NHS as a Theological Institution' *British Medical Journal* 319 (1999). Available online at: https://doi.org/10.1136/bmj.319.7225.1588. See also David Barer, 'The NHS: National Religion or National Football' *British Medical Journal* 352 (2016). Available online at: https://doi.org/10.1136/bmj.i1023. On the compassionate culture of English hospices, see Alan Baron, John Hassard, Fiona Cheetham, Sudi Sharifi, *Inside the Compassionate Organization: Culture, Identity, and Image in an English Hospice* (Oxford: Oxford University Press, 2018).

37. 'Care and Compassion?: Report of the Health Service Ombudsman' Great Britain. *Parliamentary and Health Service Ombudsman*, Available online at: https://www.ombudsman.org.uk/sites/default/files/2016-10/Care%20and%20Compassion.pdf

38. M. Flynn and D. Mercer, 'Is compassion possible in a market-led NHS?' *Nursing Times* 109 (2013), 12–14.

39. Merali, 'NHS managers'. See also A. Hewison and Y. Sawbridge et al., 'Leading with compassion in health care organisations: The development of a compassion recognition scheme-evaluation and analysis' *Journal of Health Organization and Management* 32 (2018), 338–354. Available online at: https://doi.org/10.1108/JHOM-10-2017-0266

40. Carole Branch and Dean Klinkenberg 'Compassion Fatigue Among Paediatric Healthcare Providers' *The American Journal of Maternal/Child Nursing* (2015), Available online at: https://doi.org/10.1097/NMC.0000000000000133

41. Paquita C. de Zulueta 'Developing compassionate leadership in health care: an integrative review' *Journal of Healthcare Leadership* 18 (2015), 1–10.

42. Katherine Curtis, Ann Gallagher, Charlotte Ramage et al, 'Using Appreciative Inquiry to develop, implement and evaluate a multi-organisation 'Cultivating Compassion' programme for health professionals and support staff' *Journal of Research in Nursing* 22 (2017), 150–165.

43. Peter Frost et al, 'Narratives of Compassion in Organizations' in Stephen Fineman (ed), *Emotion in Organizations* (London: Sage, 2000), 25–45.

44. Peter Frost et al, 'Narratives of Compassion', 26.

45. Peter Frost et al, 'Narratives of Compassion', 35.

46. H. Opdebeeck, H. and A. Habisch, 'Compassion: Chinese and western perspectives on practical wisdom in management' *Journal of Management*

Development 30 (2011), 778–788. Available online at: https://doi. org/10.1108/02621711111150272

47. Opdebeeck and Habisch 'Compassion'.

48. '[…] [A]s a responsible entrepreneur I have to try as hard as I can to create jobs for the unfortunate. Creating a service business like Malan Noodle was one of the solutions I came up with (Jianxin, 2008, p. 56).' Cited in Opdebeeck and Habisch 'Compassion'.

49. Opdebeeck and Habisch 'Compassion'.

50. Opdebeeck and Habisch 'Compassion'.

51. Opdebeeck and Habisch 'Compassion'.

52. Opdebeeck and Habisch 'Compassion'.

53. M. Henkel, 'Academic values and the university as corporate enterprise' *Higher Education Quarterly* 51 (1997), 134–143.

54. Henkel, 'Academic', 135.

55. Guven Ozdem, 'An Analysis of the Mission and Vision Statements on the Strategic Plans of Higher Education Institutions' *Educational Sciences: Theory and Practice* 11 (2011), 1887–1894.

56. Sheila Furey, Paul Springer and Christine Parsons, 'Positioning university as a brand: distinctions between the brand promise of Russell Group, 1994 Group, University Alliance, and Million+ universities' *Journal of Marketing for Higher Education* 24:1 (2014), 99–121. Available online at: https:// doi.org/10.1080/08841241.2014.919980

57. Sally Kuensberg, 'The discourse of self-presentation in Scottish university mission statements' *Quality in Higher Education* 17 (2011) 279–298. Available online at: https://doi.org/10.1080/13538322.2011.625205

58. https://www.exeter.ac.uk/ourstrategy/values/

59. https://www.exeter.ac.uk/ourstrategy/values/

60. They cite six discursive trends within this moment: 'The concept of globalization itself; neoliberalism; the mixed economy of welfare, with its related issues of corporatism, managerialism, and efficiency; living with increasing diversity and difference; community/civic engagement; and postmodernist perspectives on knowledge itself.' Frank Gaffikin and David C. Perry, 'Discourses and Strategic Visions: The U.S. Research University as an Institutional Manifestation of Neoliberalism in a Global Era' *American Educational Research Journal* 46 (2009), 115–144. Available online at: https://doi.org/10.3102/0002831208322180

61. Gaffikin and Perry, 'Discourses', 116.

62. Gaffikin and Perry, 'Discourses', 116.

63. Gaffikin and Perry, 'Discourses', 124.

64. 'Scholars, especially those working with oppressed and marginalised learners and those involved in community and international development are calling for a much broader understanding of "knowledge" through which

we might learn to develop our humanity, to recognise global inequality and to enact a principled response to it in which personal development is not just an individual privatised acquisition of knowledge. Rather, knowledge is a gift to be shared with both global and local forms of active and collaborative citizenship valuing indigenous and experiential learning.' M. Henkel, 'Academic values and the university as corporate enterprise' *Higher Education Quarterly* 51 (1997), 134–143.

65. Gaffikin and Perry, 'Discourses', 124.
66. Other values of Rhodes University are *Academic freedom, Institutional autonomy, Excellence, Collegiality, Social Justice and Respect for each other, Equity and Redress, Development and wellbeing, Stewardship, Advancing the Public Good.* The values as a whole are much more human focussed in relation to equity, wellbeing, and advancement of public good and social justice. See https://www.ru.ac.za/institutionalplanningunit/idp/missionvalues/
67. Jìmí O. Adésínà, 'Realising the Vision: The Discursive and Institutional Challenges of Becoming an African University' *African Sociological Review* 9 (2005), 23–39.
68. Adésínà, 'Realising', 25.
69. Adésínà, 'Realising', 25.
70. Adésínà, 'Realising', 25.
71. Adésínà, 'Realising', 37.
72. https://www.exeter.ac.uk/ourstrategy/values/
73. Jason Kanov et al, 'Compassion in Organizational Life' *American Behavioral Scientist* 47 (2004), 808–827, 810.
74. Kanov et al, 'Compassion', 817.
75. T. Maginess, & A. MacKenzie, 'Achieving moralised compassion in Higher Education' *Journal of Perspectives in Applied Academic Practice*, 6 (2018), 42–48. https://doi.org/10.14297/jpaap.v6i3.370
76. Maginess and MacKenzie, 'Achieving'.
77. Maginess and MacKenzie, 'Achieving'.
78. Maginess and MacKenzie, 'Achieving'.
79. Maginess and MacKenzie, 'Achieving'.
80. Irena Papadopoulos, Sue Shea, Georgina Taylor, Alfonso Pezzella and Laura Foley 'Developing tools to promote culturally competent compassion, courage, and intercultural communication in healthcare' *Journal of Compassionate Health Care* 3 (2016). Available online at: https://doi.org/10.1186/s40639-016-0019-6
81. Gaffikin and Perry, 'Discourses'.
82. Andre L. Delbecq, 'Organizational compassion: a litmus test for a spiritually centred university culture' *Journal of Management, Spirituality and Religion*, 7 (2010) 241–249, DOI: https://doi.org/10.1080/1476608 6.2010.499998

83. Kanov et al, 'Compassion', 817.
84. Lisa Langstraat and Melody Bowdon, 'Service-Learning and Critical Emotion Studies: On the Perils of Empathy and the Politics of Compassion' *Michigan Journal of Community Service Learning* (2011) 5–14.
85. See http://www.bridgecollective.org.uk
86. https://www.sense.org.uk/get-support/centres-education-and-day-services/
87. https://www.exeter.ac.uk/grandchallenges/
88. https://www.worcester.ac.uk/about/university-information/who-we-are/a-compassionate-university.aspx
89. https://www.worcester.ac.uk/about/university-information/who-we-are/a-compassionate-university.aspx
90. https://www.worcester.ac.uk/about/university-information/who-we-are/a-compassionate-university.aspx
91. https://www.worcester.ac.uk/about/university-information/who-we-are/a-compassionate-university.aspx
92. The University of Derby, too, has recently fore-fronted compassion and care as a core institutional value, building on its institutional expertise in relation to wellbeing and mental health in this area: 'We are a University of first choice for students who want a caring, aspirational environment where they can equip themselves for the career they choose. We have been delivering Compassion Focussed Therapy over past years. We have a Centre of Excellence for Research in Compassion, Mindfulness and Mental Health.' It is also a signatory on the Charter of Compassion. https://charter-forcompassion.org/university-of-derby
93. https://www.westminster.ac.uk/about-us/our-university/our-purpose-mission-and-values
94. http://ccare.stanford.edu/stanford-compassionate-university-project/
95. Juliet Trail and Tim Cunningham, 'The Compassionate University: How University of Virginia is Changing the Culture of Compassion at a Large' *Journal of Perspectives in Applied Academic Practice* 6 (2018). Available online at: https://jpaap.napier.ac.uk/index.php/JPAAP/article/view/358/511
96. James Gregory, 'Engineering Compassion: The Institutional Structure of Virtue' *Journal of Social Policy* (2015), 339–356.
97. Andre Delbecq, 'Organizational compassion: A litmus test for a spiritually cantered university culture' *Journal of Management Spirituality & Religion* 3 (2010), 241–249.
98. Eleanor Casella, 'Lockdown: On the Materiality of Confinement' in Adrian Myers and Gabriel Moshenska (ed), *Archaeologies of Internment* (New York: Springer, 2011), 285–95.

CHAPTER 4

Compassionate Curricula? Northern and Southern Epistemologies and Cognitive [In-]Justice

Raewyn Connell in her timely and challenging book *The Good University: What Universities Actually Do and Why It's Time for Radical Change*[1] urges higher education institutions to examine how they create and perpetuate privilege and exclusion. She insists that interrogation of global economies of knowledge (which at present are largely inequitable) could ultimately ground hope that another (more compassionate?) university is possible.[2] She observes how leading research institutions, journals, and research grants are too often centred in North America and/or Western Europe. Anglophone scholarship still largely dominates academic publishing, and Western authors still exclusively populate many module reading lists. This state of affairs is linked to a heritage in which imperial restructuring led to asymmetrical global distributions within knowledge economies: 'While the colonies became a vast data mine, the imperial metropole (to use the French term for the colonizing centre) became the main site[s] where data was accumulated, classified, and published.'[3] Moreover, in the universities of the metropole, research was transformed into disciplines ('applied sciences, or technologies, such as engineering, pharmaceuticals, medicine, agronomy, and geological mapping') which in turn re-shipped knowledge to the colonised world and employed it within colonial practices such as excavation of natural resources.[4] In this sense, for Connell, patterns of 'northern hegemony' and 'southern extraversion'—'being oriented to sources of authority outside [one's] own society'[5]—were

L. J. Lawrence, *Refiguring Universities in an Age of Neoliberalism*, Palgrave Critical University Studies, https://doi.org/10.1007/978-3-030-73371-1_4

historically set and still haunt the shaping of research-based knowledge and education today.[6] Eurocentric knowledge systems set the unmarked universal position within the academy. Moreover, the 'white man's Bible' itself became a potent tool of colonial expansion and Eurocentric ideology.[7]

Colonial knowledge economies formed, and continue (in many instances unquestioned) to scaffold, the design and curation of curricula, within university degree programmes.[8] Curricula all comprise 'a selection from the archive of available knowledge'[9] and in turn form and figure learning outcomes and student identities and epistemologies—what knowledge is and how it is attained—in particular ways. Three types of curricula are often cited within curriculum scholarship: first, 'the explicit curriculum', which comprises module expectations, assessments, readings, and thematic coverage; second, 'the hidden curriculum' in which students become aware of the norms and values assumed within a discipline's or institution's culture; and third, the 'null curriculum', denoting that which is omitted, neglected, forgotten, and/or unspoken (this, as will be seen, is of particular significance in relation to north/south epistemologies). Some note that the explicit curricula have often replicated European industrial systems and principles in patterning an outcomes-based approach of 'curriculum as planned' rather than 'curriculum as experienced'.[10] Yet 'curriculum as experienced' could offer fresh and experimental opportunities for staff and students to pluralise their learning and teaching, be made aware of different traditions of knowing, and allow them to start to interrogate the 'hidden curriculums' and 'null curriculums' of their own universities, contexts, and subject fields. Curriculum designers must honestly ask themselves: what are the consequences of an epistemological hegemony which pervades educational systems?[11] Whose context, voice, and methods are privileged here? Who or what contexts are excluded? What can be done to address this?[12] In asking such questions one begins to see how curricula have the power to negatively perpetuate 'epistemic injustices' in relation to global knowledge economies, but also, when appropriately reflective and other-regarding—compassionate—are able to sensitise students to these injustices, take action to address them, and inculcate alternative 'epistemic virtues'.[13] Such practices enact 'cognitive justice'—a principle forming the basis of a democratic 'dialogue amongst knowers and their knowledges'.[14] Martha Nussbaum identified such competencies as 'compassionate imagining' essential for equipping students for democratic action in public life, through humane and just treatment.[15] In Nussbaum's terms:

> In order for compassion to be present, the person must consider the suffering of another as a significant part of his or her own scheme, goals and ends. She must take that person's ill as affecting her own flourishing. In effect, she must make herself vulnerable in the person of another.[16]

All this involves students and academics questioning meanings, visualising different modes of operation, transforming perceptions, and consciously promoting more democratic models of regard and critical engagement within their research and education.[17]

This chapter will trace some of the ways in which the disciplines in which I primarily work—biblical studies and disability studies—have perpetuated and/or destabilised northern epistemological hegemony. Although rooted in illustrations from these specific fields, I hope some issues raised here will have broader or allied applicability within other disciplinary domains. I will employ insights from southern theory to probe (a) curricula and north-south global inequalities; and (b) curricula and forgotten/invisible disabled bodies. It is worth stating at the outset my own context and location as a white, female, able-bodied, British, academic employed at a UK research-intensive institution, who has also conducted research in a southern context (in Namibia, Africa). What follows constitutes a reflexive analysis of both the privilege (and precariousness) afforded by my own context and embodiment, and the ways in which my research, and the curricula which I (and others like me) then curate for students, could itself risk concealing contexts and embodiments through unmarked neoliberal and neo-imperialist transcripts. It also offers some ways in which these epistemic injustices could be exposed and challenged, and more compassionate imaginaries could be developed within curriculum designers and students.

Curricula and North-South Global Inequalities

Southern theory, coined by feminist and postcolonial theorist Raewyn Connell, traces the outcomes of knowledge economies patterned by colonial histories and north-south global inequalities.[18] 'Southern' here is not wholly conceived geographically, but rather 'symbolically' to denote spaces of marginality vis-à-vis centres of power and wealth.[19] As Avril Bell notes, 'what makes theory "southern" is not so much *where* we are working as that we work from a political, critical, and historically-informed *awareness* of where we are'.[20]

Southern theory has an important role to play in destabilising and limiting the dominant and dominating 'global north' contexts, and patterns of knowing, within both research and teaching.[21] Context is commonly understood as 'the circumstances that form the setting for an event, statement, or idea, and in terms of which it can be fully understood and assessed'.[22] Within the academy, 'invisible' or 'forgotten' contexts are often used as shorthand labels for those contexts perceived to be marked by marginalisation, oppression, limited access to power, and/or representation. Such contexts are ones which the liberation paradigms of social justice, rather than the Enlightenment-driven rational, logical, objective interpretations, often locate themselves within. Contexts that count, however, cannot be critically gauged by academics and students, without due attention also being paid to the metropolitan academic contexts which have inevitably patterned and shaped knowledge encounters within the academy; nor too can consideration of 'invisible' and 'forgotten' contexts be undertaken without reference to their own statuses within processes, narrations, learning, and teaching (the so-called unspoken 'null curriculum' of northern epistemological hegemony). This issue has increasingly been on the radar of my own discipline. The Society of Biblical Literature's 'Ideological Criticism' section in 2019, for example, ran a joint session with the American Academy of Religion's 'Sacred Texts, Theory, and Theological Construction' to explore 'unexamined contexts' defined as 'those contexts taken for granted even when readers try to make explicit their contexts. A focus *on our own contexts, not those of other cultures.*' They urged academics to name and interrogate those contexts, for example, 'academic settings, masculinity, the dominant race, ableism, cisgenders, "liberal" assumptions'. And to ask 'Why is there resistance to contextualizing these contexts? [What] pitfalls [are there] in doing contextuality? How might our (lack of) response to hidden contexts expand or limit scholarship?'[23] Reflective too of this aim is the hosting of a recent event by the Society of Biblical Literature on 'Black Scholars Matter'.[24]

Since the #RhodesMustFall campaign in South Africa garnered global attention—in the UK Oxford University particularly witnessed allied demonstrations—the call to examine (often undeclared) contexts of power, privilege, and oppression within higher education has gained increasing traction. In the wake of George Floyd's death and Black Lives Matter protests too, there have been renewed calls to take down imperial statuary across university campuses and acknowledge imperial and slave-trader inheritances of these institutions.[25] So too have calls to 'decolonise' the curriculum in different institutions across the world been voiced. This comprises challenging those intellectual norms which discount indigenous knowledge and methodologies, and proactively accord equality to these.[26] Recent research has traced representation and decolonisation in reading lists across UK higher education institutions. It finds (unsurprisingly) the dominance of white, male, Eurocentric authors; moreover, these reading lists often do not reflect diverse student profiles, but rather more often the dominant demography of celebrated Western intellectual forebears and/ or northern academic staff. Authors of the report powerfully illustrate how reading lists are political tools and have important roles to play not only in decolonising curricula but also in deconstructing global inequalities.[27] Brenda Leibowitz too in her study of 'decolonisation' of the curriculum in higher education institutions in South Africa also reflects on some of the hazards of implementing cognitive justice as a guiding principle in 'curriculum reflection and redesign' and reading lists.[28] Pointedly, she reveals that much literature on decoloniality used in South Africa has been formulated in fields and disciplines within the West. Whilst Frantz Fanon and Edward Said are well-known theorists in critical pedagogies, few South African perspectives are ever employed in this regard.[29] Problematically, therefore:

> By and large theory on teaching and learning with regard to schooling or higher education, has been produced in the West, and within the discourses and paradigms emanating from the West. Whilst in the field of academic development and teaching and learning much literature, bibliographic or case study research has been produced in the global South, certainly from South Africa, the 'big ideas' on which this literature rests remains Western. . . . There is thus no substantive 'decolonised' or 'decolonial' theory, to guide the transformation of the curriculum.[30]

There is something of a risk in re-inscribing views that southern perspectives (not co-opted by the North) tend to be characterised as grassroots and therefore ignoring the rich and varied intellectuals (including currently) from non-Western traditions. Connell warns against the tendency of the metropole to castigate southern intellectual enquiries to the past: 'the Indian intellectual is [frequently] forced to relegate local bodies of thought to the past – to treat them as "traditions" [curiosities?] of historical and ethnographic interest.'[31] Leibowitz also highlights identities of educationalists which still are often indelibly shaped by Western, humanist, and Cartesian, Enlightenment perspectives.[32] As such, often curricula risk being conceived as grids into which disembodied knowledge is cast without due attention being paid to epistemological, experiential, and affective dimensions: 'The assumption that one can design a curriculum around what knowledge is, and not around how people come to know, is a problem.'[33] In a related vein, she warns against the commodification of knowledge as 'capital' akin to economic 'output'. She reveals how Pierre Bourdieu's notion of social 'capital' has leaked into metaphors of the curriculum as commodity, rather than a device for critique. In response, she champions 'epistemic justice' which requires diverse knowledges being brought into relation, not in any relativistic sense but rather aware of their own context, their own part in silencing other 'life-giving' alternatives and encouraging seeing southern perspectives as subjects in their own right, rather than 'objects on the fringes of Europe'.[34]

In light of such perspectives, as a Departmental Director of Education at the University of Exeter, I led the reshaping of Theology and Religion degree programmes. Staff were encouraged to reflect on developing more inclusive curricula with regard to race, ethnicity, and gender. The epistemological norm within the existing Theology and Religion programmes was ethnocentrically conceived, with 'great [Western, white] men' featuring as intellectual forebears[35] and female and non-Western authors hardly featuring at all. 'De-centring' the curriculum was rectified, however, not only by conscious promotion of marginalised voices in core modules but also by 'critical pedagogies' which sought to make students aware of social privileges conferred within the discipline and classrooms 'naturalized by patriarchy, colonialism and modernity'.[36] For decolonising the curriculum, as campaigners in Cambridge University UK, for example, warned, cannot be achieved by tokenistic gestures ('including a few non-European voices in historical xenophobic reading lists'),[37] but rather the conscious practice of 'decolonial resistance' which explicitly raised for students within their curricula the role colonialism still plays within structural inequalities, and the necessity for recompenses by Europeans to ex-colonies through conscious interruption of European ways of being, and a conscious retrieval of indigenous perspectives.[38]

Revising the core biblical studies components of the Theology and Religion programmes at Exeter in view of such perspectives, we realised students were also encountering another sort of 'centrism': namely the dominance of historical-critical methods of reading texts (a method born out of Eurocentric, Enlightenment rationality). With this in mind, the new core level 1 module which I co-designed (Bible: Past and Present) intentionally set out to challenge the dominance of this model, by approaching the biblical canon through themes (race, bodies, land, and gender) rather than types of literature/books (law, prophecy, gospels, and epistles) or hermeneutical methods, which inevitability perpetuated the dominance of Eurocentric historical readings by marking advocacy interpretations (feminist, postcolonial, decolonial, queer, etc.) as 'other'. Thematic foci allowed students to explore not only what texts 'meant' (in their ancient contexts) but also most importantly how they continue to 'mean' in diverse social, political, cultural, and popular receptions (including southern contexts), without privileging one methodology or location.

So-called Contextual Bible Study (CBS) was also employed within the curriculum, as an example of public and collective reading practice, originating in southern thought and practice, to challenge power structures for students and sensitise them to coloniality.[39] Students undertook training in facilitation and participation within these communal encounters, and some, throughout their programmes and dissertations, chose to undertake their own live Contextual Bible Study research projects. In its participatory methodology and epistemic privileging of voices outside the global north's academy, CBS could itself be seen as drawing on rich 'southern' traditions of education, including Brazilian educator Paulo Freire's critically acclaimed *Pedagogy of the Oppressed* (1968) and his conception of liberation/freedom as a dialogical practice.[40] Students were introduced to the history of the Contextual Bible Study movement which was nurtured in the townships of South Africa during the apartheid era as a force of liberation. The movement, like base community readings in Latin America, sought to engage interpreters with no specific training in biblical study, in contemplative conversation with the text and value readers' experience as a stimulant for both knowledge and social praxis. In *Ujamaa CBS Bible Study Manual*,[41] it is stated that two types of questions lead the so-called Contextual Bible Study process. First are 'community/folk consciousness questions' which draw on the experience and feelings of the participants. Second are 'critical consciousness questions' that include reference to literary, historical, and sociological paradigms. The sessions follow the same procedure and notably, akin to the liberation paradigm, have a bias towards the perspective of communities on the borders of society, and an explicit emphasis on praxis as the outcome of biblical interpretation. African interpretations including struggles with apartheid and Western forms of Christianity 'that vilified traditional cultures and religions'[42] and black theologies resistant to racial and ethnic oppression are made explicit for students through this methodology. In relation to South America, Ernesto Cardenal's now famous collection of responses to biblical narratives amongst *campesinos* in Nicaragua, *The Gospel in Solentiname*, is also used as a notable example of such an approach. In the collections, presented in dialogues, the community groups interpreted Jesus politically, seeing his revolutionary and counter-cultural ethos as a pattern for societal critique in their own situation. Every Sunday Cardenal initiated conversations about the gospels in which participants began to see the vision of the Kingdom as one in which the exploited were liberated from oppression and all goods were held in common. Moreover, these interpretations in Cardenal's opinion 'taught us that the word of God is not only to be heard, but also put into practice'.[43] The community produced a number of artistic representations of biblical narratives including the massacre of the infants, where the slaughterers were decked in the uniform of Samoza Debayle's National Guard. At all times the focus was on practical exegesis: theology, salvation, and Christology were not seen as ahistorical, but rather potent stimulants for social change.

One issue particularly raised for students within such exercises is the nomenclature of 'global' readings within biblical studies ('global' frequently functioning within professional biblical studies as a byword for 'global South') where the sounding of vernacular voices has been most explicitly pursued in professional biblical interpretation. Interrogating this terminology within the discipline, students consider Walter Dietrich and Ulrich Luz's edited volume *The Bible in A World Context: An Experiment in Contextual Hermeneutics.*[44] The contributions written from the perspective of various authors in Costa Rica, Nigeria, and Japan, respectively, all petition for exegesis that is academically informed, pastorally sensitive, and engaged with grassroots Christian communities. Daniel Patte's *The Global Bible Commentary* likewise initiated specifically 'contextual' readings of biblical books through a tripolar method of interaction between (a) the scriptural text, (b) the believers' life context, and (c) the believers' religious perceptions of life ('believers' incidentally always being conceived in a communal as opposed to individualistic sense). Students see that whilst one of the great contributions of CBS has been to bring forth so-called hidden/forgotten voices that had previously been muted, one of the great shortcomings has been that these 'contextual' voices are still often pitted against a mythical 'context-less' (northern) scholarly guild. Pablo Richard tellingly believes that 'behind the scholars of the First World

there is a library. Behind the scholars of the Third World there are conti-
nents of poor and marginalised people.'45 The strict divisions set up
between community readings and so-called scholarly readings mask a fal-
lacy. For all these readings are themselves 'context-full' of particular ideological perspectives and suppositions. Alissa Jones accordingly bemoans
the consigning of 'vernacular voices' to the ghetto.46 Randall Bailey, similarly, in a critical review of the *Global Bible Commentary*, chastised the
editors particularly on this point. He provocatively asks:

> What would happen to a reading of Genesis from the standpoint of the Brits
> who saw God having given them dominion over all and the imperative to
> subdue the whole land? I guess I am wondering if this approach to contex-
> tuality is within the framework that it is only the darker people who are
> contextual. Is this colonization of knowledge? . . . We have to ask, when will
> the 'white voice' become contextualised and put on a level playing field with
> other contextual voices?47

Within the CBS encounter, these identities are oft-times manifest through
the distinctions made between so-called ordinary [contextual] readers and
what Sarojini Nadar pointedly refers to as the 'invisible [context-less]
intellectual'.48 She warns,

> What concerns me after years working in this field is that in most academic
> reflections and analyses of CBS ... the focus is not on how participants are
> challenged to change and transform their interpretations of the Bible or
> their analysis of the social context in which they find themselves. Instead the
> preoccupation is rather bland, and dare I say romantic, description of both
> the participants in the Bible study and the intellectual. These descriptions of
> the participants variously range from "oppressed", "poor and marginalised"
> "other" "ordinary" to "survivors". Descriptions of the intellectual range
> from "trained reader" to "socially engaged biblical scholar" to
> "activist-intellectual".49

Valerie Clifford and Catherine Montgomery in their studies of internationalised curricula too note that the terminology of 'global' has been
contested on grounds that it harbours certain Western colonial conceptions so too the practical 'lack of a global state to which people could hold
citizenship'.50 They also reveal that attempts to 'internationalise' curricula
by merely listing southern voices in reading lists do little to enhance students' world perspectives and cross-cultural knowledge or to address

'diversity in the classroom and others' perspectives'.[51] More critical was direct interaction with methodologies, resources, perspectives, and voices from southern contexts.[52]

The economy of knowledge production is also raised for students and bears on the question of which 'contexts count'? Southern theorists warn of the claims to universality often assumed in the global north's authorial voice which meant 'in practice, if research is conducted in the metropole there is no need for any geo-political reference, whereas if you are writing from the periphery it is necessary to specify your location'.[53] Southern voices are also often frequently flattened or homogenised in curricula and publications as an anti-type of northern perspectives, and/or a people who speak monolithically in one voice. Indeed, Cardenal's *Gospel in Solentiname* is offered to students as an example of one (if not the only) publication to date in contextual biblical studies in print to present raw, full transcripts of the sessions, including different named participants. More often the researcher 'writes up' the CBS encounters, curating the material in specific ways, using carefully selected voice quotations (often due to compliance with institutional research ethics presented 'anonymously') to support specific points, often situated within global north intellectual frameworks and discourses. Swadener and Mutua pose a timely warning about how such processes risk producing 'discourses that inscribe and render Others powerless by producing a discourse that "author-ises" certain people to speak and correspondingly silences others, or at least makes their voices less authoritative'.[54] Research ethics, anonymity, and confidentiality too are contextualised for the students as being embedded in Enlightenment ideals. Southern theory alerts researchers to ways in which research participants agency can be deeply rooted in their names. Kristen Perry in research with Sudanese refugees realised just this:

> In some cases, name-changing can be its own form of oppression. Forcing individuals to change their names has, in fact, been a common technique of oppression used in the Sudan. Bok's captor forced him to convert to Islam and changed his name to Abdul Rahman; Bok reclaimed his own name after he escaped from slavery. In my research with the 'Lost Boys' – indeed, this term, while used by many of the youth to refer to themselves, was bestowed upon them by a Western journalist who compared them to the orphans in *Peter Pan* – Chol told me about a name-changing experience his uncle encountered while studying at a university in Khartoum, Sudan's capital. Choli's uncle continually found himself failing at the bottom of the class,

although he studied hard and knew the material. When he complained about this, an acquaintance suggested he change his name to something more Arab-sounding; after Chol's uncle changed his name, he suddenly found himself at the head of the class. Given these contexts, it is understandable why many Sudanese refugees might take a dim view toward having their names changed.[55]

Southern theory research on higher education has also probed the ways in which 'English language dominates academic publishing and how attempts to challenge Western knowledge production can be (mis)read as failure to achieve the "world" standard set up by the North/metropole'.[56] Zodwa Motsa, from a decolonial position, exposes the 'epistemicide and linguicide of knowledges and languages'. Citing an African proverb she starkly writes: 'until the lion tells his/her own story, the hunter will always have the best part of the story.'[57] Similar to the Writing Culture debates of the 1980s in anthropology, researchers must guard against 'authorial egoism'[58] and need self-consciously to relate 'what they see to their own experiences' more explicitly, rather than assuming a neutral and hidden authorial persona.[59]

Students are made aware that imperialism and language is not only relevant to biblical reception and interpretation but also important in relation to historical-critical scholarship of ancient texts in New Testament studies. Decolonising would mean learning about the privileging of Greek and Latin over and against Armenian or Georgian, for example, delimiting the discipline's engagement with texts and traditions outside the Protestant (and even Catholic) canon[60]—thus, working towards a model of biblical studies that not only keeps a focus on ancient historical texts, languages, and contexts, but also works to decolonise its epistemology.

Students are made aware that even the selection of themes and contexts planned and executed by global north researchers inevitably follow patterns of 'valid' research questions which will likely attract funding from research bodies. In the UK, these are often framed around research 'impact' agendas (in social/economic terms). In an allied vein Beth Swadener and Kagendo Mutua reflect on the US academy's complicity in 'cultural imperialism of research funding agencies, particularly in, but not limited to "developing" regions of the world and their role in defining "valid" (read positivist) research'.[61] Nadar warns of the possible implications of such trends where 'CBS reflection in the academy [is used] as a research tool, to allow scholars to be "peeping toms" into the lives of the poor'.[62] Is it, she provocatively asks, 'easier for the poor to pass through the eye of the CBS needle than the rich'?[63] This is surely a valid and discomforting criticism: if the aim, however, is to bring about reflective change in all participants (including the research/facilitator) within the CBS encounter, perhaps there are ways to mitigate concerns regarding intrusion and exploitation.

On a more structural level, Nontando Hadebe also offers important reflections on neo-colonial and neoliberal dynamics within theological curricula and programmes in an African context.[64] She too bemoans their propagation of 'the hegemony of western knowledge'[65] and documents how African theologians defy such forces. In a colonial situation, in which Christian missionary forces subdued indigenous religious traditions, the quest for the transformation of theology programmes must be rooted in inclusion and epistemic justice. Hadebe states:

> The epistemic exclusion in theological education has since its inception been African Indigenous knowledge, gender and lived experiences of Africans. Naidoo (2013) describes the central characteristic of theological institutions in Sub-Saharan Africa as 'foreignness': 'The history of theological education in this region has been characterised basically by foreignness, that is, foreign theological content, methodology and languages. In recent years theological educators have realised the need to take African culture seriously in order to produce a relevant theology for the African people' (p. 6). One of the consequences of the foreignness of theological education is that it detaches students from their context and compromises their ability to respond to the needs of the parishioners and communities in which they serve.

Hadebe also berates the 'commodification' of degree programmes to serve capitalist ends. She notes that widespread 'trading' of theological training and what she calls 'Christian consumerism' (involving higher education providers exporting modules from one context to another through satellite campuses, franchises, etc.) putting particular pressures on higher education institutions in her context[66]:

> Former colonies face additional challenges because the 'product' traded in higher education is western knowledge that further entrenches its hegemony that was established during the colonial and apartheid eras. Consequently, identity, Africanisation, contextualisation and decolonialisation represent resistance in pursuit of transformation that serves the wider social context and not the narrow interests of the market. Theological

education in Africa is embedded in this context and therefore faces similar challenges.[67]

Other Western institutions (with economic and corporate interests) frequently talk (with not unproblematic undertones of capitalism, neo-colonialism, and neoliberalism)[68] about 'marketing', 'selling', and/or 'capturing' an international market.

In light of such critiques, Rafe McGregror and Miriam Sang-Ah Park more boldly call for the entire 'deconstruction' of the 'neo-colonial curriculum'.[69] They employ Frantz Fanon and Çiğdem Kağitçibaşi to explore how this sort of deconstruction could be applied, 'by the prioritisation of theory and practice that [is] sensitive to context'.[70] This involves a destabilising of the neo-colonial curricula normative in the global north that often plays on neoliberal priorities to increase economic reward.[71] They too are highly critical, for example, of the 'rapid increase of international branch campuses' of Western institutions: 'the neoliberal definition of excellence in higher education in economic terms is depriving institutions of the autonomy to determine the curriculum in the global South, which exacerbates the situation.'[72]

Higher education institutions in Africa and across the south need to be situated within southern lived experiences and operate consciously with respect to the specific social context in which they operate, rather than a neoliberal market model imported from the West.[73] Hadebe is clear, however, that African epistemologies should not obliterate Western epistemologies, but rather question their hegemony. She proposes 'pluriversalism' as an alternative epistemological standpoint. This offers:

> a counter-paradigm that attributes equal status to multiple forms of knowledge … and militates against the anti-pluralism of hegemonic western knowledge that recognises only one system of knowledge and advocates instead for multiple systems of knowledge that have equal recognition.[74]

As such, the revised curriculum at Exeter also encouraged students to engage directly with power and privilege in the discipline from their different backgrounds. Students wrote weekly self-reflections and wiki contributions on their own locations (and the privileges these variously offered) and those of the methodologies and authors encountered. Not only did this make students engage in dialogue in a public forum with each other, but also made them sensitive to their various complicities with northern power and epistemologies. This collaborative electronic environment also broke away from the lone historical exegete model and started to embody biblical interpretation as a shared (and civil) endeavour.[75] This sort of reframing of the field replaces the competitive and individualistic neoliberal models prevalent in many curricula with an emancipatory, radical, democratic, and pedagogical model that fosters co-operation.[76] In a review of the new programme, student representatives undertook an analysis which testified to the strengths of the programme in 'facilitating a critical awareness of a diversity of standpoints' and appreciation for opportunities for 'gracious engagement with those with different opinions and life experiences from one's own',[77] though undoubtedly much reflection and reform in this area is still needed.

CURRICULA AND FORGOTTEN/INVISIBLE BODIES

Certain bodies, particularly those perceived as non-normative or disabled, have also frequently been rendered invisible within curricula and intellectual enquiries framed and curated by northern epistemologies and able-bodied researchers. Nirmala Erevelles in her study of curricula notes that disability studies has had little attention within curriculum theory and dominant northern epistemologies are still patterned on the 'vision of the ideal [and able] man'.[78] Ideas of supremacy based on race, gender, and evolutionary hierarchy often structured the colonised as 'backward, infantile and animal like'; as such there can be no significant division between 'the racialized subaltern' and the 'disabled subaltern' in the colonial system.[79] In view of such heritages, it is unsurprising that curricula across the academy risk functioning as exclusionary 'normalizing text[s]'[80] which prevent the construction of emancipatory epistemologies.[81] Erevelles proposes that curricula could play an important part in redressing this divide, in creating encounters which are culturally sensitive, and prioritise, as the cultural minority model of disability promotes the voice of experience rather than the biomedical model of bodily deficiency. This constitutes persons with disabilities sharing their own experiences, cultures, and modes of communication from within their own locations and contexts.

I offer both an option module on disability studies and religion, and contribute on disability to the Liberal Arts programme at Exeter, based in part, on my previous research with members of the British Deaf community, who largely identify themselves as a minority language group (using British Sign Language [BSL], as per the 'minority' model of disability) rather than a people who cannot hear properly (as per the 'medical' model of disability). In introducing students to this area, they are made aware of historical instances of the disempowerment of the Deaf (particularly in reference to their own language) and how this is often experienced as analogous to political colonisation defined as 'a process of physical subjugation, language, culture and mores and the regulation of education on behalf of colonial goals'.[82] Missions to Deaf people founded in the late nineteenth century opposed and vetoed the use of sign language. 'Hearing' missionaries tried to educate with a strong dose of patriarchal paternalism and as such 'seemed to be carrying out a form of cultural imperialism as much as they were spreading the gospel'.[83] As a result of these dynamics, Davis and others have drawn comparisons between colonial racial stigmatisation and Deaf stigmatisation as 'outsiders'.[84] Reacting to these oppressive trends, the 1970s witnessed the rise of the Deaf Pride movement in Northern Europe and America. Deaf Pride involved a recovery of lost (literally silenced) moments of Deaf history, and British Sign Language was at last recognised as a discrete language with its own structure, grammar, and regional variations.[85] This led to the development of cultural dynamics of 'Deaf World' and 'Deaf Way', where sign language was freely used.[86] The colonised were at last openly resisting the oppressive structures that had previously 'silenced' them. The accessibility (or rather inaccessibility) of texts within BSL has though continued to perpetuate an 'outsider' status, even in times of Deaf pride. Whilst the works of Shakespeare are in part now available in BSL, the Bible still is not, although a BSL version is currently in production (as and when time, resources, and funds permit).[87] Hannah Lewis in her steps towards the construction of *Deaf Liberation Theology* brings out the importance of contextual interpretations by the Deaf quite forcefully when she openly states: 'I am not really interested in what hearing people, however involved with Deaf people they might be, have said about what Deaf people think and what a theology of the Deaf would look like!'[88] The import of her claim is that the 'hearing' foreigners need to take careful notice of what the Deaf community's 'signs source' on its own terms has to teach us.

Raising awareness among students of how cultures have sustained ableism (prejudice against non-normative bodies) and sane privilege (invisible advantages accrued to those who have never experienced or been diagnosed or perceived as mentally ill)[89] is key. A group presentation in my option module 'Deviant Bodies? Disability Studies and the New Testament' seeks to achieve this by producing a student-designed 'inclusive' presentation (note the language of 'inclusion' as opposed to 'accessibility' which according to disability studies often leaves normative structures unchanged/unquestioned) to an audience with a 'disability' of their choosing. Students have variously produced sessions designed to engage those with sensory impairments, autism, dyslexia, anxiety, and so on. This enables students to think not only critically and carefully about the subject matter and content they deliver, but also crucially the medium and encounter they construct.[90] In challenging ableism and sanism, the module sensitises students to the limitations of a deficit model of disability (x can't do y because they are disabled) and rather encourages students to try and capture voices of experience (what disability studies calls the 'minority model') to try and think about how different people experience the world. So, for example, a group presentation on autism did not assume the triad of deficits surrounding communication, metaphor, and literalism so often associated with the condition, but rather in light of Temple Grandin's[91] and Tito Mukhopadhyay's[92] autobiographical works focused on sensory awareness in the classroom and visual language.

Whilst examples such as the above of the cultural or 'minority group' model of disability which seeks to garner 'insider' views of complex personal identities and shared rich heritages have an important role to play in challenging ableism and reasserting value in personhood, actual reflection within disability communities hitherto has been scarce and almost exclusively employed in the global north.[93] A review of my own reading lists for the modules I teach attest to this imbalance.[94] This inevitably risks errantly 'universalising' aspects of these d/Deaf experiences into southern spaces. Moreover, 'the agendas of disability pride and celebration in the metropole may appear to stand in stark contrast to the need to prevent mass impairments in the global South'.[95] Helen Meekosha in her work on 'Decolonising disability: thinking and acting globally' also points out that:

> There has been a one-way transfer of ideas and knowledge from the North to the South in this field ... contemporary disability studies constitutes a form of scholarly colonialism, and needs to be re-thought taking full account of the 400 million disabled people living in the global South ... Disability studies *almost never* cites non metropolitan thinkers and *almost never* builds on social theory formulated outside the metropole .[96]

My research on disability in Namibia has alerted me to starkly different experiences of disability in Southern Africa to British contexts.[97] Namibia has policies on community inclusion and inclusive education, and indigenous cultural narratives surrounding conditions are various. Cynthy Haihambo and Elizabeth Lightfoot reveal that belief in 'supernatural causes of disability, such as witchcraft, and/or in the role of improper relationships of family members as causes of disability' impact negatively on experiences of people with disabilities within that context. As such 'inclusion policies' are much more likely to be fruitful if built 'upon positive aspects of cultural beliefs about disability'.[98] Work with d/Deaf experience and Namibian Sign Language (NSL) is also very different to working in British contexts. Many deaf children and adults in rural Namibia have not had access to signed language.[99] The Finnish Association of the Deaf, in collaboration with Namibian National Association for the Deaf (NNAD), have recently been seeking to redress this by training interpreters, producing an NSL dictionary, and raising awareness of deaf issues (including a deaf theatre group performance for school children across Namibia, a documentary on deaf workers, and NSL educational materials).[100] Little, to my knowledge, has been done with NSL translations or interpretations of biblical material hitherto, though some attempts to 'translate' the South African Signed Bible (only itself released in 2019) with Namibian specific signs are ongoing.[101]

More starkly, the processes and practices of (neo-)colonialism have also produced disabled bodies in southern spaces which are rarely acknowledged in disability studies' literature and/or curricula in the metropole: 'war and civil strife, nuclear testing, growth of the arms trade, export of pollution to "pollution havens" and the emergence of sweat shops'.[102] It was in Namibia, for example, that the infamous Nazi eugenicist Eugen Fischer honed trials in 'field research'.[103] Many Namibian skulls were brought back for testing in Europe in the colonial era, for use in research to defend European superiority. The Namibian government has recently petitioned for the return of these body parts which are still to this day retained in European university repositories. The Namibian authorities plan to afford the skulls and bones 'a burial at Heroes' Acre outside the capital Windhoek'.[104]

Connell herself also underlines that disability in the south needs to be situated within social, political, and economic contexts of violence, capitalist accumulation, and material aspects of disability. For her 'global society has to be understood as embodied, and social embodiment as a reality-forming (onto formative) process, not a system-maintaining one'. Moreover, 'intellectual, cultural and social resources of colonised and postcolonial societies'[105] must be disclosed as these offer critical sites for 'disability politics'. There is, she contends, a conspicuous incongruity between disability studies actively challenging one type of normativity, while practicing another. Connell also proposes some more inclusive practices for designing curricula—including interacting with southern literature, poetry, and film, and 'world-centred' rather than 'metropole centred' approaches to disability.[106]

In introducing these contexts to students, it is also vitally important that southern experiences are not filtered through northern frameworks which flatten them, most often seen in the problematic '"ubiquitous 'poster child' narratives of dependency and pity" and represented in pictures of the "disabled beggar"'.[107] In 'Reimagining personal and collective experiences of disability in Africa', Colleen Howell, Theresa Lorenzo, and Siphokazi Sompeta-Gcaza, for example, note that social models of disability need to take seriously indigenous resources for constructive disability models, not just cultural stigma and oppression. They cite the African conception of *Umntu ngumntu ngabantu* (You are who you are because of others) in this regard and suggest that students be encouraged to represent pictorially through posters and presentations, not only the experience of an individual body but also collective responsibility and values, and broader south-south and north-south networks.[108] Accordingly, they construct an African model of disability advocacy and compassion:

> Human beings do not thrive when isolated from others; therefore this [African] framework requires the consideration of values such as: personhood, morality, respect, human dignity, group solidarity, compassion and collective unity. Africa is a melting pot of differences and an African model of disability should be ageless, universal, transcultural, indigenous and humanitarian while fostering social consciousness and disability confidence.[109]

Not acknowledging (or alerting students) to how the epistemologies and practices of the north impact southern bodies, nor how southern perspectives can offer rich constructive standpoints, is not only problematic but also uncompassionate. By engaging with southern sources and experiences, for example, reviews of films and literature produced in the south, students are able to concretely experience a 'pedagogy of discomfort' which alerts them to their privilege of their own contexts, and the ways in which their own contexts have unconsciously or otherwise ethnocentrically silenced, or damaged, others. In my own module students write disability-critical reviews of a South-African produced film *Son of Man*,[110] and the Namibian production, *Katutura* (a township in Windhoek),[111] both featuring cultural and religious narratives surrounding disability, including contested legacies of Christian Western missionary endeavours. Clifford and Montgomery call such encounters 'transformative learning' which purposefully defy dominant and dominating views and assumptions, to instigate access to non-dominant perspectives, and 'encourage new ways of thinking'.[112]

COMPASSIONATE CURRICULA?

In answering the question 'which contexts count within higher education curricula?' the short answer is of course all of them, but one must also be alive to the ways and means by which 'some contexts have counted more than others'. The Anglo-American metropole, and its able-bodied intelligentsia, though often unmarked in discourse, has perhaps (albeit invisibly and hidden) counted far too much. Connell believes that 'the criterion of a good university is its deep diversity', engaging democratically with plural knowledge economies.[113] She berates 'the textbookized curriculum (to coin a horrible name for a horrible phenomenon)' which often 'confronts the student as a pre-determined body of information, techniques and rules'[114] and is undergirded by northern hegemonic power. This 'curriculum as planned' (/product), as opposed to 'curriculum as experienced', often functions 'by consent, below the radar, establishing a regime of common sense in which alternatives can hardly be imagined'.[115] As such, it often leaves unquestioned inequitable knowledge economies and perpetuates exclusion and epistemic injustice. João M. Paraskeva names such processes as 'curriculum epistemicide':

> a deeply embedded belief in the subhumanity of the "Other" continues to linger in the Western mind-set of even its most liberal champions' ... despite all the well-intentioned campaigns and proclamations, the politics of human rights based wittingly or unwittingly on what Paulo Freire termed 'false generosity' has failed miserably to transform the underlying global apparatus, which remains in full bloom within schools and society.[116]

Decolonial reshaping and democratising of curricula for students in view of this is central. In reflecting here on my own social, political, and disciplinary contexts and practices through the lens of southern theory, I have been sensitised to the ways in which the domination of northern epistemologies play out in teaching—explicit, hidden, and null curricula—and research. By engaging students in these sorts of critical and creative enquiries, and by providing them with tools to interrogate assumptions grounding their explicit, hidden, and curricula's complicity with colonialism, one is able to instil within them a 'epistemic disobedience'.[117] Such curricula forefront intercultural issues of power and epistemic injustice and question neoliberal models of education which perpetrate marginalisation and exclusion.[118] To enable and facilitate students to develop compassionate imaginaries and sensitise them to epistemic (in)justice academics need to carefully locate research and curricula within the context of 'project[s] of decolonization that engage with indigenous ways of knowing',[119] being, and living. Pedagogically, these curricula would also offer students critical experiences and skills to cultivate within themselves the collaborative and compassionate forms of thinking needed to be 'democratic agents'[120] within the world.

NOTES

1. Raewyn Connell, *The Good University: What Universities Actually Do and Why It's Time for Radical Change* (Zed Books, 2019). See also Raewyn Connell, 'Southern theory and World Universities' *Higher Education Research & Development* 36:1 (2017), 4–15, Available online at: https://www.tandfonline.com/doi/abs/10.1080/07294360.2017.1252311
2. Connell, *Good*, 9.
3. Connell, *Good*, 75.
4. Connell, *Good*, 77.
5. Connell, 'Southern', 14.
6. Connell, *Good*, 78. She also notes, 'It is not surprising that in Africa, the Islamic world and East Asia, the research-based knowledge formation is often called "Western Science". That is a common view in Europe and North America too, where it is comfortably assumed that "the West" invented modern knowledge and then gifted it to the rest of the world. In fact, the knowledge economy in which the research-based formation emerged is not so much Western as Imperial. The wider world played a crucial role in its history from the beginning.' Connell, *Good*, 73.
7. R.S. Sugirtharajah, 'A Brief Memorandum on Postcolonialism and Biblical Studies' *Journal for the Study of the New Testament* 21 (1999), 3–5. Available online at: https://doi.org/10.1177/0142064X9902107301.

Also Jeremy Punt, 'Postcolonial biblical criticism in South Africa: some mind and road mapping' *Neotestimentica* 37 (2003), 59–85, and Fernando Segovia and Stephen Moore, *Postcolonial Biblical Criticism: Interdisciplinary Intersections* (London: T&T Clark, 2005).

8. Anders Breidlid, *Education, Indigenous Knowledges, and Development in the Global South* (Oxford/New York: Routledge, 2012), 1–2. Connell notes that 'Curriculum from a Latin word meaning "running" has come to mean the content of a course of study. (The Latin root also means "chariot") ... There is fascinating historical literature on how subjects like geography, linguistics or medicine were assembled by academic entrepreneurs. Their work made fresh selections and combinations of existing knowledge, accompanied by exclusions and suppressions. The exclusion of women's healing knowledge, during the development of modern medical curricula is a famous example.' Connell, *Good*, 43.

9. Connell, *Good*, 44.

10. L. Le Grange, 'Decolonising the University Curriculum' *South African Journal of Higher Education* 30/2 (2016), 1–12.

11. Breidlid, *Education*, 2.

12. On the politics of citation and reading lists, see Carrie Mott & Daniel Cockayne, 'Citation matters: mobilizing the politics of citation toward a practice of 'conscientious engagement'' *Gender, Place & Culture* 24:7 (2017), 954–973. Available online at: https://doi.org/10.1080/0966369X.2017.1339022; Kiran Phull, Gokhan Ciflikli, Gustav Meibauer, 'Gender and bias in the International Relations curriculum: Insights from reading lists' *European Journal of International Relations* 25:2 (2019), 383–407. Available online at: https://doi.org/10.1177/1354066118791690; Neema Begum and Rima Saini, 'Decolonising the Curriculum' *Political Studies Review* Volume 17:2 (2019), 196–201. Available online at: https://doi.org/10.1177/1478929918808459

13. Ronald Barnett, 'Knowing and becoming in the higher education curriculum' *Studies in Higher Education* 34:4 (2009), 429–440, 429. Available online at: https://www.tandfonline.com/doi/abs/10.1080/03075070902771978

14. Van der Velden cited in Brenda Leibowitz, 'Cognitive justice and the higher education curriculum' *Journal of Education* 68 (2017). Available online at: http://www.scielo.org.za/scielo.php?script=sci_arttext&pid=S2520-98682017000100006

15. Martha Nussbaum, *Upheavals of Thought: The Intelligence of Emotions* (Cambridge: Cambridge University Press, 2001), 229.

16. Nussbaum, *Upheavals*, 319.

17. Nussbaum, *Upheavals*, 319. See also Y. Waghid, 'Universities and Public Goods: In Defence of Democratic Deliberation, Compassionate Imagining and Cosmopolitan Justice' in E. Bitzer (ed), *Higher Education in South Africa: A Scholarly Look Behind the Scenes* (Stellenbosch: Sun Media, 2009), 71–83. See also Roxanne Rashedi, Thomas G. Plante, and Erin S. Callister, 'Compassion Development in Higher Education' *Journal of Psychology and Theology* 43/2 (2015), 131–139. They note that 'Early research demonstrated that higher education has a significant and lasting impact on a person's values, attitudes, and beliefs (Feldman & Newcomb, 1969). More recent research has examined the long-term effects of higher education—the lasting attitudes, beliefs, and activities of students several years after graduating (Pascarella & Terenzini, 1991) … a college education shapes a student's cognitive, moral, and psychosocial characteristics. Thus, college is an optimal time to focus on compassion cultivation.' Plante et al, 'Compassion', 134–135.

18. Raewyn Connell, 'Using Southern Theory: Decolonizing Social Thought in Theory, Research and Application' *Planning Theory* (2013) 13(2), 210–223.

19. See contributions in Emma Mawdsley, Elsje Fourie, Wiebe Nauta (eds) *Researching South-South Development Cooperation: The Politics of Knowledge Production* (London: Routledge, 2019).

20. Bell cited in Catherine Manathunga and Barbara Grant 'Editorial: Southern Theories and Higher Education' *Higher Education Research and Development* Vol 36 (2017) 1–3, 1.

21. Debbie Epstein & Robert Morrell 'Approaching Southern Theory: Explorations of Gender in South African Education' *Gender and Education* 24 (2012), 469–482.

22. *Oxford English Dictionary*, Available online at: https://www.oed.com/

23. My italicisation. Available online at: https://www.sblsite.org/meetings/Congresses_CallForPaperDetails.aspx?MeetingId=35&VolunteerUnitId=321

24. https://www.sbl-site.org/meetings/blackscholarsmatter.aspx

25. 'George Floyd protests: Oxford demo to target statue of imperialist at university' *Sky News* (9th June 2020), Available online at: https://news.sky.com/story/george-floyd-protests-oxford-demo-to-target-statue-of-imperialist-at-university-12003330. 'Uncomfortable Oxford' ran a series of blogs on statues in the weeks following the George Floyd protests. Available online at: https://www.uncomfortableoxford.co.uk/. Some Oxbridge Colleges are also undertaking research into their colonial past (e.g. former donors whose money came from slavery): for example https://www.sjc.ox.ac.uk/discover/about-college/st-johns-and-colonial-past/. They, of course, are not the only institutions with these

sorts of legacies. Cambridge University has commissioned a study into the ways in which it has both profited and resisted the Atlantic slave trade, during colonialism. See Myriam Francois, 'It's not just Cambridge University—all of Britain benefited from slavery' *The Guardian* (7th May 2019). Available online at: https://www.theguardian.com/commentis-free/2019/may/07/cambridge-university-britain-slavery

26. Rafe McGregor and Miriam Sang-Ah Park, 'Towards a deconstructed curriculum: Rethinking higher education in the Global North' *Teaching in Higher Education* 24(3) (2019), 332–345. Available online at: https://doi.org/10.1080/13562517.2019.1566221

27. 'Only 7% of Social Science authors reviewed were BAME researchers, versus a student population which is 39% BAME for UK domiciled students; 50% of reviewed Social Science authors were female, versus a student population which is 66% female; 99% of reviewed Social Science authors were affiliated to European, North American or Australasian universities, versus a postgraduate student population which is 67% overseas students (69% of which are non-European); 90% of reviewed Science authors were from European, North American or Australasian universities. Whilst national data doesn't exist, 32% of students at the university from which the reading list was taken were from outside the EU.' See K. Schucan Bird and L. Pitman, 'How diverse is your reading list? Exploring issues of representation and decolonisation in the UK' *Higher Education* (2019). Available online at: https://doi.org/10.1007/s10734-019-00446-9

28. Leibowitz, 'Cognitive'.

29. A similar point is made in relation to Brazilian authors and sources by Ines B. Oliveira who notes the 'epistemicide, cognitive [in]justice, ecology of knowledges, and itinerant curriculum theory … especially, Paraskeva's relevance to the area of "curriculum and everyday school life studies" that has emerged in the Brazilian field of curriculum studies, with potentials to influence the intellectual work of Northern curriculum theorists.' Ines B. Oliveira, 'Itinerant Curriculum Theory Against Epistemicides: A Dialogue Between the Thinking of Santos and Paraskeva' *Journal of the American Association for the Advancement of Curriculum Studies* 12/1 (2017). Available online at: https://doi.org/10.14288/jaaacs.v12i1.189708

30. Leibowitz, 'Cognitive'.

31. Raewyn Connell, *Southern Theory* (Cambridge: Polity, 2007), xi.

32. Leibowitz, 'Cognitive'.

33. Leibowitz, 'Cognitive'.

34. Makgoba and Seepe cited in Leibowitz, 'Cognitive'. Open access journals and resources also have an important part to play in this regard in encour-

aging southern authors to be producers, rather than consumers (or worse mere subjects) of published research.

35. See M. Hunter, 'Decentering the White and Male Standpoints in Race and Ethnicity Courses' in A. A. Macdonald and S. Sánchez-Casal (eds), *Twenty-First-Century Feminist Classrooms. Comparative Feminist Studies Series* (New York: Palgrave Macmillan, 2002). Also E. Schüssler Fiorenza, *Democratizing Biblical Studies: Toward an Emancipatory Educational Space* (Louisville: Westminster John Knox, 2009).

36. M. Trelstad, 'The Ethics of Effective Teaching: Challenges from the Religious Right and Critical Pedagogy' *Teaching Theology and Religion* 11 (2008), 191–202.

37. 'Many students and academics have formed working groups to reconsider how existing curricula simultaneously excludes the epistemologies of indigenous people and fails to situate white authors and their theories in a colonial context. However, to rectify this, tokenistic gestures of inclusion are not sufficient. For example, campaigners have critiqued the Politics department for haphazardly adding Fanon and Gandhi to the end of an introductory Politics module without considering the positionality of these authors to the rest of the course. Campaigners argue that adding authors to an ever growing reading list does very little to seriously consider the impact of colonialism in the history of European political thought.' https://www.varsity.co.uk/features/16143

38. https://www.varsity.co.uk/features/16143

39. 'Coloniality is a term used to describe the continuation of colonialism, albeit in different forms, in former colonies after independence. Ndlovu-Gatsheni (2012:1) defines coloniality as the "invisible power structure that sustains colonial relations of exploitation and domination long after the end of direct colonialism". That power according to Grosfoguel (2011:15) is exercised in the "cultural, political, sexual and economic oppression/exploitation of subordinate racialised/ethnic groups by dominant racial/ethnic groups with or without the existence of colonial administrations in contemporary global colonisation". Thus, economic systems that produce and perpetuate inequalities in contemporary Africa have their roots in colonial/apartheid legacies. However, this does not discount the endemic corruption and mismanagement of resources by the ruling elite in contemporary Africa that has further exacerbated the current economic crisis. In addition, some of the oppressive hierarchies such as gender inequality and heterosexual bias are reinforced by Christian and cultural beliefs.' Nontando M. Hadebe, 'Commodification, decolonisation and theological education in Africa: Renewed challenges for African theologians' *HTS Theological Studies*

73/3 (2017). Available online at: http://www.scielo.org.za/scielo. php?script=sci_arttext&pid=S0259-94222017000300050

40. Paulo Freire, *Pedagogy of the Oppressed (30th anniversary ed.) (New York: Bloomsbury, 2000)*.

41. http://ujamaa.ukzn.ac.za/Libraries/manuals/Ujamaa_CBS_bible_ study_Manual_part_1_2.sflb.ashx

42. Hadebe, 'Commodification'.

43. Ernesto Cardenel, *The Gospel in Solentiname*, vol. 4, trans. D. Walsh (Maryknoll: Orbis Books, 1982), 272.

44. Walter Dietrich and Ulrich Luz (eds), *The Bible in a World Context: An Experiment in Contextual Hermeneutics: An Experiment in Contextual Hermeneutics* (Grand Rapids: Eerdmans, 2002).

45. Pablo Richard, 'Jesus: A Latin American Perspective' in Daniel Patte (ed), *The Global Bible Commentary* (Nashville: Abingdon Press, 2004), 338.

46. Alissa Jones cited in Helen John, 'Conversations in Context: Cross-Cultural (Grassroots) Biblical Interpretation Groups Challenging Western-centric (Professional) Biblical Interpretation.' *Biblical Interpretation* 27.1 (2019): 36–68.

47. Randall Bailey, 'Whatever happened to Good Old White Boys? A Review of the Global Bible Commentary' Available online at: https://www. vanderbilt.edu/AnS/religious_studies/GBC/proscons.htm

48. Sarojini Nadar, 'Beyond the "ordinary reader" and the "invisible intellectual": Shifting contextual bible study from liberation discourse to liberation pedagogy' *Old Testament Essays* 22/2 (2009), 384–403. Available online at: http://www.scielo.org.za/scielo.php?script=sci_ arttext&pid=S1010-99192009000200009

49. Nadar, 'Beyond', 388.

50. Valerie Clifford & Catherine Montgomery, 'Designing an internationalised curriculum for higher education: embracing the local and the global citizen' *Higher Education Research and Development* 36(6) (2017), 1138–1151, 1139. Available online at: https://doi.org/10.108 0/07294360.2017.1296413

51. Clifford and Montgomery, 'Designing', 1140.

52. MOOC (Massive Open Online Course) platforms have offered some opportunities in this regard, allowing learning to be scaled up and, in some cases, material to be user-generated which is especially important for garnering voices of experience in the south. For example, a free MOOC run by the University of Exeter on climate change has been able to engage learners on campus with other individuals from across the world (though access to technology is still an issue in some contexts). See Tim Lenton, Damien Mansell, and Exeter Geography alumnus Liam Taylor's MOOC. Details available at: https://lifesciences.exeter.ac.uk/ research/ess/mooc/ also Twitter @ClimateExeter and Facebook. Of

course, whilst the MOOC is itself free, the institution is still capitalising on the labour/experience of those producing user-generated material, and not paying them for it.

53. Connell discussed in Helen Meekosha 'Decolonising disability: thinking and acting globally' *Disability and Society* 26 (2011), 667–682. Available online at: https://doi.org/10.1080/09687599.2011.602860

54. Kagendo Mutua and Beth Blue Swadener, *Decolonizing Research in Cross-Cultural Contexts: Critical Personal Narratives* (New York: State University of New York Press, 2011), 31.

55. Kristen Perry, "'I Want the World to Know': The Ethics of Anonymity in Ethnographic Literacy Research", in G. Walford (ed) *Methodological Developments in Ethnography (Studies in Educational Ethnography, Vol. 12)* (Bingley: Emerald Group Publishing Limited, 2007), 137–154. Helen John's study in Namibia also retained informant's names at their request. See Helen John, *Biblical Interpretation and African Traditional Religion: Cross-Cultural and Community Readings in Owamboland Namibia*, Biblical Interpretation Series Vol 176 (Brill, 2019).

56. Adisorn Juntrasook and James Burford, 'Animating Southern Theory in the Context of Thai Higher Education' *Higher Education Research and Development* 36 (1) (2017), 21–27. Available online at: https://www.tandfonline.com/doi/full/10.1080/07294360.2017.1249069.   See also Sheila Trahar, Adisorn Juntrasook, James Burford, Astrid von Kotze and Danny Wildemeersch, 'Hovering on the periphery? 'Decolonising' writing for academic journals' *Compare: A Journal of Comparative and International Education* 49:1 (2019), 149–167. Available online at: DOI: https://doi.org/10.1080/03057925.2018.1545817

57. Zodwa Motsa, 'When the Lion Tell the Story: A Response from South Africa' *Higher Education Research and Development* 26 (2017), 28–35. Available online at: https://www.researchgate.net/publication/311565769_When_the_lion_tells_the_story_a_response_from_South_Africa

58. Andrea Stöckl, 'Ethnography, Travel Writing and the Self: Reflections on Socially Robust Knowledge and the Authorial Ego' *Forum: Qualitative Social Research* 7 (2006). Available online at: https://doi.org/10.17169/fqs-7.2.113

59. Helen John's recent work on what she calls 'Cross-Cultural Biblical Interpretation' is one compelling example of such an approach. See Helen John, *Biblical*. Also paying attention to the multiplicity of contexts involved in the CBS encounter is H. de Wit, 'Intercultural bible reading and hermeneutics' In H. de Wit, L. Jonker, M. Kool, & D. Schipani (eds), *Through the Eyes of Another: Intercultural reading of the Bible*

(Elkhart: Institute of Mennonite Studies – Vrije Universiteit, 2004), 477–492.

60. At Exeter we are fortunate to have staff with research interests and linguistic competence in such traditions. See Emma Loosley, *Architecture and Asceticism: Cultural Interaction between Syria and Georgia in Late Antiquity* (Leiden: Brill, 2018).

61. Beth Blue Swadener and Kagendo Mutua, 'Decolonizing Performances: Deconstructing the Global Postcolonial' in Norman K. Denzin, Yvonna S. Lincoln, Linda Tuhiwai Smith (eds) *Handbook of Critical and Indigenous Methodologies* (Sage Publishing, 2008), 31–44, 31.

62. Nadar, 'Beyond' 393.

63. Nadar, 'Beyond' 393.

64. Hadebe, 'Commodification'.

65. Hadebe, 'Commodification'.

66. 'The social and political policies that make for starving children, battered women, and the evils of rising fascism remain in place as people learn through prayer to find the tranquillity to live with corrupt political and social structures instead of channelling their distress and anger and anxiety into energy for constructive change (Jantzen 1994:201).' Hadebe, 'Commodification'.

67. Hadebe, 'Commodification'.

68. See Monica Heller, Bonnie McElhinny, *Language, Capitalism, Colonialism: Toward a Critical History* (Toronto: University of Toronto Press, 2017).

69. Rafe McGregor & Miriam Sang-Ah Park (2019) 'Towards a deconstructed curriculum: Rethinking higher education in the Global North', *Teaching in Higher Education* 24:3 (2019), 332–345. Available online at: DOI: https://doi.org/10.1080/13562517.2019.1566221

70. McGregor and Sang-Ah Park, 'Towards'.

71. They talk, for example, about the neo-colonial impulse by Western universities, to found satellite campuses elsewhere in the world. McGregor and Sang-Ah Park, 'Towards'.

72. McGregor and Sang-Ah Park, 'Towards'.

73. Hadebe, 'Commodification'.

74. Hadebe, 'Commodification'.

75. MOOCs have also provided means to engage north/south voices in collaboration, though the availability of technology in some areas could risk another form of oppression (so-called digital exclusion).

76. Fiorenza, *Democratizing*.

77. Theology and Religion Staff/Student Liaison Committee, University of Exeter, feedback.

78. Nirmala Erevelles, 'Understanding curriculum as normalizing text: disability studies meet curriculum theory' *Journal of Curriculum Studies* 37:4 (2005), 421–439, 425. Available online at: DOI: https://doi.org/10.1080/0022027032000276970

79. Erevelles, 'Understanding', 425.

80. Erevelles, 'Understanding', 425.

81. Erevelles, 'Understanding', 421.

82. Hannah Lewis, *Deaf Liberation Theology* (Aldershot: Ashgate, 2007), 32.

83. P. Hitching, *The Church and Deaf People* (Milton Keynes: Paternoster Press, 2003), 23.

84. See Leonard Davis, *Enforcing Normalcy: Disability, Deafness and the Body* (London: Verso, 1995), 78.

85. See Lewis, *Deaf*, 26.

86. Lewis, *Deaf*, 22.

87. http://www.bslbible.org.uk/

88. Lewis, *Deaf*, 6.

89. P. Wolframe, 'The Madwomen in the Academy, or, Revealing the Invisible Straitjacket: Theorizing and Teaching Sanism and Sane Privilege' *Disability Studies Quarterly* Vol 33 (2013). Available online at: http://dsq-sds.org/article/view/3425/3200

90. J. Campbell, L. Gilmore and M. Cuskelly, 'Changing Student Teachers' Attitudes Towards Disability and Inclusion' *Journal of Intellectual & Developmental Disability* Volume 28 (2003), 369–379. See also Louise J. Lawrence, 'Scribes Trained for the Kingdom of Heaven: Reflections on Reading the Bible for Politics in Community, Secondary and Higher Education Contexts in Scotland' *Discourse* Vol 5 (2006), 99–122.

91. Temple Grandin with M. Scariano, *Emergence: Labeled Autistic* (Florida: Costello, 1986).

92. Tito Mukhopadhyay, *The Mind Tree* (New York: Arcade Publishing, 2003).

93. See Louise Lawrence, *Sense and Stigma in the Gospels: Depictions of Sensory-Disabled Characters* (Oxford: Oxford University Press, 2013). Also M. Hewerdine, 'Studying the New Testament using a Disability Hermeneutic: Notes for Contextual Bible Studies' MA Dissertation, Queens Foundation for Ecumenical Theological Education, Birmingham, UK (2011). Available online at: https://www.academia.edu/2252176/_Studying_the_New_Testament_using_a_Disability_Hermeneutic_Notes_for_Contextual_Bible_Studies_

94. Reference guides on disability and southern thought and experience will be a welcome resource in this respect: 'Established and emerging scholars alongside advocates adopt a critical and interdisciplinary stance to probe, challenge and shift common held social understandings of disability in established discourses, epistemologies and practices, including

those in prominent areas such as global health, disability studies and international development. Motivated by decolonizing approaches, contributors carefully weave the lived and embodied experiences of disabled people, families and communities through contextual, cultural, spatial, racial, economic, identity and geopolitical complexities and heterogeneities. Dispatches from Ghana, Lebanon, Sri Lanka, Cambodia, Venezuela among many others spotlight the complex uncertainties of modern geopolitics of coloniality; emergent forms of governance including neoliberal globalization, war and conflicts; the interstices of gender, race, ethnicity, space and religion; structural barriers to redistribution and realization of rights; and processes of disability representation.' Shaun Grech and Karen Soldatic, *Disability in the Global South: The Critical Handbook* (Switzerland: Springer, 2016). https://www.researchgate.net/publication/321540655_Disability_in_the_Global_South_The_Critical_Handbook

95. Meekosha, 'Decolonising', 669.
96. Meekosha, 'Decolonising', 669.
97. Lawrence et al, 'Disability and Embodiment in Namibia: Religious and Cultural Perspectives' A University of Exeter and University of Namibia partnership project funded by the UK's Arts and Humanities Research Council. For further details see project blog, available online at: http://blogs.exeter.ac.uk/disabilitynamibia/
98. Cynthy Haihambo and Elizabeth Lightfoot, 'Cultural Beliefs Regarding People with Disabilities in Namibia: Implications for the Inclusion of People with Disabilities' *International Journal of Special Education* 25/3 (2010), 76–87. Available online at: University of Minnesota Digital Conservancy, http://hdl.handle.net/11299/171770
99. Davíð Bjarnason, Valgerður Stefánsdóttir and Lizette Beukes 'Signs speak as loud as words: deaf empowerment in Namibia' *Development in Practice* 22 (2012), 190–201. Available online at: https://doi.org/10.1080/09614524.2012.640986
100. Bjarnason et al., 'Signs'.
101. See Bible Society statement on signed translations across the globe at: https://www.biblesociety.co.za/index.php/take-action/projects/19-projects/80-english-bible-for-the-deaf
102. Meekosha, 'Decolonising', 669. Likewise, 'The civil wars and genocide that have swept many postcolonial countries in the twentieth and twenty-first centuries producing mutilation and impairments barely rate a mention in mainstream disability studies literature.' Meekosha, 'Decolonising', 669. Others too note 'A more common argument that these scholars have advanced, is that while Western countries seek to universalize their disability ideology and development agenda, they, through their neoliberal

capitalist activities such as wars, environmental pollution, and hazardous industrial activities continue to be a major cause of impairment in the global South. These critical disability studies scholars argue that despite accounting for over 80 percent of the global population of disabled people, the global South remains at the periphery of "development policy, research and programs, and virtually excluded from the Western-centric disability studies" (Grech, 2011:87). In addition, they emphasize how the "universalization" of Western-founded disability paradigms has negative impacts, especially on the global South where experiences of disability may be profoundly different.' Privilege Haang'andu, 'Transnationalizing Disability in Embedded Cultural-Cognitive Worldviews: The Case of Sub-Saharan Africa' *Disability and the Global South* 5/1 (2018), 1292–1314, 1292. Available online at: https://disabilityglobalsouth.files.wordpress.com/2018/02/dgs-05-01-06.pdf

103. See Susan Arndt, 'Blinded by Privilege: The West and the Rest Under Lockdown', *De Gruyter Conversations* Spring 2020. Available online at: https://blog.degruyter.com/white-privilege-in-the-time-of-covid-19/

104. 'Namibia Wants Back Skulls Held at German Universities' *DW Made for Minds*. Available online at: https://www.dw.com/en/namibia-wants-back-skulls-held-at-german-universities/a-3729704

105. Raewyn Connell, 'Southern Bodies and Disability: Rethinking Concepts' *Third World Quarterly* 32 (2011) Available online at: https://doi.org/1 0.1080/01436597.2011.614799

106. Raewyn Connell, 'Masculinities in global perspective: hegemony, contestation, and changing structures of power' *Theory and Society* 45/4 (2016), 303–318. Available online at: https://doi.org/10.1007/s11186-016-9275-x

107. Meekosha cited in Colleen Howell, Theresa Lorenzo and Siphokazi Sompeta-Gcaza, 'Reimagining personal and collective experiences of disability in Africa' *Disability & the Global South* 6/2 (2019), 1719–1735, 1720.

108. 'While most of the students stressed the inherent rights of a disabled person as an individual, they also emphasised the collective responsibility of the community towards, as one student put it, "solving the challenges of disability". Such community responsibility involved "Nondisabled people form(ing) alliances with disabled people to advocate for their rights, management of personal support, liaise with other services and advocate for removal of barriers in the local environment" (Justus Mckenzie Nthitu), while another student used the African proverb "Together we can lift an elephant" (Patrice M Malonza) to capture the importance of the collective in responding to disability." Reimagining personal and collective

experiences of disability in Africa.' Howell, Lorenzo and Sompeta-Gcaza, 'Reimagining', 1723.

109. Howell, Lorenzo and Sompeta-Gcaza, 'Reimagining', 1724.
110. Directed by Mark Dornford-May, *Son of Man* (2006) is a South African interpretation of the life of Jesus. This was the first South-African film to be unveiled at the Sundance festival. I am deeply indebted to Victoria Omotoso's research on this film's cross-cultural reception in her PhD thesis at the University of Exeter which I have co-supervised. She has also helped me at various points delivering reflective material on this film to students in my modules.
111. *Katatura* (2015) is a Namibian drama, directed by Florian Schott.
112. Valerie Clifford and Catherine Montgomery, 'Designing an internationalised curriculum for higher education: embracing the local and the global citizen' *Higher Education Research and Development* 36(6) (2017), 1138–1151.
113. Connell, *Good*, 43.
114. Connell, *Good*, 45
115. Connell, *Good*, 46.
116. João M. Paraskeva, *Curriculum Epistemicide: Towards an Itinerant Curriculum Theory* (Oxford/New York: Routledge, 2015), x.
117. N. Martin Nakata, Victoria Nakata, Sarah Keech and Reuben Bolt Nura Gili, 'Decolonial goals and pedagogies for Indigenous studies' *Decolonization: Indigeneity, Education and Society* Vol 1 no 1 (2012), 120–140.
118. Clifford and Montgomery 'Designing'.
119. Xuan Thuy Nguyen 'Critical Disability Studies at the Edge of Global Development: Why Do We Need to Engage with Southern Theory?' *Canadian Journal of Disability Studies* 7 (2018). Available online at: https://doi.org/10.15353/cjds.v7i1.400
120. Noah De Lissovoy, (2011) 'Pedagogy in Common: Democratic education in the global era' *Educational Philosophy and Theory*, 43:10 (2011), 1119–1134, 1119. Available online at: https://doi.org/10.1111/j.1469-5812.2009.00630.x

Compassionate Campus Climates: Confronting Privilege and Prejudice with Compassionate Citizenship

The death on 25 May 2020 of George Floyd—an African-American man in Minneapolis, who handcuffed, face down on the road, pleaded, 'Please, I can't breathe', whilst a white police officer kneeled on his neck for over eight minutes—has (re-)ignited anti-racism protests, responses, and performative actions across the world.[1] Higher education institutions released statements in response to the events, many of which rehearsed their commitment to equality, diversity, and inclusion, and the 'Black Lives Matter' cause. Some have criticised these assertions as 'toothless': 'an unholy alchemy of risk management, legal liability, and trustee anxiety'.[2] Tahmina Choudhery in her frank assessment of university media statements pointedly asked, 'Why do you suddenly care now?' She writes:

The conversations have all gone something like this:

University:	"We have a commitment to exposing and challenging racial inequality"
Students:	"Why don't you have a single black professor then?"
University:	"We stand together with our black students, staff, and communities"
Students:	"I literally dropped out of your university because you took no action against racist bullying"
University:	"We are proud of our diversity and welcome students from 140 different countries"

L. J. Lawrence, *Refiguring Universities in an Age of Neoliberalism*, Palgrave Critical University Studies, https://doi.org/10.1007/978-3-030-73371-1_5

Students:	"This vague statement isn't even the bare minimum, why don't you use words like race or black?"
University:	"We have a Zero Tolerance approach to any harassment and work hard to create a welcoming and diverse experience"
Students:	"Why don't you ever take any actual action to support PoC, to diversify your curriculum or to listen to our concerns?"[3]

Jonathan Flowers, writing in *The Chronicle of Higher Education*, also dismisses many institutional edicts as what Sara Ahmed would categorise as 'the reduction of diversity to "image work"',[4] the 'shiny veneer of diversity',[5] and 'equality and diversity pride'.[6] Ahmed's ethnographic research among 'diversity practitioners' in UK and Australian universities notes that strategic focus on diversity (pledging rather than being bound, managing rather than challenging) often works against diversity becoming embedded and habitual within an institution. So much so, that the metaphor of 'brick [white?] walls' is often used, and racism is accordingly seen as something to be gotten 'over'[7] in institutional life. More-'over', Ahmed warns that 'speaking about racism is … heard as an injury not to those who speak, but to those who are spoken about'[8] as such those who experience racism are all too often perceived as, or feel they are, challenging or difficult within an institution.

Such feelings were made explicit in my own institution in March 2020 when an article entitled 'This is what unpalatable student activism costs' was published by a female student of colour at the University of Exeter. It documented the visceral and explicit sexualised threats and racist abuse she had been subject to both on campus and online.[9] She felt compelled to publically document her experience after a year of feeling 'quite outstandingly – alone' not 'as an act of reckless misconstrued activism: but simply because staying silent mean[t] putting it aside and being expected to go on as normal'.[10] Two years earlier, screenshots were posted of racist, sexist, and bigoted messages circulated within a University of Exeter Bracton Law Society private WhatsApp group.[11] Both incidents employed words, as critical race theorists would identify, as 'weapons to ambush, terrorize, wound, militate, and degrade',[12] and as vehicles of hate:

> Verbal and written words, and symbolic acts, that convey a grossly negative assessment of particular persons or groups, based on their race, gender, ethnicity, religion, sexual orientation, or disability. It is not limited to face-to-face

confrontations or shouts from the crowd. It may appear on shirts, on posters, on classroom blackboards, on student bulletin boards.[13]

Incidents such as the above, alongside more casual and indirect expressions of discrimination, are regrettably not infrequent within the higher education sector. An inquiry directed by the Equality and Human Rights Commission (EHRC) notes that racism (and other forms of prejudice) is a common experience for many within UK universities.[14] In the US, too, evidence of such incidents are widespread.[15] So also is the recognition that discrimination and bigotry cannot be combated without due acknowledgement of how certain groups exert power and privilege within colleges and university: 'including the power to define racism and its injury and to impose a cultural norm that will be the premise of debate as well as social life'.[16]

Institutional climate—'how students experience their campus environment'[17]—is a critical element. Negative climates hinder educational attainment and developmental outcomes.[18] Jodi Linley notes that contributing dimensions of negative campus climates include historical legacies of exclusion, lack of structural diversity (demographics of student enrolment), psychological dimensions (connecting negative experiences to mental ill health of students), and behavioural dimensions (the ways in which students interact with one another).[19] It is particularly behavioural dimensions which relate to harassment and aggression. Linley cites three forms of campus aggressions: invalidations (disregard for the thoughts, emotions, or experiences of others), insults (offensive, vulgar, and insolent disrespect for a persons' traditions or identities), and assaults (including hateful speech and 'purposeful discriminatory actions').[20] More broadly, she also highlights a frequently perceived disconnect for (minoritised) students between an institution's claimed dominant values surrounding diversity and inclusion (such as those reiterated in the wake of George Floyd's death), and their own encounters on campus: 'students of color can feel a sense of belonging among their racial or ethnic subculture while simultaneously feeling alienated from the larger institutional environment.'[21] Alison Phipps, more cynically, points out the chasm felt between individuals and the branding of universities in this regard:

> On billboards and in glossy magazines, to be marketable means to appear unblemished: and the 'brand naming' of the university ... mean[t] that not only must the institution be polished, but all flaws must be airbrushed out.[22]

Recognising that campus climates can be perceived differently according to different identities and group membership, Robert Reason and Susan Rankin submit that whilst in many institutions racial and ethnic diversity of college-going populations has increased, this diversification without intentional education about issues of identity and difference may result in negative exchanges and outcomes.[23] They contend that planned multicultural experiences for students and intentional policies and programmes that foster respectful and honest interactions[24] are critical in developing positive and compassionate campus climates. In creating more open and safe environments, institutions can start to ensure more democratic experiences and developmental outcomes for all their students.

This sort of positive intentional action has marked responses within the University of Exeter to the hostile incidents which opened this chapter. Anti-racism rallies and campaigns were swiftly organised in 2018, united by the inclusive and defiant mantra 'We are all Exeter'.[25] Formal internal investigations were also conducted, and expulsions and sanctions were taken against perpetrators. But these actions alone, without addressing broader cultural change, were seen to be insufficient. As such the university launched the Provost Commission to eliminate all forms of harassment and discrimination across its campuses, and to advocate, construct, and implement initiatives to promote a more open, diverse, and safe environment for all.[26] Darryl Brown notes that such institutional transformations require authentic dialogue free from suspicion and a broad commitment to compassion: 'a sentiment of community strong enough to enable each group to entrust its fate to the good faith and decency of the other'.[27] He notes that in acknowledging injustice, 'we can begin to reform institutions in which the repression of race-specific [or other minoritized bodies'] experience will be replaced by acknowledgement and empowerment'.[28]

Accordingly, in this chapter, I will seek to identify the underlying power, prejudice, and privilege dynamics which at least in part can be seen to undergird the aggressive incidents at Exeter and allied cases more broadly within the sector. The ways in which (toxic) online material also impacts face-to-face campus relationships will be probed. I will then chart selected preventative and constructive interventions initiated under the auspices of the Provost Commission at Exeter centred on (a) Induction and Awareness and (b) Anti-racist Pedagogies and Learning and Teaching, in particular, as these were implemented within my own discipline. These interventions were specifically designed to develop what Martha Nussbaum refers to as 'compassionate citizenship'—'an awareness of cultural difference ... in order to promote respect for another that is the essential underpinning for dialogue'[29]—within an affirmative and progressive campus climate.[30] These interventions also underscore Seyla Benhabib's named dynamics essential for developing democratic citizenship: the fostering of a collective identity, a sense of the responsibilities of membership, and the championing of social rights and benefits of all.[31] Citizenship is a concept which can break down institutional 'walls' of which Ahmed speaks. Authentic citizenship also compels, discomforting as it may be, honest attention and authentic self-reflection on one's own positionality alongside the 'stories of others',[32] including those subject to the attacks which opened this chapter. Much written on campus discrimination tends to present decontextualised institutional cases, perhaps for fear of organisational reputation (it is interesting how the Bracton Law WhatsApp group incident is, for example, now frequently referred to as a 'scandal').[33] However, Phipps notes the critical importance of candid institutional self-reflection with regard to privilege, prejudice, and power relations, for these ultimately shape the campus climate for all within a university.[34] Exeter's story is a powerful exemplar of such a discomfortingly self-reflective approach.

PRIVILEGE AND PREJUDICE ON CAMPUS

The University of Exeter is a sizeable and diverse organisation with staff from over 80 countries and students from over 130 countries.[35] It is part of the Russell Group (a collection of 'research intensive' elite universities in the UK) which on average have lower black student numbers than other institutions (less than 4% compared with UK average of 8%).[36] It has formal commitments to increasing the diversity of its student population through recruitment, widening participation initiatives, and the Centre for Social Mobility.[37] Greater diversity, however, does not simplistically equate to a more inclusive campus climate without intentional education about issues of diversity and identity within its existent student body.[38] Indeed, Exeter has been seen by many both within and external to its campuses as marred by racism.

Critical race theory provides important tools to think with in relation to harassment and aggression against minoritised bodies and identities on campus. Linley notes that, first, issues of power, dominance, and normative identities (such as whiteness in historically white-dominated campuses or 'laddish' masculinities) need frank and critical interrogation. Second, minoritised 'individual's narratives' need to be made explicit and heard by others as 'legitimate and authoritative knowledge' which can usefully 'redirect ... the dominant gaze'[39] and unmask prejudices and predetermined biases within contexts. The author of 'This is what unpalatable student activism costs' voiced as much when she openly stated:

> I do not want sympathy. I do not want solidarity when all solidarity is a whispered word that makes you feel revolutionary. I want this to not occur again, and I am not being falsehearted or martyrish in saying "it's fine if it's me, change it for the future" – but that it should not have happened at all.[40]

Theorists note that acknowledging power and privilege is important in combatting prejudice, harassment, aggression, and discrimination, because it is often these ideologies which scaffold and maintain patterns of social hierarchy:

> Harassment occurs as those in more powerful, dominant social groups attempt to oppress targeted social groups. Women, LGBT students, and students of color experience harassment at greater rates than male, straight, or white students because of their lack of power in the social system. Harassment occurs as individuals from dominant groups attempt to maintain their social power; harassment also occurs as members of target groups attempt to advance their relative position at the expense of other target groups.[41]

Privilege can be understood through Peggy McIntosh's vivid metaphor as 'an invisible, weightless knapsack of special provisions – unearned assets of which one is often oblivious'.[42] Such privileges can also undergird prejudicial attitudes towards non-privileged or minoritised groups, in particular contexts, which can at times be made manifest in extreme forms such as the hate speech incidents at Exeter, but also (often unwittingly or casually) through discourse, processes, and practices.[43] Within higher education, 'hyper-privilege' is often accorded to those who are white and male. These identities accordingly hold the most systemic power to either sustain or contest prejudice on campus.[44] White privilege and its associated economic power[45] ('advantages[s accrued] as a white middle-class person'[46]) is often cited in this respect. Frances Henry and Carol Tator trace the 'impact of hegemonic whiteness and the process of racialization that continue[s] to function in the academy'.[47] Diane Lynn Gusa too in her study of 'White Institutional Presence: The Impact of Whiteness on

Campus Climate' emphasises the significance of race by examining the culture of whiteness within mainly 'White institutions'. White mainstream ideology, and what she terms white institutional presence (WIP) (which often undergirds white supremacy),[48] is shown to have the following main features: white ascendancy ('thinking and behaviour that arises from White mainstream authority an advantage ... a sense of superiority a sense of entitlement, domination over racial discourse and white victimization')[49], monoculturalism and white blindness ('racial ideology which protects white identity and privilege')[50], and white estrangement ('distancing of whites physically and socially from People of Color').[51] Politically, too, neoliberalism has reinforced the structures of access to the advantages of mentoring, patronage, and power that whiteness brings, and as such, neo-liberalism frequently 'fails to acknowledge racism by reinforcing the notion that neoliberalism is for the good of the whole of society, rather than a select few'.[52]

In reference to campuses, David Brunsma, Eric Brown, and Peggy Placier point out the 'walls of whiteness' offer protection from 'attacks on white supremacy'; they also submit 'that walls of class privilege, patriarchy, heterosexism, and ableism also "shield" [certain] students' from critical self-questioning or self-analysis. As such, 'most white students emerge from college with their walls of whiteness essentially unchallenged, unscathed, and often strengthened'.[53] Nolan León Cabrera, too, in his exposure of 'whiteness'[54] noted that white student interviewees in his research could see limited evidence of racism and actually at times identified themselves as the 'true victims of multiculturalism (i.e. reverse racism)', a sentiment he sees grounding an entitlement for white students to maintain 'homogenous campus sub-environments':

> This sense of racial victimization corresponded to the participants blaming racial minorities for racial antagonism (both on campus and society as a whole), which cyclically served to rationalize the persistence of segregated, white campus sub-environments. Within these ethnic enclaves, the participants reported minimal changes in their racial views since entering college with the exception of an enhanced sense of 'reverse racism,' and this cycle of racial privilege begetting racial privilege was especially pronounced within the fraternity system. [55]

Annemarie Vaccaro similarly in her feminist analysis of sexism and racism in universities notes frequent male hostility towards equity initiatives[56] and 'resentment toward[s] a liberal bias'.[57] The online comments on the Exeter Bracton Law Society WhatsApp group ('Dodgy blokes soc')—'if you ain't English, go home', 'we need a race war'[58]—could be evidence of such a mind-set. So too could the harassment (mainly via anonymous re-routed e-mails) of the student of colour which has similarities to those racialised hostilities experienced elsewhere in predominantly white institutions.[59]

Laddism/laddish masculinities (often comprising misogynist repartee, 'objectification of women and pressure around quantities and particular forms of sexual interaction and activity'[60]) as a source of everyday sexism and rape culture too are a potent force in campus prejudice. The 'lad' was the subject of the UK National Union of Studies 2010 report 'Hidden Marks: A Study of Women Students' Experiences of Harassment, Stalking Violence and Sexual Assault'[61] and their 2013 report 'That's What She Said: Women Students' Experiences of "Lad Culture" at Universities'.[62] In both these reports, undergraduate laddishness was typified by excessive intake of alcohol, sport clubs, heterosexual bravado, sexual conquests, and adopting casual approaches to university work and study.[63] Ruth Lewis, Susan Marine, and Kathryn Kenny in their feminist activist work[64] with 33 women based in higher education institutions across the UK and US note accordingly how universities can be constructed as unsafe spaces for women:

> [With] the university as a hotbed of laddism, there is a risk that the university – a site of potential empowerment and liberation for women (and men) – becomes re-positioned as a danger zone. The limited focus on danger and safety belies the potential of universities to enhance human freedoms through intellectual endeavour.[65]

Whilst laddism has traditionally been associated in British contexts with working-class social locations, in reference to universities, it has also incorporated a persuasive focus on 'white middle- and upper-class men', which presents an opportunity to reflect on different embodiments of laddish masculinities 'instead of positioning them as universal/default or obscuring their specific behaviours and practices with vague notions of hegemony'.[66] Furthermore, laddish masculinities at elite universities are often manifest through 'domineering demeanours' often used to threaten or scare women or groups perceived as 'other', 'rather than [just being anti-social or] disruptive'.[67] Ruth Lewis et al. make two inferences with regard to laddism's construction: first, 'lad culture in universities can be conceived of as part of a backlash to women's encroachment on traditionally male environments'.[68] The middle-class lad is not relegated or side-lined, but he may sense he is, and as such:

> the aggressive sexism perpetrated in social spaces by privileged men can be seen as an attempt to preserve or reclaim territory, contextualized in relation to the backlash against feminism more broadly, and the idea of higher education 'feminization' in particular. Related to the performances of educational dominance mentioned in the previous section, it is possible to see hostile sexism in the social sphere as a defensive response from men accustomed to topping the ranks. Broader 'widening participation' agendas in higher education may also be pertinent, since extant laddism often incorporates classism and racism as well.[69]

Second, she also warns that the portrayal of campuses as unsafe for young women 'runs the risk of a neoconservative paternalistic response' where the aim of the institution is characterised as 'protect[ing] young women from marauding, excessive masculinity' rather than challenging its underlying causes.[70] Such responses also perpetuate dangerous stereotypes of masculine sexual predatory behaviours and women as 'responsible for preserving sexual restraint' and as such risk 'limiting rather than expanding women's freedoms'.[71] The author of 'This is what unpalatable student activism costs' attests to such limitations when she recalls:

> I was offered a "welfare support caseworker" in meetings, and I could ask for mitigation "if I needed it." I refused. I was shown safe paths to take and given a rape alarm. The rape alarm astounded me. I had not been assaulted yet, at this point. The sheer defeatism in it frightened me. I was being sexually harassed, possibly stalked, and being sent threats of rape and murder – constantly. Was this my pound of flesh, then? An offer of an extension and a rape alarm?[72]

Of course the ill effects of whiteness and laddism are often shifting, contextual and differently performed and enacted in various social arenas and spaces. Kevin Gin et al. note that whilst micro aggressions occur more regularly within face-to-face settings, cyberspace facilitates more overt aggressions that can 'include photos and references to physical violence, demeaning equivocations, slurs' and as such 'these incidents are not micro, but represent blatant discrimination'.[73] The online forums, including user-anonymous platforms, become spaces of discrimination in which social dynamics which contour campus cultures are amplified and played out:[74]

> bestow[ing] privileges to users to liberate themselves from the constraints of accountability that normally mediated the facilitation of hostile comments in online forums. The results of removing these inhibitions led to statements that were often shocking to encounter and read.[75]

Overt harassment, aggression, and discrimination in online forums cause students to feel uncertainty about the genuineness of peer relations on campus and that 'the experience of living in a state of paranoia [or racial/gender battle fatigue] has the potential to contribute to beliefs that [they] are under constant surveillance by White members of the campus community'.[76] The author of 'This is what unpalatable student activism costs' accordingly testifies to the emotional and mental toll that harassment and aggression took on her:

> If mental health is a buzzword then let me press the buzzer. I cannot function on this campus. I begin sweating and hyperventilating in crowded, student-heavy areas of campus. I hadn't needed trigger warnings previously: yet now racialized slurs or scenes of sexual violence even in films, books, whatever – sets my heart beating because I can't help thinking of this. I can't walk with a raised head – I constantly look at the floor. I have seen someone that I think – it could be them, and I have to be sick, immediately. I'm constantly shivering, even when it isn't cold. I adore going out and partying and having a laugh: now I can't go on a single night out without being immensely tense and constantly on the lookout. There is not one day since last March that I had not thought about all of this.[77]

Such incidents not only have a deep and persistent effect on wellbeing, but also the 'demoralisation brought by abuse' can lead to 'ghettoization, as collective defensiveness and an urge to find safety in numbers strengthen group identification'[78], isolation, or at times withdrawal altogether from what is experienced as a negative and oppressive institutional climate. This is compounded if the individual subject to the harassment feels unsupported or let down by the institution. Researchers focusing on institutional responses to alleged harassment cases frequently note what has been termed a feeling of 'institutional betrayal'. This is a phenomenon when an individual who relies on the protections of an institution experiences a rupture in that support or feels their voice has not been heard or sufficiently responded to.[79] The author of 'This is what unpalatable student activism costs', for example, voiced her dismay at being asked to share abusive and sexually explicit messages about her body with male senior management, also the way in which she felt silenced by the entire process.[80]

> The University had assured me, in my very first meeting, how "lucky" I was that I had such a stable support network, and that my issue reached their ears immediately. I was lucky. I had a support network, I had friends, I had a partner who would die for me. This was why I was constantly asked to go to the police, or to pursue this, or to keep forwarding these on, or to keep these in my inbox: because what if it happened to *someone else*? That was the line of justification: what if others were targeted. I had to sit there, receiving a barrage of vitriol and threats, listening about *what if it happened to someone else*? What would that someone else look like? Less vocal? Less prone to journalistic ventures? White? Would that be the someone that I endure this for? ... But I did what was told, by almost everyone, for a year. I stayed quiet about this except with people I unequivocally trusted. I didn't expose anything. If members of the press approached me about anything unrelated or tangentially related, I directed them to the University. I have played at being a marionette for a year in the hopes of something ceasing, or myself somehow coming out of this unscathed because I did what they said and kept it quiet. But the police said once they can't do anything and I can't keep running to them over it. Perhaps I have attacked the institution too much, however. Perhaps they are tired of it.[81]

Others warn that the swift censoring and expulsions of perpetrators of abuse by institutions are often right and proper, though action taken on a case-by-case basis, and disciplinary measures meted out only to individuals who get caught, will never be sufficient to change an institutional culture or climate:[82]

> When universities do take action it is usually in a punitive and individualistic fashion that both fails to address the roots of problems and has tremendous potential to exacerbate other inequalities ... In contrast to [the] picture of the violent serial rapist the theorisation [here] suggests that many acts of sexual violence at university stem from a variety of more spontaneous boundary-crossings shaped by intersectional cultures of masculinity and scaffolded by the patriarchal and neo-liberal rationalities of the institution.[83]

Phipps notes that survivors often have few options, but to speak out in what she terms the 'outrage economy of the corporate media'.[84] Again, the author of 'This is what unpalatable student activism costs' gives voice to such sentiments when she writes:

> [If someone is in] an institution, and is being suffocated, threatened – do not placate them and say the only onus is with the police. Instead, engage in antiracist movements rather than tokenistic campaigns ... The message is not to be kind, and love one another and espouse the Institutional Values: it's to look racism in the eye and take concrete action. A decolonized University is an actively antiracist one. This does not mean a campaign: this means not staying silent, or encouraging silence about something so horrific that is evidently going on in this environment. This is going on at this institution, these are the thoughts certain individuals on this campus have: that should be acknowledged, and understood.[85]

What is important here is that institutional response is not merely seen as neoliberal brand preservation, 'airbrushing', and/or 'bolster[ing] punitive technologies'.[86] Actually, both this student's account and the leaking of the Bracton Law Society's racist postings have already become within the institution 'affective political force[s]'[87] which have aroused institutional outrage, agitation, and disgust and have stimulated and enforced ongoing critical reflection on how to foster a more positive climate. In their article on allied mediations of gender and sexual violence, Phipps et al. note how voices of resistance can reclaim digital media (often the means of their abuse) as a 'generative activist space' to form 'affective solidarities'.[88] The University of Exeter has, I believe, taken these voices very seriously and made it an ongoing priority to manifest its 'affective solidarity' with those subject to harassment and prejudice and address instances of abuse. Moreover, the university has, as will be seen, initiated activities and interventions designed to implement broader cultural changes, including a decolonising network, and anti-racist boards with student and staff representation, which make important steps towards embodying an other-regarding and compassionate campus climate, though there is of course still a long way to go on this.

Confronting Privilege and Prejudice with Compassionate Citizenship

In May 2018, the Provost at Exeter founded a commission (comprised of students, academics, and professional services) to advocate and action resources, policies, and interventions to ensure that Exeter was 'an open, diverse and safe university community for all'.[89] Research reveals that 'a power-and-privilege-cognizant approach requires campus climate issues be examined from a systemic perspective' as 'no single intervention is powerful enough to affect institutional change'.[90] As a result, the commission worked closely with Equality, Diversity and Inclusivity teams and other relevant parties across the institution. Other prominent initiatives, including the setting up of a decolonial network, were facilitated at the initiation of staff, students, and people of colour within the institution.

In response to the Bracton Law Society WhatsApp group incident, a key priority in the earliest phase of the commission was to improve and augment systems and tools for reporting harassment. 'Exeter Speaks Out' was initiated. Institutional 'Speak Out Guardians' were appointed 'to act in an independent and impartial capacity', 'help create an open culture which is based on listening and learning', 'provide expertise in developing a safe culture within the University community', 'oversee the governance and management of reported issues', 'make sure university effectively responses to concerns and supporting staff and students who raise them', and provide leadership and support to the pre-existing Dignity and Respect Advisor network.[91] A bystander/intervention training toolkit was also introduced and championed within the campus community.[92] Bystander interventions denote those actions and interventions 'taken by "ordinary" people in response to incidents of interpersonal or systemic harassment',[93] discrimination, and abuse. It works through training and development of individuals as 'pro-social citizens',[94] empowered to challenge and confront perpetrators based on appropriate knowledge, compassionate social norms, and other-regard for peers:[95]

> These include being aware of a situation in which someone is being victimized, making a prior commitment to help, having a sense of partial responsibility for helping, believing that the victim has not caused the situation to occur, having a sense of self efficacy in possessing the skills to do something, and to have seen others modeling such pro-social behaviour.[96]

In evaluations of this intervention elsewhere, bystander approaches have been positively linked with more developed empathetic and compassionate responses to others and more awareness and transformed attitudes towards bullying and harassment.[97] The courage to call out discrimination on online forums is also important in this respect. Kevin Gin et al. note that:

> Antiracist education and discourse regarding how all students can engage in actions that advance justice and equity in social media environments, while simultaneously dismantling home territories that harbor racism would further contribute to the elimination of White supremacy that has acted as the dominant mechanism of racialized oppression in online spaces.[98]

Researchers in higher educational contexts too have probed interactions and encounters during university years which harbour 'the potential to be transformative', 're-shape attitudes and values',[99] and 'develop cross-cultural competencies'.[100] The university is a space in which (discursively at least) a liberal ethos is forwarded and ideals of equality and democratic citizenship should be upheld as models.[101] The University of Exeter accordingly pledged to:

> Continue to build trust with our community and encourage reporting so that we can take informed action. We cannot take for granted that our students and staff have lived in diverse communities before arriving at Exeter— we need to raise understanding, change attitudes and develop skills. Some members of our community do not feel included, respected, and safe. We need to be more aware of people's cultures and experiences (and to be more 'culturally competent').[102]

Working in collaboration with colleagues in Georgetown University's 'National Centre for Cultural Competence',[103] Exeter appointed a number of its own staff to manage projects under the auspices of this institutional partnership and to facilitate organisational change. Cultural competence is understood as 'a defined set of values and principles, behaviours, attitudes, places and structures' which enable effective cross-cultural work with the capacity to 'value diversity', 'conduct self-assessment', 'manage the dynamics of difference', 'acquire and institutionalize cultural knowledge', and 'adapt to diversity and the cultural contexts of the communities they serve'.[104] Laurence Kirmayer notes how cultural competence has been adopted largely in medical care literature, where it perhaps risks essentialising cultural identities as static and unchanging.[105] Following developments in anthropology, he notes that culturally competent actions must instead acknowledge that cultures are fluid, dynamic, contextual, and increasingly hybrid. He proposes that cultural identities must accordingly be understood in terms of 'interactions with multiple networks or communities' with each 'struggl[ling] to define, position, constrain and exploit the other'.[106] As such cultural competence 'foregrounds issues of power and politics of identity and otherness' and how these inequalities of power can be addressed.[107] A key area of attention in this regard has been culturally competent collaboration between the University, its own culture, and its local environment. Research notes that 'academic citizenship' should extend beyond campuses to develop a sense of institutional presence and being as a 'placeful university'. This provides:

> an opportunity to re-imagine the possibilities of the university to integrate with people and society through dialogue and placeful-ness. Accordingly, supporting academic citizenship entails designing for the placeful university – a university that invites and promotes openness, dialogue, democracy, mutual integration, care and joint responsibility. Consequently, a comprehension of the placeful university is developed in the article to make the potentiality of academic citizenship for the future university emerge.[108]

An annual Exeter Respect on Campus Festival, spearheaded by the Student's Guild on campus, was begun in 2018, and an 'Individuality Speaker Series' was initiated in order to bring champions of inclusion and equality to the city to speak. Professor Tawara Goode, Director of the National Centre for Cultural Competence at Georgetown University (US), and Zrinka Bralo, the CEO of Migrants Organise, were among those who came to speak and function as role models in this area. This vision also compelled the institution to consider its campus spaces (both material and ideological) as arenas in which deliberative, culturally competent, compassionate, and cosmopolitan collaborations could be experienced. It also acknowledged that citizenship involved consciousness raising and empowerment to call out discrimination and renounce hateful words and actions.[109] With these insights in mind as the commission's work evolved main areas of action emerged which included (but were no means limited to) (a) awareness and induction and (b) inclusive learning and teaching.

(a) Awareness and Induction

Lani Guinier talks of 'admission [/induction] rituals as political acts' and 'high-stake moments of civic pedagogy' in which individuals can be moulded and shaped into an organisation's values and outlook.[110] Institutional commitments to equality and diversity were highlighted in fresher's week through institutional slides and media and (in the business school) an online orientation MOOC including inclusion, which students were invited to complete prior to arrival on campus. Associated public engagement activities included the physical displaying of maps of the world in central campus spaces where students were encouraged to pin locations of where they came from and public messaging surrounding the 'We are all Exeter' campaign.

Different disciplines were also encouraged to develop their own initiatives which would champion inclusion and diversity awareness during induction. Within the Theology and Religion department, we adopted an 'Exeter Diversity Trail' to introduce diverse stories of the city over time and which was designed in collaboration with students as a 'change agent project'.[111] The county of Devon in which Exeter is located is a predominantly white area ('with only 5.1% of BAME people (including "White other") reported in the 2011 Census. However, it is likely this figure is more in the region of 8 to 10% for some parts of Devon (2017)')[112]—a fact that is often picked up on in student chat rooms where Exeter is frequently stereotyped as a white, middle-class enclave.[113] Heritage trails, however, are increasingly recognised as significant educational tools and initiatives for not only transforming ideas surrounding a particular place and its global interconnections and histories—'seeing a city in new ways by [promoting] attention to the process of examining and acknowledging layers of cultural production'[114]—but also as a shared and collective activity as a positive means to encourage bonding and cultural competence within a diverse learning community. Building on similar student-learning projects elsewhere centred on community engagement, coupled with critical pedagogy of race and identity,[115] the Exeter diversity trail sought to voice and connect hidden local histories and curate a place-specific experience for students. For, as others have noted:

> Locating ethnic and women's history in urban space can contribute to what might be called a politics of place construction, redefining the mainstream experience, and making visible some of its forgotten parts.[116]

Students had to find particular objects within the local Royal Albert Memorial Museum (RAMM), also the original site of what became the University, and learn about this particular museum's place within Victorian object collecting and colonialism. They also visited places of worship in the city including the mosque, and the synagogue (one of the oldest in the whole UK) and the Jewish cemetery, and learned about trade, migration, and travel; slavery and abolitionism; Windrush Generation histories; global cuisine in the city; and disability histories including the Exeter Royal Academy for the Deaf, and WESC Foundation (formerly the West of England School and College for children with little or no sight). This facilitated student engagement with their location and encouraged reflection on how 'all spaces are racialized [and constructed] via a complex of relations and practices'. [117] The trail lasted two hours and student teams (based on personal tutor groups) were encouraged to tweet pictures of themselves at various points along the trail. Students were made aware that the trail would allow them to 'practic[e] techniques for analysing community histories' and to encounter the 'complex' human stories of the city. Importantly, as in other similar trails designed to inculcate intercultural competence, at no point were the individuals and stories presented in the trail as 'abstract victims' or triumphant over-comers, but rather 'figures and groups [to some extent like them] negotiating a complex and culturally produced landscape with complex outcomes'.[118] Students were also encouraged to document their own stories and present them in a variety of media on a shared platform. The Exeter diversity trail constituted a participatory approach which engaged students as democratic actors with their peers and as agents in their own learning. As an activity, it moved beyond a didactic model of inclusion and diversity, and rather actively allowed certain sentiments to be confronted critically together with other students in their group. As such, the activity introduced some of the qualities needed for compassionate, other-regarding citizenship, which not only mattered in the historical past but also crucially in the encounters and relationships of the city (of which they each had a part to play) in the present.[119]

(b) Anti-Racist Pedagogy, and Learning and Teaching

Whilst Chap. 4 has documented moves to incorporate decolonial thought and southern epistemologies within programmes, anti-racist pedagogy is not limited to decolonising curriculum content. Rather, it involves wholesale reflection on one's own social position and how this effects encounters and interactions both within and outside the classroom. Reading the self and acknowledging:

> both faculty and students are on the journey of learning leads to sharing power and building a sense of community in the classroom. To admit that the faculty are 'also in the process of learning' and to acknowledge their oppressed identity as well as their complicity in the oppression of others is a political act.[120]

A working group (on which I served) was tasked with developing anti-racist and inclusive pedagogies—'teaching that is as helpful as possible to the widest possible range of students—teaching that works well for students with different physical and psychological conditions, different skills, enthusiasms and cultural backgrounds, different "learning styles" and worldviews'[121]—within education. First, increasing awareness within learning encounters to ensure safety and respect for all and foster 'an inclusive environment in which problematic language and behaviours are called out and corrected immediately'[122]—questioning assumptions, pre-suppositions, and stereotypes related to particular characteristics—was seen as central. So too was alerting students and educators to issues around language of difference (class privilege, patriarchy, heterosexism, Eurocentrism, and ableism), the differences between banter and bullying, and how some idioms have damaging roots of which speakers are often unaware.[123] This calling out of issues was done in a constructive way that 'provided strong, supportive ally-ship while also allowing the offending party to learn and grow without feeling embarrassed or hostile'.[124] These frameworks were used in part to identify and dismantle what others have termed 'the walls of whiteness' in a student's experience: 'pedagogical imperatives that must be incorporated into the educational experience at college if there is any hope of breaking through these walls of justification, ideology, and "common sense".'[125]

Second, transformative inclusive practice was foregrounded, and ground rules for facilitating open and safe environments of democracy and respect were advocated. In Theology and Religion, we adopted a 'Covenant of Presence' (a tool often used in leadership development) within our modules as an intervention to establish and develop other-regarding and co-creative relationships within our learning community.[126] Building on Stephanie Crumpton's work on sensitive discussions around sexual trauma, the covenant of presence sought to cultivate a safe and respectful tone for learning encounters and establish ethical norms for discourse.[127] Students agreed to presume welcome to one another; to come as equals; to value every member in all their diversity; to defer judgement and instead turn to wonder and curiosity (asking why do they think that? why do I have such intense reactions in this regard?); to share the air and encourage everyone to participate and have a voice; to reserve the right to say 'no' to sharing experiences which are difficult in appointed class time; to engage sensitively with others in social media and online forums; and to have courage to call out those who did not abide by these citizenship principles. Compassionate group work was also encouraged. Theo Gilbert has been at the fore-front of the development of this pedagogical technique and its associated assessment within group work and seminars.[128] Micro-skills of compassion which he identified include 'the noting and addressing of distress and/or disadvantaging in group work' and how 'demonstrable, compassionate behaviours' can foster enhanced 'levels of inclusivity and critical thinking'.[129] These include compassionate curation of dialogue (inviting quieter students to participate in group discussions, not dominating conversation, using eye contact and body language appropriately to foster a positive and inclusive group environment, etc.). Such techniques draw on a body of research which underscores the importance of affective capacities within students, and compassion and empathy as 'moral disposition[s] that contribute[s] to a sense of fairness and an interest in others' well-being'.[130] It also echoes anti-racist pedagogies which aim to construct a sense of community and a decentring of authority in pedagogical space:

> A classroom which focuses on the learning process, collaboration among classmates, and dialog will help students understand the importance of allies and support when struggling with difficult projects or concepts. These interpersonal relationships as well as critical analytical skills discussed above become important in anti-racist organizing. An example of empowering students through collaborative learning is deconstructing racism and critiquing problems, and then 'rebuilding' by asking and articulating what an anti-racist society would look like. It is problematic to only focus on dismantling racism and assuming that everyone has a common understanding of an anti-racist society. Working towards a goal requires a vision, and talking only about the problems of racism leaves students feeling powerless. Again, what is important is the collaborative process, the dialog between students, as they discuss the world they want to strive for.[131]

Compassionate Campus Climates: Confronting Privilege and Prejudice

The social activist bell hooks talks about the power of those voices within organisations who share their experiences of exclusion.[132] The voices of those subject to the hostile and discriminatory incidents at Exeter recounted at the start of this chapter, undoubtedly continue to force the institution to critically and constructively reflect on its responsibility, complicity, and culpability in perpetuating unspoken assumptions of privilege and prejudice within the student body, and the realities of a campus climate perceived very differently by students according to their own experiences. 'I want this not to occur again'[133] was a striking declaration by the student who had suffered, especially her insight that this was not just from a desire to protect others in the future but from a sense that her own well-being was tied up with it not happening again. Discussion here also perhaps shows most clearly the evidence for neoliberalism in the policy choices universities have set in front of them. By naming privilege and prejudice, and not limiting action to penal sanctions on individuals, but rather seeing problems of discrimination as more broadly structural and social, much more culturally competent engagement and deep dialogue within an organisation can be generated.[134] It was no doubt these voices too that inflected the University of Exeter's Vice-Chancellor's statement released in the wake of George Floyd's death. Unlike many institution's statements, there was a notable sense of a recognition of failures, humility, regret, and contrition:

I write this message with a real sense of humility because I want to start by saying something about the horrific death in the US of George Floyd. Because of my own white identity, and despite my revulsion at his killing, it is impossible for me to feel the same pain and sense of injustice that so many of our Black and Minority Ethnic students and colleagues feel … I hope it goes without saying that this is a time for us to confront racism, to call it out in our communities and to stand up for what is right. We must stand shoulder to shoulder together and state that racism is wrong and must stop. But saying things like this is less important than listening to the views and concerns of our Black and Minority Ethnic students and colleagues, and then, crucially, acting. That listening and that acting has to begin in our own university community. Everyone reading this message knows that we have not made the progress that we want. To my personal shame, there have been abhorrent incidents here, and we have not been able, so far, to stop these incidents before they happen. So, to state the obvious, we must do everything in our power to root out all forms of racism and hate crime in our community. But as I have said, I am acutely aware that it is not just our words but our actions that matter and we must be visibly and actively anti-racist: not merely non-racist, but actively anti-racist. Right now I also know that colleagues and students are traumatised by recent events and need support and compassion more than anything else, so I urge you to reach out to our support services and each other. Please do recognise that your colleagues and your students may be hurting through what is going on and look out for each other. I urge all colleagues and leaders to bring up and talk about issues of racism, this burden should not rest on our black and minority ethnic colleagues. Tackling racism is for all of us.[135]

The internal interventions proposed and actioned under the auspices of the Provost Commission at Exeter built on those viewpoints which have identified universities as 'the perfect laboratories for students "to develop new capacities for learning across differences"'[136] and in so doing embody a compassionate citizenship which empowers them to critically reflect on their own positionality, and call out and confront unjust and abusive uses of power against others within their learning community. Of course, there is still a long way to go. Anti-Asian discrimination in the city of Exeter broke out in response to the Coronavirus outbreak in March 2020. Strong (place-full) collaboration between civic authorities and the university enabled a swift, collaborative, and collective city/campus response. An Open Letter tackling hate crime and racism signed by local authorities, the police, and the University Vice-Chancellor states:

We are proud of our diverse community in Exeter and the huge benefits people from around the world bring to our city and society. Regardless of race, background, belief or nationality everyone has a right to thrive in Exeter and feel welcome in the place they have made their home ... We will stand together to tackle hate crime and hateful people, and in equal measure promote and celebrate diversity to ensure that love and respect always conquers hate. Please work with us and support us to make Exeter the best city to live in the world.[137]

Compassion grounded this response, and the above interventions, as a practice of reasoning and social solidarity: 'It provides the conditions for human rights, equality and social justice, anti-racism, anti-homophobia and anti-xenophobia'[138] and, when understood in terms of justice, seeks to pursue the challenging but essential work to ensure that everybody feels they belong (physically, ideologically, and psychologically) as citizens within a positive and affirming campus climate.

NOTES

1. For responses across the UK and Europe to the death of George Floyd, see IRR New Team 'Responses Across the UK and Europe to the Death of George Floyd' Institute of Race Relations (4th June 2020). Available online at: http://www.irr.org.uk/news/responses-across-the-uk-and-europe-to-the-death-of-george-floyd/
2. Jason England and Richard Purcell, 'Statements by college leaders reflect an unholy alchemy of risk management, legal liability and trustee anxiety' *The Chronicle of Higher Education* (8th June 2020). Available online at: https://www.chronicle.com/article/Higher-Ed-s-Toothless/248946
3. Tahmina Choudhery, 'We Can't Separate the Issues of Race and Reopening Universities' WONKHE (3rd June 2020). Available online at: https://wonkhe.com/blogs/we-cant-separate-the-issues-of-race-and-reopening-in-universities/
4. Ahmed cited and discussed in Jonathan Charles Flowers, 'The Coming Campus Protests: College leaders will be judged by their actions—not their words' Chronicle of Higher Education (10th June 2020). Available online at: https://www.chronicle.com/article/The-Coming-Campus-Protests/248967?cid=wsinglestory_41_1
5. Sara Ahmed, On Being Included: Race and Diversity in Institutional Life (Durham: Duke University Press, 2012), 113.
6. Ahmed, On Being, 109.
7. Ahmed, On Being, 22.
8. Ahmed, On Being, 147.
9. NS, 'This is'.
10. NS, 'This is'.
11. 'Law Students "frustrated" with Bracton Law Society President' Expose (2018). Available online at: https://exepose.com/2019/05/10/law-students-frustrated-with-bracton-law-president/. See also 'Bracton Law Society Scandal' Wikipedia Available online at: https://en.wikipedia.org/wiki/2018_Bracton_Law_Society_Scandal
12. Eric Heinze, Hate Speech and Democratic Citizenship (Oxford: Oxford University Press, 2016), 2.
13. Kaplin cited in John Downey and Frances Stage, 'Hate Crimes and Violence on College and University Campuses' Journal of College Student Development 40 (1999), 3–9, 3.

14. 'The report, "Tackling Racial Harassment: Universities Challenged" sur-
    veyed more than 1000 students and conducted in-depth interviews with
    students and staff. It found that 20% of those students had been physically
    attacked, while 56% of students who had been racially harassed had expe-
    rienced racist name-calling, insults and jokes, physical attacks and racist
    material and displays often linked to student society events.' See https://
    www.refinery29.com/en-gb/racism-discrimination-university-uk
15. Carole Corcoran and Aisha Thompson 'What's Race Got to do, Got to
    do With It?' Denial of Racism on Predominantly White College
    Campuses' in Jean Lau Chin (ed), The Psychology of Prejudice and
    Discrimination: Racisms in America (Westport: Praegar, 2004), 137–176.
16. Darryl Brown, 'Racism and Race Relations in the University' Virginia
    Law Review 76 (1990), 295–335.
17. Robert D. Reason and Susan R. Rankin, 'College Students' Experiences
    and Perceptions of Harassment on Campus: An Exploration of Gender
    Differences' College Student Affairs Journal 26 (2006), 7–29. Available
    online at: https://files.eric.ed.gov/fulltext/EJ902800.pdf. On campus
    climate, see also Fatma Nevra Seggie & Gretchen Sanford, 'Perceptions
    of female Muslim students who veil: campus religious climate' Race,
    Ethnicity and Education 13 (2010), 59–82.
18. Reason and Rankin, 'College Students', 7.
19. Jodi Linley, 'Racism Here, Racism There, Racism Everywhere: The Racial
    Realities of Minoritized Peer Socialization Agents at a Historically White
    Institution' Journal of College Student Development 59 (2018), 21–36.
20. Linley, 'Racism', 24.
21. Linley, 'Racism', 24.
22. Alison Phipps, 'Reckoning up: sexual harassment and violence in the neo-
    liberal university' Gender and Education 32 (2020), 227–243, 230.
    Available online at: https://doi.org/10.1080/09540253.2018.1482413
23. Robert D. Reason and Susan R. Rankin, 'Differing Perceptions: How
    Students of Color and White Students Perceive Campus Climate for
    Underrepresented Groups' Journal of College Student Development
    46 (2005), 43–61. Available online at: https://muse.jhu.edu/article/
    177605
24. Reason and Rankin, 'Differing', 43–44. See also Barbara Perry 'No big-
    gie: The denial of oppression on campus' Education, Citizenship and
    Social Justice 5 (2010), 265–279. Available online at: https://doi.
    org/10.1177/1746197910387543. Note Schlosser and Selacek's point
    that 'Shifts in the demographics in North American colleges and universi-
    ties over the past decades have created much more diverse and multieth-
    nic campuses. Some praise these trends for creating more dynamic
    environments. However, not all are happy with the "infiltration" of tradi-

tionally white, male enclaves, such that newcomers are met with hostility, even violence. In our campus hate crime study conducted at adjoining college and university campuses in Ontario, we found widespread awareness that minority students were frequent victims of hate crime and discrimination. In an interesting paradox, however, this did not translate into a parallel awareness that racism, or sexism, or homophobia were problems for the campus in question. In other words, while students may observe racist behaviour, they do not "see" it—that is, they do not register the structured embeddedness of campus oppression.' Lewis Z. Schlosser and William E. Sedlacek, 'Hate on Campus: A Model for Evaluating, Understanding, and Handling Critical Incidents' About Campus: Enriching the Student Learning Experience 6 (2001), 25–27.

25. '#WeAreAllExeter has been realised to celebrate the diversity that exists on our campus and in our city. We are a community of people from different places, with different experiences and different passions, and yet, we are all Exeter. Everybody here at the University of Exeter has a story and we want you to share yours with us, or learn more about your friends and fellow students and their lives.' Exeter Guild, https://www.exeterguild. org/weareallexeter/. In the US, too, campaigns of this sort have been initiated: 'hashtags such as #BlackOnCampus and #ConcernedStudent1950 facilitated increased visibility of the hostile racial climate toward Black students at the University of Missouri, and Harvard University's #ItooAmHarvard was developed as a means to raise awareness of minoritized student experiences at the institution (Kahn, 2014). Multiple SOC at MU leveraged this hashtag activism and endorsed #BlackLivesMatter as a means to contextualize what Bonilla and Rosa (2015) referred to as a "particular interpretive frame" that served to raise awareness of the prevalence of racism within the MU online environments (p. 5). The engagement with and endorsement of hashtags by students in this study further reified the contemporary form of online activism observed within higher education.' Kevin J. Gin, Ana M. Martínez-Alemán, Heather T. Rowan-Kenyon and Derek Hottell 'Racialized Aggressions and Social Media on Campus' Journal of College Student Development 58 (2017), 159–174. Available online at: https://muse.jhu.edu/article/650712/pdf

26. Kevin Rawlinson, 'Exeter University Expels Students Over Racism Row' The Guardian (1st May 2018). Available online at: https://www.theguardian.com/education/2018/may/01/exeter-university-expels-students-over-racism-row

27. Brown, 'Racism' 295–335.

28. Brown, 'Racism' 295–335.

29. Martha Nussbaum, Cultivating Humanity: A Classical Defense of Reform in Liberal Education (Cambridge/London: Harvard University Press, 1997), 68.
30. Yusef Waghid, 'Compassionate citizenship and education research article' Perspectives in Education 22 (2004), 41–50.
31. Seyla Benhabib, The Claims of Culture: Equality and Diversity in the Global Era (Princeton, New Jersey: Princeton University Press, 2002), 134. Cited in Waghid, 'Compassionate', 41.
32. Sharon K. Anderson and Valerie A. Middleton, Explorations in Diversity: Examining Privilege and Oppression in a Multicultural Society (Brooks/Cole Cengage Learning, 2011), 1.
33. Phipps, 'Reckoning'.
34. Phipps, 'Reckoning'.
35. http://www.exeter.ac.uk/media/universityofexeter/humanresources/edi/equalitydata/EDI_Annual_Report_v2.2_-_20190827.pdf
36. https://www.bbc.co.uk/news/education-44226434
37. http://www.exeter.ac.uk/departments/communication/studentrecruitment/wideningparticipation/
38. Reason and Rankin, 'Differing' Perceptions: How Students of Color and White Students Perceive Campus Climate for Underrepresented Groups' Journal of College Student Development 46 (2005), 43–61. Available online at: https://muse.jhu.edu/article/177605
39. Linley, 'Racism', 24.
40. NS, 'This is'.
41. Reason and Rankin 'College Students', 22.
42. McIntosh 1989, cited in Anderson and Middleton, Explorations, 1.
43. Jane M. Simoni and Karina L. Walters 'Heterosexual Identity and Heterosexism Recognizing Privilege to Reduce Prejudice' Journal of Homosexuality Vol 41 (2008), 157–172. Available online at: https://doi.org/10.1300/J082v41n01_06. See also Kim A. Case, 'Raising White Privilege Awareness and Reducing Racial Prejudice: Assessing Diversity Course Effectiveness' Teaching of Psychology 34 (2007), 231–235. Available online at: https://doi.org/10.1080/00986280701700250
44. Nolan L. Cabrera, 'Beyond Black and White: How White, Male, College Students See Their Asian American Peers, Equity & Excellence in Education' Equity and Excellence in Education 47 (2014), 133–151, 134. Available online at: https://doi.org/10.1080/10665684.2014.900427
45. Zeus Leonardo, 'The Color of Supremacy: Beyond the Discourse of 'white privilege'' Educational Philosophy and Theory 36 (2004), 137–152.
46. Sharon Anderson and Valerie Middleton 'An Awakening to Privilege, Oppression and Discrimination' chapter 1 in Sharon Anderson and

Valerie Middleton (eds), Explorations in Diversity: Examining the Complexities of Privilege, Discrimination and Oppression (Oxford: Oxford University Press, 3ed, 2018), 5–10, 5.

47. Frances Henry and Carol Tator, 'Introduction: Racism in the Canadian University' Frances Henry and Carol Tator (eds), Racism in the Canadian University: Demanding Social Justice, Inclusion, and Equity (Toronto: University of Toronto Press, 2009), 3–21, 3.

48. Leonardo, 'The Color'.

49. Diane Gusa, 'White Institutional Presence: The Impact of Whiteness on Campus Climate' Harvard Educational Review 80 (2010), 464–490, 472.

50. Gusa, 'White', 477.

51. Gusa, 'White', 478.

52. Bhopal Kalwant, White Privilege: The Myth of a Post-Racial Society (Bristol: Policy Press, 2018), 5.

53. 'In the United States, the idea of the "white university" has been around since Harvard University opened its doors in 1636 – in Europe, much longer. Scholarly literature to refer to an institution of higher education whose histories, traditions, symbols, stories, icons, curriculum, and processes were all designed by whites, for whites, to reproduce whiteness via a white experience at the exclusion of others who, since the 1950s and 1960s, have been allowed in such spaces.' David L. Brunsma, Eric S. Brown and Peggy Placier, 'Teaching Race at Historically White Colleges and Universities: Identifying and Dismantling the Walls of Whiteness' Critical Sociology 39 (2012), 717–738.

54. Cabrera, 'Exposing', 30–55.

55. Cabrera, 'Exposing', 30.

56. Annemarie Vaccaro, 'What Lies Beneath Seemingly Positive Campus Climate Results: Institutional Sexism, Racism, and Male Hostility Toward Equity Initiatives and Liberal Bias' Equity and Excellence in Education 42 (2010), 202–215. Available online at: https://www.tandfonline.com/doi/full/10.1080/10665680903520231

57. Vaccaro, 'What' 202–215.

58. https://en.wikipedia.org/wiki/2018_Bracton_Law_Society_Scandal

59. Gin et al. 'Racialized'. Cabrera notes that 'One method of whiteness normalizing is the disproportionately high representation of whites in higher education, especially in four-year institutions … To the extent that a college degree represents increased earning potential and access to high-power social networks, the concentrated awarding of this valued commodity to whites serves to reinforce the existing racial paradigm … Other methods include an institutional stance on racism that is reactive instead of proactive, the exclusion of diversity in the mission statement, concentration of institutional power in white (often male) administrators,

minimal representation of faculty of color, and a reliance upon "traditional pedagogies" that disregard teaching across racial difference ... On the student level, there are a number of ways in which white supremacy is reified in higher education. A salient example is the fraternity/sorority system because students have the explicit ability to select members, frequently excluding people of color from participation.' Cabrera, 'Exposing', 32.

60. Ruth Lewis, Susan Marine and Kathryn Kenney, "I get together with my friends and try to change it': Young feminist students resist 'laddism', 'rape culture' and 'everyday sexism" Journal of Gender Studies 27 (2018), 56–72. Available online at: https://doi.org/10.1080/0958923 6.2016.1175925

61. Alison Phipps and Isabel Young, '"Lad culture" in higher education: Agency in the sexualization debates' Sexualities 18 (2015), 459–479. 'This article reports on research funded by the National Union of Students, which explored women students' experiences of "lad culture" through focus groups and interviews. We found that although laddism is only one of various potential masculinities, for our participants it dominated the social and sexual spheres of university life in problematic ways. However, their objections to laddish behaviours did not support contemporary models of "sexual panic", even while oppugning the more simplistic celebrations of young women's empowerment which have been observed in debates about sexualization. We argue that in their ability to reject "lad culture", our respondents expressed a form of agency which is often invisibilized in sexualization discussions and which could be harnessed to tackle some of the issues we uncovered.' Phipps and Young, 'Lad Culture', 459.

62. NUS, 'That's What She Said: Women Student's Experiences of 'Lad Culture' at Universities' (2013). Available online at: https://www.nus.org.uk/PageFiles/12238/Thats%20What%20She%20Said%20-%20 Full%20Report%20(1).pdf.

63. 'Degrees of Laddishness: Laddism in Higher Education' SRHE Feb 2014 – DRAFT. Available online at: https://eprints.lancs.ac.uk/id/eprint/68650/2/Dempster_and_Jackson_srhe_for_press.pdf/

64. Lewis et al.., 'I get together', 56–72.

65. Lewis et al.., 'I get together', 56.

66. 'The rugby players, drinking and debating society members from elite universities who exemplify contemporary laddism ... bring to mind the men and masculinities typified by the Bullingdon Club, a centuries-old all-male exclusive dining club at Oxford University which boasts high-profile former members including British Prime Minister David Cameron. Bullingdon dinners have historically been typified by copious amounts of

alcohol and have erupted into violence, and at the club's informal gatherings which have been open to women, they have been made to whinny on all fours while men brandish hunting horns and whips ... Problematic practices and behaviours linked with similar elite masculinities are also at the centre of conversations in the US around sexism and "rape culture" in fraternities.' Alison Phipps, '(Re)theorising laddish masculinities in higher education' Gender and Education 29 (2017), 815–830, 821. Available online at https://doi.org/10.1080/09540253.2016.1171298

67. NUS 2013 report cited in Phipps '(Re)theorising', 822.
68. Lewis et al.., 'I get together', 56.
69. Phipps '(Re)theorising', 823.
70. Lewis et al., 'I get together', 58.
71. Lewis et al., 'I get together', 58.
72. NS, 'This is'.
73. Gin et al., 'Racialized', 160. See also Rebecca L. Stotzer, Emily Hossellman 'Hate Crimes on Campus: Racial/Ethnic Diversity and Campus Safety' Journal of Interpersonal Violence 27 (2011), 644–661.
74. Stotzer and Hossellman, 'Hate Crimes', 644.
75. Gin et al., 'Racialized', 164. 'Cyberbullying has been defined as "an aggressive act or behaviour that is carried out using electronic means by a group or an individual repeatedly and over time against a victim who cannot easily defend him or herself" ... the reported reasons for attacking a person online involve the bullies' need for power and dominance within a group, the perceived vulnerability of the target, perceived provocativeness on the part of the target (usually as a justification for the aggression on the part of the bully), and interpersonal animosities.' Carrie-Anne Myers and Helen Cowie, 'Bullying at University: The Social and Legal Contexts of Cyberbullying Among University Students' Journal of Cross-Cultural Psychology 48 (2017), 1172–1182.
76. Gin et al., 'Racialized', 171.
77. https://medium.com/@ns1997/this-is-what-unpalatable-student-activism-costs-5d06f653a84f
78. Lorraine Brown and Ian Jones, 'Encounters with racism and the international student experience', Studies in Higher Education 38 (2013), 1004–1019. Available online at https://doi.org/ https://doi.org/1 0.1080/03075079.2011.614940
79. Lewis et al. 'I get together' 56–72.
80. Other silencing or airbrushing techniques include 'complainants may be discouraged from pursuing allegations; or allegations may be acted upon, but alleged perpetrators allowed to withdraw quietly'. Alison Phipps, 'Reckoning up: sexual harassment and violence in the neoliberal univer-

sity' Gender and Education 32 (2020), 227–243. Available online at: https://doi.org/10.1080/09540253.2018.1482413

81. NS, 'This is'.

82. 'The individualised and reactive approaches of the universities are, in some ways, understandable because they are basing their responses on what they know and what they are told. The places and spaces where lad culture is most evident – e.g. bars and nightclubs - are not spaces where most university staff go, so what staff know about lad culture is shaped by what students tell them. And Universities are rather notoriously secretive about [problems] ... people will very quickly tell you of the areas where they're successful. It takes quite a lot of probing for anybody to say actually we have a real problem with drink or with drugs ... I think we should wash dirty linen in public on the grounds that dirty linen exists everywhere to a certain extent, and it's better washed really.' Alison Phipps, Jessica Ringrose, Emma Renold and Carolyn Jackson, 'Rape culture, lad culture and everyday sexism: researching, conceptualizing and politicizing new mediations of gender and sexual violence' Journal of Gender Studies 27 (2018), 1–8. Available online at https://doi.org/10.108 0/09589236.2016.1266792

83. Anitha, Sundari and Ruth Lewis, Gender based violence in university communities: policy, prevention and educational interventions in Britain (Bristol: Policy Press, 2018), 51.

84. Phipps, 'Reckoning' 227–243.

85. NS, 'This is'.

86. Phipps, 'Reckoning', 228.

87. #MeToo is perhaps the best-known feminist activism in this sphere. See Kaitlynn Mendes, Jessica Ringrose, Jessalynn Keller, '#MeToo and the promise and pitfalls of challenging rape culture through digital feminist activism' European Journal of Women's Studies 25 (2018), 236–246.

88. Nicollini discussed in Phipps et al., 'Rape culture', 1–8.

89. https://www.exeter.ac.uk/provostcommission/#a2

90. Reason and Rankin, 'College', 629.

91. https://www.exeter.ac.uk/speakout/campaigns/speakoutguardians/

92. See R. A. Fenton, H. L. Mott, K. McCartan and P. Rumney, The Intervention Initiative. Bristol: UWE and Public Health England (2014). 'The Intervention Initiative is a free resource for universities and further education settings in England, developed in 2014 by the University of the West of England on receipt of a grant from Public Health England. It is an evidence-based educational programme for the prevention of sexual coercion and domestic abuse in university settings, through empowering students to act as prosocial citizens.' https://socialsciences.exeter.ac.uk/ research/interventioninitiative/about/about/#a0

93. See 'The Challenging Racism Project' listed in the Charter of Compassion. https://charterforcompassion.org/igb-anti-muslim-bigotry/the-challenging-racism-project

94. E. J. Cassell, 'Compassion' in C. R. Snyder & S. J. Lopez (eds), Handbook of Positive Psychology (Oxford: Oxford University Press, 2002), 434–445.

95. 'Bullying is a major public health problem faced by youth today. This randomized controlled study evaluated a brief, counselor-led bystander bullying intervention for elementary school students with a history of occasionally bullying (N = 54). The intervention—stealing the show, turning it over, accompanying others, and coaching compassion (STAC)—is designed to train students to intervene as peer advocates when they witness bullying situations at school. Students in the STAC intervention group reported a significantly lower level of bullying perpetration compared to students in the wait-list control group. Findings suggest that training students who bully to be peer advocates may be a promising approach to bullying prevention.' Aida Midgett, Diana M. Doumas, Rhiannon Trull and Jamie Johnson, 'Training Students Who Occasionally Bully to Be Peer Advocates: Is a Bystander Intervention Effective in Reducing Bullying Behavior?' Journal of Child and Adolescent Counseling, 3:1 (2017), 1–13. Available online at: https://doi.org/10.1080/23727810.2016.1277116

96. John D. Foubert, Matthew W. Brosi and R. Sean Bannon, 'Pornography Viewing among Fraternity Men: Effects on Bystander Intervention, Rape Myth Acceptance and Behavioral Intent to Commit Sexual Assault, Sexual Addiction & Compulsivity' 18:4 (2011), 212–231. Available online at: https://doi.org/10.1080/10720162.2011.625552. See also Anne Kleinsasser, Ernest Jouriles, Renee N., McDonald and David Rosenfield, 'An online bystander intervention program for the prevention of sexual violence' Psychology of Violence Vol 5(3) (2015) 227–235.

97. A. B. Dessel, K. D. Goodman, M. R. Woodford, 'LGBT discrimination on campus and heterosexual bystanders: Understanding intentions to intervene' Journal of Diversity in Higher Education, 10(2) (2017), 101–116. Available online at: https://doi.org/10.1037/dhe0000015

98. Gin et al., 'Racialized', 172.

99. Johan Andersson, Joanna Sadgrove, and Gill Valentine, 'Consuming campus: geographies of encounter at a British university' Social & Cultural Geography, 13:5 (2012), 501–515. Available online at: https://doi.org/10.1080/14649365.2012.700725

100. Uma Jayakumar, 'Can Higher Education Meet the Needs of an Increasingly Diverse and Global Society? Campus Diversity and Cross-Cultural Workforce Competencies' Harvard Educational Review 78

(2008), 615–651. Available online at: https://doi.org/10.17763/hae r.78.4.b60031p350276699
101. Andersson et al., 'Consuming' 501–515.
102. http://www.exeter.ac.uk/media/universityofexeter/humanresources/ edi/equalitydata/EDI_Annual_Report_v2.2_-_20190827.pdf
103. https://nccc.georgetown.edu/
104. https://nccc.georgetown.edu/
105. Kirmayer, 'Rethinking' cultural competence' Transcultural Psychology 49 (2012), 149–164. Available online at: https://doi.org/10.1177/ 1363461512444673
106. Kirmayer, 'Rethinking', 149–164.
107. He adopts the languages of 'cultural safety' coined in New Zealand in response to Maori discontent over injustice. Kirmayer, 'Rethinking', 149–164.
108. Rikke Toft Nørgård & Søren Smedegaard Ernst Bengtsen, 'Academic citizenship beyond the campus: a call for the placeful university' Higher Education Research & Development 35:1 (2016), 4–16, 4. Available online at: https://www.tandfonline.com/doi/abs/10.1080/0729436 0.2015.1131669
109. Nuraan Davids and Yusef Waghid, 'Higher education as a pedagogical site for citizenship education' Education, Citizenship and Social Justice 11 (2016), 34–43.
110. Lani Guinier 'Admission Rituals as Political Acts: Guardians at the Gates of our Democratic Ideals' Harvard Law Review 117 (2003–2004). Available online at: https://heinonline.org/HOL/Page?collection=jour nals&handle=hein.journals/hlr117&id=141&men_tab=srchresults
111. The trail was inspired in part by the Telling Our Stories, Finding Our Roots initiative. This 'website is a resource for multicultural education and exploration highlighting the diversity in Devon and Exeter's local history. The product of our community research project exploring multi-culturalism and diversity in Exeter, supporting Black History Month and Exeter's Respect festival with information on our story-telling events, local history, films and schools activities. Part of a Heritage Lottery funded project, "Telling our Stories, Finding our Roots: Exeter's Multi-Coloured History" is run by Devon Development Education at the Global Centre in Exeter.' http://www.tellingourstoriesexeter.org.uk/ index.php?page=guided-tour
112. https://www.devon.gov.uk/equality/communities/race
113. See thread in the Student Room 'Is Exeter ethnically diverse?' https:// www.thestudentroom.co.uk/showthread.php?t=854885
114. Susan Carson, Lesley Hawkes, Kari Gislason & Kate Cantrell, 'Literature, tourism and the city: writing and cultural change', Journal of Tourism

and Cultural Change 15:4 (2017), 380–392. Available online at: https://doi.org/10.1080/14766825.2016.1165237

115. Natchee Barnd, 'Constructing a Social Justice Tour: Pedagogy, Race, and Student Learning through Geography', Journal of Geography 115:5 (2016), 212–223. Available online at: https://doi.org/10.1080/00221341.2016.1153132

116. Dolores Hayden, The Power of Place: Urban Landscapes as Public History (MIT Press, 1997), xii. See also Susan Carson Creative Writing and Literary Studies, Creative Industries, QUT (Queensland University of Technology), Victoria Park Road, Kelvin Grove, Brisbane, QLD 4059 Australia; Lesley Hawkes Creative Writing and Literary Studies, Creative Industries, QUT (Queensland University of Technology), Victoria Park Road, Kelvin Grove, Brisbane, QLD 4059 AustraliaCorrespondencel. hawkes@qut.edu.au; Kari Gislason Creative Writing and Literary Studies, Creative Industries, QUT (Queensland University of Technology), Victoria Park Road, Kelvin Grove, Brisbane, QLD 4059 Australia; and Kate Cantrell Creative Writing and Literary Studies, Creative Industries, QUT (Queensland University of Technology), Victoria Park Road, Kelvin Grove, Brisbane, QLD 4059 Australia, 'Literature, tourism and the city: writing and cultural change' Journal of Tourism and Cultural Change 15:4 (2017), 380–392. Available online at: https://doi.org/10.1080/14766825.2016.1165237. Pages 380–392 Received 08 Oct 2015; Accepted 04 Mar 2016; Published online: 04 Apr 2016

117. Barnd 'Constructing' 215.

118. Barnd 'Constructing' 215.

119. Yusef Waghid, 'Education for responsible citizenship: Conversation' Perspectives in Education 27 (2009), 85–90. Also Barnd 'Constructing' 223.

120. Kyoko Kishimoto, 'Anti-racist pedagogy: from faculty's self-reflection to organizing within and beyond the classroom', Race Ethnicity and Education, 21:4 (2018), 540–554. Available online at: https://doi.org/10.1080/13613324.2016.1248824, 542.

121. Definition from Advance HE (2011) cited in https://as.exeter.ac.uk/tqae/inclusiveteaching/

122. Definition from Advance HE (2011) cited in https://as.exeter.ac.uk/tqae/inclusiveteaching/

123. https://as.exeter.ac.uk/tqae/inclusiveteaching/

124. https://as.exeter.ac.uk/tqae/inclusiveteaching/

125. Brunsma et al., 'Teaching', 717–738.

126. Nadyne Guzmán, 'The Leadership Covenant: Essential Factors for Developing Co-creative Relationships Within a Learning Community'

Journal of Leadership Studies Volume 2 (1995), 151–160. Available online at: https://doi.org/10.1177/107179199500200412

127. Stephanie Crumpton, 'Trigger warnings, covenants of presence, and more: Cultivating safe space for theological discussions about sexual trauma' Teaching Theology and Religion 20 (2017), 137–147. Available online at: https://onlinelibrary.wiley.com/doi/abs/10.1111/teth.12376. Susannah Cornwall was instrumental in infusing this intervention within our curriculum at Exeter. She introduced the covenant within her module on queer theologies, and students were very appreciative of the respectful and democratic tone it set for their discussions as co-citizens of the module.

128. Theo Gilbert, 'When Looking Is Allowed: What Compassionate Group Work Looks Like in a UK University' in P. Gibbs (ed), The Pedagogy of Compassion at the Heart of Higher Education (Switzerland: Springer, 2017), 189–202.

129. Gilbert, 'When Looking', 189–202.

130. Bruce Maxwell, 'Pursuing the Aim of Compassionate Empathy in Higher Education' in P. Gibbs (ed), The Pedagogy of Compassion at the Heart of Higher Education (Switzerland: Springer, 2017), 33–48, 33.

131. Kishimoto, 'Anti-Racist', 549.

132. bell hooks cited in Annemarie Vaccaro, 'What', 202.

133. NS, 'This is'.

134. Vaccaro, 'What' 202.

135. Steve Smith, 'Message from the Vice-Chancellor to staff and students' (5th June 2020). Available online at: https://www.exeter.ac.uk/coronavirus/communications/vc5june/

136. Vaccaro, 'What' 202.

137. https://www.exeter.ac.uk/news/university/title_781838_en.html

138. Mano Candappa, Madeleine Arnot and Halleli Pinson, 'Compassion, Justice and Sanctuary: Can Asylum-Seeking and Refugee Students "Belong" in British Schools?' Paper presented at the British Educational Research Association Annual Conference, University of Manchester, 2–5 September 2009. Available online at: http://www.leeds.ac.uk/educol/documents/192216.pdf

Compassion and Kindness: Refiguring Discourses of Student Mental Health and Wellbeing

A recent news article entitled 'The Way Universities are Run is Making Us Ill: Inside the Student Mental Health Crisis'[1] traced escalations in British Universities over the last ten years of student anxiety, depression, breakdown, withdrawals on account of mental ill health, and suicides.[2] Many take as given the 'deep crisis affecting universities' producing a 'psychosocial and somatic catastrophe' manifest in 'experiences of chronic stress, anxiety, exhaustion, insomnia, and spiralling rates of physical and mental illness'.[3] Financial pressures, disruptive transitions, the impact of technology, and drug and alcohol abuse have all been cited as potential contributing factors, so too has the fact that 'a growing proportion just seem terrified of failure, and experience the whole process of learning and assessment as an unforgiving ordeal that offer[s] no room for creativity or mistakes'.[4] Discursive reliance on tropes of crisis, pathology, and vulnerability, illustrated in this news article, are not uncommon in wider discourses surrounding student mental (ill) health and wellbeing within the sector. There is also a tendency to configure mental (ill) health within a medical model as an established condition outside the influence of academic institutions and/or programmes. As a result, interventions are likely to focus on service provision and not pay critical attention to existent institutional policies, curriculum, and social structure that indelibly form and figure the character of the organisation and student experiences within it.

L. J. Lawrence, *Refiguring Universities in an Age of Neoliberalism*, Palgrave Critical University Studies, https://doi.org/10.1007/978-3-030-73371-1_6

Prompted by emergent insights such as these, my own institution set out in 2018 to initiate a 'Wellbeing Review' chaired and directed by our Deputy Vice-Chancellor of Education.[5] Following the *Universities UK Stepchange: Mental Health in Higher Education Framework*,[6] the review purposefully set out to engage a whole institutional approach[7]: this was designed to advance a comprehensive methodology to mental health and wellbeing of both students and staff in the institution.[8] Under the living, learning, and community streams, and gaining insights from National Student Survey (NSS) data and comments, programme survey data, withdrawal data, and student and staff voices, particular areas for attention were identified: (a) discourses surrounding student mental (ill) health and wellbeing within the institution and (b) whole campus ethos and interventions, with compassion and kindness in particular advocated. Whilst up to this point, institutional energies in the area had been concentrated on better access to medical interventions and providers, this review prompted new attention to social models of wellness and (among other areas) brought specific attention to curriculum, assessment, and teaching to promote student wellbeing.[9] Central to this review was the insight that cultures designed to prevent mental (ill) health were central and that 'most [students] aren't looking for therapy or an expert but "a compassionate human [or community] who can help them make sense of things"'.[10] The institution was compelled in this light to 'relate to students authentically and compassionately'[11] with critical attention given to the assumptions underlying narratives surrounding student mental (ill) health and wellbeing that were often (albeit unconsciously) employed, and to turn attention to creating alternative discourses, interventions, and philosophies that could advance whole institutional care, compassion, and equality for all, if and when, former discourses/structures/practices were found wanting.[12] There was acceptance that certain students will require specific medical attention and interventions, yet for many students it is the culture and practices of an institution which were seen to provide a suitable context in which to live, thrive, and enhance wellbeing.

Situating this specific institutional review in the broader context of the sector, alongside insights from an area in which I work, disability studies, first this chapter will seek to probe and interrogate some of the discourses surrounding student mental (ill) health and wellbeing in higher education. In particular, tropes which reflect the ways in which the neoliberal academy has constructed individualised and pathologising discourses surrounding those perceived as other to a rational, and 'sanist' norm,[13] and forwarded therapeutising discourses which seek to secure individual identities as functioning neoliberal subjects. Second, discourses of 'compassion' and 'kindness' as 'the art of being rather than doing—a philosophy of care based on humanistic values'[14]—will be presented, particularly as they impact notions of time, affect, and affiliations. Collective compassion and kindness seek to underscore the significance of whole educational and institutional contexts in changing attitudes and alleviating stigmas and stereotypes often employed in discourses of student mental (ill) health and wellbeing. Third, and finally, practical 'compassionate' and 'kind' curricular interventions, focused on re-imagining time, productivity, and affect within the academy, will be presented which were designed within a project run by Advance HE on 'Wellbeing in the Curriculum' in which my own institution was a project partner.[15]

Discourses of Student Mental [Ill] Health and Wellbeing in the Neoliberal University

Discourses dynamically construct and shape institutional attitudes and student identities according to certain (often unacknowledged) ideological positions. Within student mental (ill) health and wellbeing discourses, hegemonic topoi which reflect asymmetrical hierarchies of power, and perpetuate certain (damaging) stereotypes, are often observable[16]: crisis, pathology, therapeutisation, resilience, and care-less-ness, as will be seen below, are all common. Discourses and collective imaginaries have concrete effects which are often replicated and imaged in institutional forms. Who is presumed at the centre, and who is an outsider? Who is assigned prominence and normativity? What 'symbols, myths and narratives' are used to represent community?[17] Enabling awareness of ideological assumptions around these discourses demands procedures of discursive 'conscientiazation'. Sue Saltmarsh, for instance, set out to disrupt 'Psy' discourses of University Mental Health Awareness Campaigns[18] in Australian Universities which constructed 'happiness, wellbeing and work-life balance as desirable [and] attainable', whilst mental ill health was constructed as 'as avoidable, manageable … [and] whose containment is treated as both devolved responsibility and celebratory occasion'.[19] She contends that too often mental health awareness campaigns utilise mental health for 'organizational gains', whilst 'ignoring, or over-simplifying, the systemic and social pressures which place the well-being of students and university workers under significant pressure'.[20] In my own institution's review, it was also felt that due attention needed to be paid to social models of mental (ill) health and wellbeing (which sensitised the institution to arenas, practices, and contexts which could hinder and/or enhance mental health and wellbeing) in addition to the hitherto near ubiquitous focus on a medical model which positioned the individual student's (or staff member's) body and mind as disordered and/or in need of treatment and therapy.

CRISIS, PATHOLOGY, AND THERAPEUTISATION

The language of 'crisis' seems prevalent in much contemporary literature on student mental (ill) health[21]; frequent too are depictions of this as an 'explosion' and/or 'epidemic' threatening to overwhelm not only individuals but also entire institutions through relentless demand on resources.[22] The UUK Stepchange framework lists as a risk the 'demand for, and costs of, student support services [which] are increasing sharply'.[23] The framework also specifically references crisis narratives as jeopardising and threatening not just institutional, but also sector-wide reputations:

> There is a public narrative of a crisis in student mental health. Headlines such as the 'Epidemic of mental illness on campus', 'Student mental health is at crisis point', 'Do British universities have a suicide problem?' characterise higher education as a toxic environment. In an alternative account, students are portrayed as vulnerable – a 'snowflake generation'. Neither of these politicised narratives help students facing mental health difficulties; nor do they address the organisational and systemic challenge of student mental health which demands a rigorous and open assessment of need, appropriate planning and investment and a robust evaluation of progress. Negative outcomes can be enormously damaging for universities: for example, the University of York's portrayal by the media following the cluster of student suicides in 2015. Positive narratives are harder to find, though increased investments are well received: for example, 'University of York invests up to £500,000 in mental health support services'.[24]

Beyond reputational maintenance, however, are the fact that discourses focused on crisis can lead to particular (often marginalising and discriminating) institutional perspectives towards those perceived as suffering mental ill health.[25] Various means by which students are tracked (in learning analytics, Teaching Excellence Framework (TEF) metrics on minority populations, etc., and on account of gender, race, social class, culture, religion, etc.)[26] and accordingly are 'identified' as 'at risk', 'vulnerable' and 'fragile' within institutions indelibly influence and shape attitudes surrounding certain student identities implicitly seen as 'other' to a presumed norm or [de-]valued as a social category. Margaret Price's book, *Mad at School*,[27] drawing on disability studies and mad studies, argues that medical discourse predominates in academia, and as such, often those students with mental (ill) health are constructed as 'out of place' in such spaces. Such assumptions all too easily equate assumed vulnerability with pathology and 'treatment':

> Therapeutic discourse means the language of disorder, addiction, vulnerability and dysfunction along with associated practices from different branches of therapy ... In practice, the government responses in several European countries already focus on building individualistic competence related to emotional well-being and mental health. In various educational settings, typical initiatives include therapeutic activities such as interventions, activities for raising self-esteem, and behavioural training.[28]

Marking out students as falling short of, or other to a sanist, rational norm also implicitly harbours prejudicial attitudes. Jennifer Poole et al. note that 'sanism is a devastating form of oppression, often leading to negative stereotyping or arguments that individuals with mental health histories are not fit to study'.[29] Indeed, the academy has long been 'so loyal to the medical model that sanist aggressions, such as pathologizing, labelling, exclusion, and dismissal have become a normal part of professional practice and education'.[30] Disability studies can sensitise the sector to the potentially 'debilitating impacts of neoliberal academia' and its attendant discourses which augment ableism and sanism[31]: 'initiatives aimed at supporting students and attending to their self-esteem are not power-free arenas.'[32] On the contrary, they often assume:

> an ideal universal student the autonomous independent (actually white, Western, male and middle-class learner) which preserves and rearticulates the rational/emotional, mind/body binary that has been subject to considerable and sustained criticism/deconstruction from feminist theorists.[33]

Furthermore, often discourses surrounding widening participation initiatives and inclusion of 'non-traditional' students evoke a 'deficit [medical] model' so much so that a 'turn to the emotional' is often perceived as 'showcasing "damaged" subjects'[34] and a suspicion that education is somehow conceived as 'therapeutic' or 'normalising'. Rhiannon Firth in her study of *Somatic Pedagogies* explores what has been termed 'therapeutic education' (drawing on the work of Ecclestone and Rawdin)[35] in which certain students are posited as 'vulnerable' or 'at risk'. Discourses identify such individuals and try to instil within them through interventions, higher 'self-esteem', 'confidence', 'emotional literacy', 'positive attitudes',[36] and 'resilience and flexibility'. Firth warns that these discourses risk 're-cast[ing] social problems as emotional ones ... and erod[ing] social ties as personal relationships [which] are increasingly featured as ... dysfunctional, abusive and dependent'.[37] She notes how such discourses risk:

> Fragment[ing] the informal networks that people might previously have drawn on for support, which in turn undermines the potential for collective political struggle. It also leads to increased dependence on professionals who are implicated in practices of surveillance as people are expected to reveal more and more of their private and inner lives ... [This] promote[s] a particular limited and limiting account of what it means to be human: a 'diminished self' ... [which] which undermines the radical and transformative power of education and of human beings.[38]

More cynically, she argues this sets the stage for 'production of [individual] conformist neoliberal subjects' and those who fall short of this image are censored, excluded, and/or treated/normalised. Neoliberalism itself has been identified as a context which 'normalizes the medicalization of human life. Because success, virtue, and happiness in liberal market society are often associated with material wealth, prestige and coming out on top.'[39] Moreover, because of this, mental ill health is firmly situated within the individual. As such the 'social realm' is rarely considered, as individuals are understood as 'self-contained agents' with bodies (and minds) which are pathologised and 'thoughts and behaviours that deviate from what the market defines as functional, productive, or desirable'.[40] Margaret Thornton in her study of discourses of wellness in Australian higher education legal academies accordingly notes how the:

> Neoliberalisation of higher education is invariably overlooked in the literature as a primary cause of stress, even though it is responsible for the high fees, large classes and an increasingly competitive job market. The ratcheting up of fees places pressure on students to vie with one another for highly remunerated employment in the corporate world. In this way, law graduates

productively serve the new knowledge economy and the individualisation of their psychological distress effectively deflects attention away from the neo-liberal agenda.[41]

As a result of this, some have called out crisis discourses as a 'crisis of mis-labelling', with the 'risk of medicalising normal emotions in well-meaning but unfocused attempts to raise awareness of mental health issues'.[42] In a similar vein arguing against pathological and therapeutic discourses, Leathwood and Hey write:

> Understanding 'therapy society', and the place and power of emotions in higher education, need not take us into the realm of self-indulgence, nor to a collusion with the production of 'the vulnerable subject', to help us to re-understand the price subjects pay and continue to pay in coming to terms with the living of inequity ... It is precisely to appreciate the ways the social comes to form and wrap around the individual self that a focus on the emo-tion and gender, class, 'race' and higher/education reveals. To enhance this exploration it is necessary to work with an imagination that is attuned to, rather than turned from, emotion ... We could perhaps then begin to better design educational systems which take into account the informal, the auto/biographic, the historical, the personal, the interpersonal as sites of learning and power/powerlessness. The intellectual effort to put these discomforting realms and their messy feelings back into the quarantine zone is suspicious and, we suggest, as much about the politics of masculinity as about the pur-poses of higher education.[43]

What seems certain is that discourses and metaphors of crisis and pathol-ogy position certain students' minds, bodies, and needs, as somehow problematic, unruly and/or unmanageable within an institution. Furthermore, while medical discourse still dominates within higher educa-tion[44] an inordinate focus on biomedical/psychological models (and indi-vidualistic frameworks) to the exclusion of collective, social, and cultural frameworks, including attention to stigma production and/or neoliberal models of time, affect, and hyper-productivity etc., are to be expected. Such discourses perilously rehearse 'sanist systems of oppression and the normalcy they reconstitute.'[45] They also remain distant from institutional 'collective politics' and rather locked into a focus on 'a set of individual-ised tools by which to 'cope' with the strains of the neoliberal academy.'[46]

RESILIENCE, TIME, AND PRODUCTIVITY

Tropes of resilience are also common in discourses surrounding student mental (ill) health and wellbeing. Resiliency is 'a flexible resistance capability ... where is it possible to adapt successfully to very strong, continuous even shocking external influence'.[47] The etymology of the word is from the Latin for jump: '"re-salire" means to jump back ... but not to break.'[48] Many have noted that neoliberalism uses mental health and wellbeing as a tool by which students can be constructed too as 'more economically productive subjects'.[49] Rationality, autonomy, responsibility, entrepreneurship, positivity, and self-confidence are among allied characteristics which 'constitute the neoliberal subject in ways consonant with neoliberal governmentality'.[50] Interesting then in this respect is the way that the UUK Stepchange framework affirmingly cites the UK government's interventions of mental health support in education, in particular Theresa May's 2017 statement that:

> Young people want to grow up to be confident and resilient, supported to fulfil their goals and ambitions. So we are placing an emphasis on building resilience, promoting good mental health and wellbeing.[51]

Social scientists have shown how social problems risk being psychologised, and influential therapeutising discourses (often forwarded in neoliberal contexts) serve to bolster these attitudes.[52] Kristiina Brunila accordingly speaks of a 'survival discourse' adopted by students who are seen by institutions, and increasingly themselves, as problematic, and who through individual autonomy can, in an age of neoliberalism, develop self-responsibility which leads to 'coping in the labour market':[53]

> Young people are described as experiencing personal struggles but, after emotional work or other types of therapeutic activity provided by programmes, they have the possibility of becoming survivors and being autonomous selves. Consequently, when the education of young people considered at risk is discussed more and more in terms of survival, direct attention to the relational, affective and emotional aspects of young people's lives as well as the psycho-social dimensions of social and educational inequality become seen as integral to socially just educational goals and practices.[54]

Vik Loveday likewise notes the '[self-]embodiment of deficiency', particularly shame, by students and the 'classed and gendered conditions [and one could add cross-cultural meanings] that coalesce in its production'.[55] This can be particularly prevalent for students undertaking professional practice courses (in medicine, law, etc.) who fear talking openly about mental ill health will 'spoil' their identity,[56] or for international students who for cross-cultural reasons may be reticent on account of shame or 'losing face'.[57]

In response to such perspectives, others have sought to 'resist resilience' and disrupt discourses of self-efficacy in higher education.[58] These caution that resilience discourses function 'in ideological tandem with a neoliberal shifting away from communal understandings of the self towards the promotion of individuals as sole, discrete, autonomous agents'[59] often tooled for employment and the labour market:

> Empowering [resilience] discourse, promoting the role of individual agency in affecting success, the subtext of this is that failure is also the fault of the individual ... Even at its most benign, resilience is always reactive rather than pro-active. In focusing on what an individual can do to change themselves, the promotion of resilience tacitly assumes social inequalities to be fixed, highlighting, as Ahmed has suggested, the deeply conservative underpinnings of the discourse.[60]

It seems quite right to point out the problems involved in isolating a characteristic such as resilience, or growth mind-sets, without considering wider social, cultural, political, or contextual factors, or questioning the policies and institutions which scaffold these.[61] Resilience inevitably has communal and collective dimensions[62] (manifest in relationships, interactions, and processes), but these are too often overlooked or undervalued in individualising models.

CARELESSNESS

'Carelessness' too has been identified as an implicit discursive dynamic in contemporary higher education and not unrelated to mental (ill) health and wellbeing therein. Kathleen Lynch hails it as a 'hidden doxa of higher education' which has been intensified by managerialism and 'individualized academic capitalism' whereby care is only recognised when it is 'professionalized'.[63] Within the Exeter Wellbeing Review, communications around mitigation, academic honesty, and so on, and the means by which students interfaced with increasingly impersonal systems and processes were particularly noted as being perceived by students as 'careless' (or due to time pressures 'lacking in care', rather than 'careless' per se) in this regard. Lynch sees 'carelessness' (often allied with efficiency) as being 'endorsed as morally worthy' in the neoliberal academy: Evocatively, she writes:

> It is enacted daily in the lifestyle of senior managers and an increasing number of academics with a 24/7 culture of availability, and migratory and transnational lifestyles. In itself this might not matter except that what has become defined as the pinnacle of all virtue, unbounded work, is now making its way down the academic employment chain. Academics at all levels expect and are expected to work unregulated and long hours; it is part of their apprenticeship. To be a successful academic is to be unencumbered by caring.[64]

Others have noted that relationships are undervalued and overlooked within higher education. For example, the UK Professional Standards Framework for Higher Education urge academics to 'develop effective learning environments and approaches to student support and guidance' and 'respect individual learners and diverse learning communities' (HEA 2013, p.3), '[but] … there is no overt and explicit mention of constructing attachments or of building bonds or the reasons for doing so, as with other professional networks'.[65] Such attitudes inevitably have implications for both staff and student wellbeing. Lynch notes how carelessness is frequently afforded a high status in higher education, and as such:

> Care and interdependency are confined to the sub-altern and relationality is denied … [the] model citizen at the heart of research and of liberal classical education is rational and public. It is a person who is being prepared for economic, political and cultural life in the public sphere but not for a relational life as an interdependent, caring and other-centred human being.[66]

Lynch notes that whilst wellbeing is often ensured by nurturing and supportive interactions and relationships, the academy rarely seeks to protect or promote such associations: this 'neglect of care as a subject for research and teaching is a serious educational deficit'.[67] She notes the eliding of emotion and affect is the heir of Cartesian views of education in which 'an autonomous, rational person … whose relationship is not regarded as central to her or his being takes centre stage'.[68] As such, she notes:

The idealization of the 'care-free' academic did not emerge with neoliberal capitalism. Neoliberalism exacerbated the demand for care-free workers, but the origins of carelessness in education lie deeper within the Cartesian thinking that underpins the very organization and scholarship of education itself.[69]

Feminist methodologies too have sought to uncover the 'master discourse' of the academy as 'normalised disembodied reason'[70] and have bemoaned the erasure of affect in higher education, including the affective dimensions of student experience. Others have intentionally begun to resist the discourses of carelessness. Sandra Wilde, for instance, laments that 'the loss of care in education is a sign of a deeper social malaise'[71] in which affiliative compassion and kindness continue to be relegated within public institutions into terrains of the 'subjective' and 'emotional' which are frequently (and erroneously) pitted against 'intellectual, technical or objective work'.[72]

> The academy has traditionally been constructed as the paradigmatic site of pure rationality devoted to the dispassionate and objective search for truth an emotion-freezone, reflecting the dominance of Cartesian dualism with its rational/emotional, mind/body, public/private, masculine/feminine split. Universities have epitomised the rational and valorised side of this dichotomy, with emotion rejected as subjective and irrational. It is not coincidental that women's entry to the academy was resisted on precisely these grounds.[73]

Others too who have probed the 'psychosocial life of the neoliberal university'[74] note how the academic world is indelibly marked by associations with 'rationality, methodological principles, objectivity and logical argument'.[75] Such perspectives inevitably position, within organisational identities, the emotional and affective dimensions of experience (particularly when these are seen as disordered as in mental ill health or compromised wellbeing) as 'alien, irrelevant, and disruptive'.[76]

REFIGURING DISCOURSES: COMPASSION AND KINDNESS

As the above attests, the effects of certain discourses surrounding mental ill health and wellbeing in the neoliberal university 'are written on [minds] and bod[ies]'.[77] A focus on individualising pathologies, resilience, productivity, and care-less procedures, however, can inordinately preoccupy 'the corporate university, not the well-being of its subject'.[78] As a result, higher education institutions need to re-imagine their identities as purposeful, compassionate, kind, and care-full organisations which are intentionally relational.[79] Other-regarding community is central for overcoming isolation, shame, and self-stigmatisation, and therefore central in enabling students not just to survive, but thrive. Compassion and kindness have of course been widely recognised as important values and foci for mental health and wellbeing; indeed, the focus for Mental Health Awareness Week in 2020 was 'kindness'. Organisers accordingly noted:

> We have chosen kindness because of its singular ability to unlock our shared humanity. Kindness strengthens relationships, develops community and deepens solidarity. It is a cornerstone of our individual and collective mental health. Wisdom from every culture across history recognises that kindness is something that all human beings need to experience and practise to be fully alive.[80]

Compassion and kindness conceived relationally also offer opportunities to overcome isolation and foster relationships and a sense of belonging.[81] Indeed, some hail 'kindness as compassion in action'.[82] Notable was the amount of times students commented positively within the NSS comments and interviews on 'feeling like someone cared', 'tutors were so kind'.[83] Applied compassion and kindness can have real and lasting effects. As a result, some have developed enabling pedagogical practices which are compassionate, care-full,[84] and/or centred in kindness,[85] as intentionally subversive of neoliberal values. Kindness is etymologically rooted in familial discourses of 'kindred'.[86] Philps and Taylor in their cultural history of the concept noted that whilst kindness had featured in public morality, it was increasingly exiled and relegated in industrialisation and became a value associated with the feminine and home, as opposed to realms of manufacturing and business:

> The relegation of the care to the private domain has profound consequences for understanding of law, citizenship and the economy, and thus in turn for education, which is understood as the preparation of students for the public life of work.[87]

In reclaiming kindness in higher education pedagogy, one is not however 'lenient, soft and prepared to overlook errors and shallowness of thoughts',[88] nor merely responding to a professionalised duty of 'due care', but rather affirming 'the recognition [that] the mutual humanity of teacher and student involves holding the self to account in the exercise of kindness'.[89] Rigour and challenge is central for higher education, but must nonetheless operate within contexts of sociality and safety. For mental health and wellbeing is situated not only in individuals but also in organisations and communities: 'To promote one you need to promote the others … individual well-being cannot be fostered in isolation from organizations that affect our lives and the communities where we live [study and work].'[90]

Compassion and kindness, too, can reconfigure institutional discourses based on individualised notions of resilience, time, and productivity. Aine Mahon in her article 'Contemplation, Compassion and the Ethics of Slowing Down' draws on the 2016 book, *The Slow Professor: Challenging the Culture of Speed in the Academy,* in which Maggie Berg and Barbara Seeber petition for the value of slowness for both staff and students in contemporary higher education: 'it is perhaps more important that we begin to demand less of our students and not more. [We need to explore as a sector] the possibilities for a less frenetic approach to university teaching and learning.'[91] She also notes the economic climate which has compelled many students to seek part-time employment alongside their study and that students' 'performances' are audited according to a presumed 'norm': attendance monitoring, participation, and self-refection are all designed to examine and track progress yet:

> The student who might wish to take their time—who may not feel ready to share their thoughts on a text or a topic in the quick-fire forum of the lecture or the seminar—will not be rewarded (or, in Macfarlane's terms, may in fact be 'vilified') as again it is not obvious that learning is taking place. In these contexts, it is all too easy for speed and visibility to trump thoughtfulness and deliberation. The same university parlance praises particular students as 'very quick' or 'very engaged' but such praise is doled out without critical consideration of what it truly means to be transformed through educational encounter. Those of us teaching at university for any length of time will attest that the same students presenting as 'very quick, very engaged' may not be the same students necessarily producing the most insightful essay at the end of the semester. And yet, we are always surprised.[92]

Riya Shahjahan as a result advocates for 'decolonizing time', bodies, and pedagogy in the Western academy.[93] He sees Eurocentric models of time (based on linear forward motion, progress, and learning outcomes) dominating neoliberal models of higher education: 'The multiplying and endless "academic tasks"—countless forms of assessments and a hyped up productivity schedule—engendered through neoliberal reforms propagate an ever-present "scarcity of time" affectively and cognitively.'[94] So much so that those bodies and mind who do not 'manage their time' or are not 'productive' (/'waste' time) are often disparaged as failing or disengaged. Time in this sense has become associated with student (and staff) moral characters and identities. Moreover, with increasing digital interaction, strict time boundaries between work and home need more rigorous protection.[95] Shahjahan notes that mind-centred epistemologies displace us from our bodies, and in response, he petitions for 're-emboy[ing] the learning environment'.[96] Re-inhabiting bodies consciously, rather than rushed schedules and tasks, try to invoke quality of attention, by incorporating class rituals (silence, physical movement, and sensory experiences) and contemplative pedagogies, as well as just minded words.

Whilst cultures of productivity are ingrained within school systems, to some extent universities have an opportunity to un-teach that, rather than instilling similar dynamics. An Asian proverb interestingly notes that being 'too busy' means the 'soul is dead'.[97] Against the neoliberal emphasis on competition, speed, and business, compassionate and kind communities are called 'to offer to each other the strong social support that underpins university and academic life as essentially human and humane endeavours'.[98] Such environments position students not as lone survivors, but communal thrivers in which 'relational, interdependent practice between two or more people' are sustained.[99] S. Gibson talks about how metrics surrounding 'student satisfaction' particularly the NSS, and so on, inevitably means that 'capacity to respond to students' needs and circumstances in a compassionate and kind way may be diminished'.[100] In contrast, a slow scholarship would develop an ethic of self-care and other-regard: 'and the creation of caring communities as a means of "finding ways to exist in a world that is diminishing"'.[101]

Looking to the future, time and affect seem two important areas to begin to refigure psycho-social dimensions of higher education systems. Institutions must recognise their complicity in perpetuating regimes which have inevitably 'got inside us', 'shape[d] our sense of self', 'produce[ed] particular affects and subjectivities (e.g. shame or anxiety)', 'erode[d] collectivity and collaboration', and 'promote[d] competition'.[102] They must also intentionally construct alternative discourses, practices, and curricula which will build more affective, affiliative, compassionate, and kind institutional characters and identities.

'COMPASSION' AND 'KINDNESS' CURRICULUM INTERVENTIONS FOR STUDENT WELLBEING

Under the auspices of an Advance HE project, 'Embedding Wellbeing in the Curriculum'[103] in which the University of Exeter was a project partner, certain compassion and kindness curriculum interventions were purposefully designed and adopted. Following Price's insights from disability and mad studies, that norms must be refigured in the academy, not primarily around the question of identifying those at risk and 'curing' mental distress through treatment, but rather the substance and practice of the curriculum itself,[104] the project team identified two areas for especial attention within the Advance HE consultancy process: (a) curriculum infusion of mental health and wellbeing-related content and (b) inclusive and compassionate learning and assessment. In engaging these areas we hoped to contribute to the 'success for all'[105] theme within the University of Exeter Education strategy and, across the institution first, promote understanding and awareness of mental wellbeing and distress; second, take account of students' own experiences of mental wellbeing and distress; third, promote effective learning, teaching, and assessment that complemented the work of existing support services.[106] The primary aim was to develop resources and interventions for education staff to enable them to design compassionate curricula which would minimise exclusionary practices. Throughout it was acknowledged that curricula, learning, and assessment do not take place outside of a context of safety alongside challenge, and we hoped the project would help us ensure that the way in which we delivered our educational challenges was grounded in a profound respect for all members of our learning community.

(a) *Curriculum Infusion of Mental Health and Wellbeing-Related Content*

Curriculum infusion refers to a strategic way to include education about real-life issues into academic content, tasks, and syllabi. Curriculum 'content' has been a key dimension in addressing inequalities of race ('decolonising the curriculum') and gender. Curriculum content, it was suggested,

could also be used to address stigma surrounding mental ill health and positively promote wellbeing. Building on the Advance HE report on
'Embedding Mental Wellbeing in the Curriculum' (2017)[107] and the
Engelhard Project at Georgetown University on Curriculum Infusion of
Compassion and Wellbeing,[108] we piloted within disciplines already identified as 'deep dive' programmes within the project a curriculum infusion of
mental health and wellbeing-related content, and have begun to construct a
repository of good practice within this area for discussion across disciplines.
The project took inspiration from the University of Exeter's already well-
established Grand Challenge on Mental Health, an extra-curricular activity
in which students from different disciplines collaborate to critically reflect
on and re-imagine solutions to questions in collaboration with external
partners. In a module on disability studies, for example, students designed
and led 'slow' seminars in which contemplative observation, reading, and
writing were integral parts of the sessions. Classics designed a 'Mindful
Classics' component of the curricula accenting contemplative pedagogies in
the teaching of antiquity. In Theology and Religion modules on spirituali-
ties, students encountered practitioners of mindfulness, meditation, and
yoga, and had opportunities to physically practice these within class too.
They also traced genealogies and affinities between these wellness practices,
ancient traditions, and their reception in contemporary contexts: both as
tools of the neoliberal self, but also politicised means through which neoliberal identities and dynamics could be subverted, and through justice bonds
of collective care with others and the environment could be developed.[109]

(b) *Inclusive and Compassionate Learning and Assessment*

We also sought to investigate some of the ways in which curriculum
design and assessments at Exeter (amount and proportionality of assessment parts in modules; different natures of assessments—exams; oral presentations; problem-solving group work; timings and practices surrounding
submission of assessments, etc.) could be negative triggers for students
who were (or perceived themselves to be) 'othered' in some way (whether
that is in regard to an Individual Learning Plan [ILP], mental health
issues, etc.). We also looked at the spread of ILPs across the institution and
worked towards 'inclusive design' of modules and assessments which
would negate the need for many of these so-called alternative provisions.
This intervention was inspired by emerging literature on pedagogies of
compassion which impel course designers to question some of the ways in
which implicitly some students feel themselves to be marginalised by

certain assessment activities and expectations.[110] We also probed how certain assessments could be more compassionately conceived and more universally designed: 'a model based on accessibility and choice, on discovering students' talents and needs, and on linking them explicitly to key curriculum goals'.[111] Asking honestly could negotiated assessments, for instance, allow all students to opt to deliver a presentation not only face to face but also via a podcast or vlog? More radically, perhaps could lifting caps on retakes, so the stakes psychologically seemed less high for students, be actioned? A number of practical interventions were also published for staff to integrate kindness and compassion within their modules to enhance student wellbeing. These were particularly timely when preparing, in light of Covid-19, for likely mixed modes of delivery for modules (face to face/online) to a student population dispersed across different locations and spaces (physical/digital.) Building on the Advance HE report 'Embedding Mental Wellbeing in the Curriculum' (2017) which adopts the New Economics Foundation's model of '5 Ways to Wellbeing' (connect, be active, take notice, keep learning, and giving), the interventions were categorised as such. It was also stressed that being up-front with students that staff had considered their wellbeing in designing the curriculum could in itself bolster confidence, safety, and reduce (self-) stigmatisation for them around this issue. The pointers designed for staff use are listed below:

(i) Connect:
Feeling connected, and having a shared identity with a learning community, is important for wellbeing.

Model kindness (the recognition we are all kin within our learning community) and compassion as a pedagogical practice in your communication with students. Be mindful of your tone in written feedback. Also, ask for mid-module feedback from them on any aspects of the subject/structure/interface of module they find difficult. You could try 'empathy mapping' your communications and curriculum (a way of signifying behaviours/feelings and a proven means to enhance wellbeing) or use empathy mapping with students to evaluate their experience of aspects of the module. Empathetic communication is an important skill for students themselves to practice to each other, particularly in online forums where communication is sometimes not accompanied by visual clues or body language.[112]

Facilitate active and meaningful contact, co-operation, and peer learning opportunities between face-to-face students and online students through group tasks, assessments, and activities (Wikis, producing crowd-sourced notes, etc.). In-class 'breakout rooms' and after-class digital discussion/social spaces for students (digital cafés; virtual student lounges on electronic module sites) could also be useful to build learning communities across different spaces. If your discipline has a peer mentor scheme, encourage your students to make use of it. Inspired by the Frome Compassionate Communities model, encourage peer community connectors to link isolated students with discipline societies, and social events on campus, and get 'peer student connectors' to accompany them in attending these events. Also make students aware of their subject representatives, allies, and inclusion champions within the student body (these individuals could even make short presentations in lectures or recordings for display on module pages).[113]

Publish a communication plan clearly setting up boundaries around time and availability (e.g. you will respond to individual enquiries or e-mails on Monday, Wednesday, and Friday only, or within two business days; your 'office hours' are X; you will give whole module updates once a fortnight, etc.). Some members of staff, especially those with caring responsibilities, may need or prefer to work outside traditional weekdays and working hours: the key is managing expectations. This is critical in alleviating anxiety for both students and staff. You may also need to think about timings: synchronous/asynchronous meetings and classes to ensure flexibility for students to participate. Also encourage reflection on digital wellbeing: 'the capacity to look after personal health, safety, relationships and work-life balance in digital settings; and understanding of the benefits and risks of digital participation in relation to health and wellbeing outcomes'.[114]

(ii) Be Active
Physical activity is important for wellbeing.

Encourage physical movement at appropriate points in class both in face to face and virtual spaces. It can be very hard to sustain motivation and attention in a sedentary position and/or with on-screen delivery. Give five minutes at regular intervals for people to get a drink or collectively stretch/touch their toes! If you want to be more creative, get students to vote on topics through physical movement.[115]

(iii) Take Notice
Forging links between learning and a student's own experiences enhances self-compassion and wellbeing.

Employ Contemplative Pedagogies. These approaches aim to foster deep engagement with material and adopt slower time 'through focused attention, reflection, and awareness'. Examples which could be used as formative exercises in modules include contemplative 'beholding' of images and objects; 'contemplative reading' (reading aloud, slow reading, rereading, annotating, performing, or memorising passages) and 'contemplative writing' (writing continuously for a predetermined amount of time or journaling about their learning journey within the module).[116]

(iv) Keep learning
Keeping learning is essential to student success and wellbeing.

Consider aspects of curriculum design which may impact positively or negatively on a student's abilities to keep learning: too many points of assessment and bunching of deadlines for assessments is often a cause of anxiety and stress. Students often also appreciate agency within design of assessments. Can you, for example, offer an 'either/or' option (e.g. either a presentation or a podcast?), bearing in mind the need to ensure each option gives students a chance to demonstrate the learning criteria. Can formative tasks be linked incrementally to the production of more 'high-stake' summative pieces?
Encourage links to be made by students to already existent subject societies and discipline events (external speakers, etc.) in face to face and digital spaces. This can allow them to 'keep learning' topics they have encountered within specific disciplines. It can also help students connect to their wider community, which is especially important if they are feeling isolated and/or are off campus.

(v) Giving
Giving is important for community and wellbeing.

Produce a digital gratitude wall. Encourage staff and students to mark three moments, people, and contributions within their module each week which they have found helpful and/or are grateful for. We often don't take notice or value each other enough. Showing gratitude means instances and actions don't pass unrecognised. Gratitude relates to mindfulness, wellbeing, and building a positive sense of community.[117]

The entire 'Wellbeing in the Curriculum Project' at Exeter sought to pay attention to students as 'affective and embodied selves' within higher education.[118] It encouraged staff to consider students in pedagogic encounters, without 'collaps[ing education] into therapeutic discourses'.[119] It also accented the role of time, affective reactions to, and dimensions of, education, for 'these in turn all play a key role in the establishment and maintenance of identity, with the associated sense of belonging'[120] all elements which institutions can play are part developing.

CONCLUSION

Whilst the semantics of 'crisis' (which opened this chapter) can, as has been illustrated here, signify imminent disaster, or for organisations 'a fundamental threat to system stability, a questioning of assumptions and beliefs, and threats to high priority goals, including image, legitimacy, profitability and even survival',[121] it can also denote a turning point, an advancement, an assembling of reserves for development, of growth, of renewal, and of change.[122] Interestingly, the word 'crisis' derives from the Greek word *krisis*, which was frequently used to denote a crossroads or turning point.[123] The Covid-19 pandemic itself can, in this sense, be hailed a site of 'crisis' which, whilst many see loading additional distress on staff and students, could itself be a defining moment in relation to mental health and wellbeing in higher education: already it has been interpreted as 'a wakeup call for those who value the quality of life and those who value financial interests regardless of the consequences to global health or human beings'.[124] Indeed, history has taught us that 'epidemics gave humans many challenges, but yet also brought with it many visible and hidden opportunities', including opportunities to build alternative, and in this instance, compassionate and kind, communities.[125] The emergence of a so-called Cornona Economy has already been theorised as helping members of organisations to co-operate and collaborate more[126] and recognise humanity as 'social-beings' rather than just individual 'human beings'. This collective dimension is seen as promising for more constructive discourses surrounding mental health and wellness[127]:

> The crisis wakened us to appreciating the value of losing physical contact due to fear of cross-contamination. The incidence made us realise how

much we love people around us and the true loyalty for those we love. This accident or incident helped to explain how we need to stick to the continual development of our social institutions so that it would impact the human action in similar crisis in the future.[128]

This chapter has demonstrated that within higher education institutions, student mental (ill) health and wellbeing discourses are too often conceived individually and pathologically within a medical model (focusing on reactive response and biomedical/psychological treatments) rather than through broader social, cultural, and discursive approaches which arguably have 'a greater capacity to effect change'.[129] Proposals here also start to encourage institutions to critically recognise their part in propagating ultimately damaging discourses premised on individual resilience, hyper-productivity, frenetic time, and the like. Whole institutional methods can stimulate an environment in which the university can provide students through their collective environment, learning communities, and co-operative and educational programmes, appropriate literacies around the qualities and values of compassion and kindness which can safeguard not only their own but also the interconnectivity of theirs' and others' mental health and wellbeing. Such approaches:

> Engage students in a transformational process by encouraging critical reflection on their learning and actions. This is as much a social process as it is a psychological one, and is clearly a relational process between teachers and students and the ideas shared. It is a process that is also intimately influenced by the wider cultural environment of the institution.[130]

Seen in this light, higher education institutions are not institutions which dispassionately (and care-less-ly) convey knowledge and skills to individuals, but also can collectively develop compassionate (care-full) and kind communities and discourses which will ultimately foster more just, equitable, and flourishing forms of education for all.[131]

Notes

1. Samira Shackle "The way universities are run is making us ill': inside the student mental health crisis' *The Guardian* (27th September 2019). Available online at: https://www.theguardian.com/society/2019/sep/27/anxiety-mental-breakdowns-depression-uk-students. In Exeter, the University wellbeing service has seen that demand has trebled since

2012: 'During its first year it was accessed by around 1000 in 2012/13. The numbers now receiving support rose to around 2400 in 2016/17.' See   https://www.devonlive.com/news/devon-news/figures-almost-treble-number-exeter-16057971

2. 'The crisis in student mental health hit the news in 2017 after a high number of suicides at Bristol University. Over 18 months, starting in October 2016, 12 students are believed to have killed themselves. While the university tried to tackle the crisis, it struggled to keep up with the rising demand for help. In November 2018, a group of students gathered on a chilly Bristol street holding placards demanding better access to psychological support. The students told reporters that despite promises of more investment in student wellbeing, services were still badly overstretched.' Shackle, 'The way universities', no pages.

3. Rosalind Gill and Ngaire Donaghue, 'Resilience, apps and reluctant individualism: Technologies of self in the neoliberal academy' *Women's Studies International Forum* 54 (2016), 91–99, 91.

4. William Davies, who has written on commercialisation of happiness, cited in Shackle 'The way universities', no pages. A recent piece in the *British Medical Journal* too talked about 'adolescent mental health in crisis': 'The young people affected are "generation Z," born in the mid 1990s and early 2000s. They grew up in the age of social media, the great recession (2008), increases in family breakdown, growth of international terrorism, and, in the UK, student debt and predicted gaps in prosperity between them and their parents. Academic pressures at school cause stress, and the UK government has focused on testing in recent years. Many of these phenomena affect both boys and girls, although some factors, such as school performance pressures and lower family income, may be more likely to affect girls.' David Gunnell, Judi Kidger and Hamish Elvidge, 'Adolescent mental health in crisis' *BMJ* (June 2018). Available online at: https://doi.org/10.1136/bmj.k2608. 'The Mental Health Report 2019' conducted by The Insight Network and Digin which interviewed students across 140 UK higher education confirms as much when it records how over half of respondents faced '"serious personal, emotional, behavioural or mental health problems for which they needed professional help"'. See Sabrina Barr, 'Almost Half of Students have Experienced a Serious Psychological Issue', *The Independent* (10th March 2020). Available online at: https://www.independent.co.uk/life-style/health-and-families/students-mental-health-university-depression-anxiety-study-a9389571.html

5. The review team worked closely with scientists and psychologists (in the Mood Disorder Centre at Exeter), clinical health professionals (clinical psychiatrists, etc., at the University of Exeter Medical School), and education leaders (in education enhancement and on a national scale, Advance HE).

6. https://www.universitiesuk.ac.uk/stepchange. A revised version was released in May 2020. See https://www.universitiesuk.ac.uk/policy-and-analysis/reports/Documents/2020/uuk-stepchange-mhu.pdf

7. Vaneeta D'Andrea and David Gosling, *Improving Teaching and Learning in Higher Education: A Whole Institute Approach* (New York: McGraw-Hill Education, 2005), 2.

8. 'The framework looks to the psycho-social model of education which goes beyond the university to include parents, employers and the NHS' https://www.embrace-learning.com/step-change-a-model-for-promoting-mental-health-in-universities/ 'Universities UK has worked in partnership with the Institute for Public Policy Research (IPPR) to strengthen the evidence-base on mental health in higher education. Their independent report – *Not by Degrees: Improving student mental health in the UK's universities* – is being published on 4 September.' https://www.universitiesuk.ac.uk/news/Pages/New-framework-for-universities-to-help-improve-student-mental-health.aspx

9. Exeter's focus was a response to wider attention in this area within the sector. See Stuart J. Slavin, Debra L. Schindler and John T. Chibnall, 'Medical Student Mental Health: Improving Student Wellness Through Curricular Changes' *Acad Med* 89(4) (2014), 573–577. In the UK, a University Mental Health Charter has been established. See https://www.studentminds.org.uk/charter.html; The Mentally Healthy Universities Programme has also been developed: 'We are working with ten local Mind and university partnerships between now and August 2021 to improve both staff and student wellbeing. The programme aligns with the whole-university approach set out in UUK's StepChange framework and the University Mental Health Charter being developed by Student Minds.' See https://www.mind.org.uk/workplace/working-with-universities/

10. Citing Nicola Byrom, Kathryn Ecclestone, 'Are universities encouraging students to believe hard study is bad for their mental health?' *Times Higher Education* (2nd April 2020). Available online at: https://www.timeshighereducation.com/features/are-universities-encouraging-students-believe-hard-study-bad-their-mental-health

11. Citing Nicola Byrom, Ecclestone, 'Are universities', no pages.

12. Sorrel Pitcher, 'Students' Constructions of Mental Illness: Using Discourse Analysis to Develop Critical Language Awareness' (2013), Thesis, Department of Psychology University of Cape Town, 4. Available online at: http://www.careers.uct.ac.za/sites/default/files/image_tool/images/117/Sorrel.Pitcher.pdf

13. Sanism can be defined as prejudice against, or marginalising of, those perceived to have 'non-normative' minds. On sanism in the academy, see Louise J. Lawrence, *Bible and Bedlam: Madness, Sanism, and New Testament Interpretation* (London: Bloomsbury, 2018).

14. Peter N. Watkins, *Mental Health Practice: A Guide to Compassionate Care* (Butterworth-Heinemann, 2008), 3.

15. I was institutional lead on the project. Exeter staff voices on the project are included in Nick Bennett, 'Mental Fitness Helps us All to Thrive: It Should be in the Curriculum' *WONKHE* (7/09/20). Available online at: https://wonkhe.com/blogs/mental-fitness-helps-us-all-to-thrive-it-should-be-in-the-curriculum/. On the science of mindful compassion in university contexts, see Kathryn Waddington, 'Creating Conditions for Compassion' in P. Gibbs (ed), *The Pedagogy of Compassion at the Heart of Higher Education* (Springer, 2017), 49–72. Teena J. Clouston 'Transforming learning: teaching compassion and caring values in higher education' *Journal of Further and Higher Education* Vol 42 (2018), 1015–1024. For an example on minimising anxiety in minority or disadvantaged university populations, see: R. N. Hao, 'Critical compassionate pedagogy and the teacher's role in first-generation student success' *New Directions for Teaching and Learning* 127 (2011), 91–98. Compassion-focussed therapies (CFT) (based on threat-derived safety strategies, goal setting, and positive reinforcement) for students in the associated contexts of pan-university cultural 'compassion' interventions will be traced. Alexander C. Wilson, Kate Mackintosh, Kevin Power & Stella W. Y. Chan 'Effectiveness of Self-Compassion Related Therapies: a Systematic Review and Meta-analysis' *Mindfulness* 10 (2019), 979–995. Also See David Veale, Paul Gilbert, Jon Wheatley, Iona Naismith 'A New Therapeutic Community: Development of a Compassion-Focussed and Contextual Behavioural Environment' *Clinical Psychology and Psychotherapy* 22 (4) (2015), 285–303.

16. Sorrel Pitcher 'Students', 4.

17. Peter A. Hall and Michèle Lamont, *Successful Societies: How Institutions and Culture Affect Health* (Cambridge: Cambridge University Press, 2009), 12.

18. Sue Saltmarsh, 'No, I'm Not OK': Disrupting 'Psy' Discourses of University Mental Health Awareness Campaigns' in Eva Petersen and Zsuzsa Millei, *Interrupting the Psy-Disciplines in Education* (London: Palgrave Macmillan, 2016), 167–183, 167.

19. Saltmarsh, 'No', 168.

20. Saltmarsh, 'No', 168.

21. 'Mental health/illness discourse currently runs rampant in higher education. Universities are declaring a "mental health crisis" on campus … and policy, access, and accommodation strategies rest on tactics that respond with notions of risk and liability.' Sarah N. Snyder, Kendra-Ann Pitt, Fady Shanouda, Jijian Voronka, Jenna Reid and Danielle Landry 'Unlearning through Mad Studies: Disruptive pedagogical praxis' *Curriculum Inquiry*

49:4 (2019) 485–502. Available online at: DOI: https://doi.org/1 0.1080/03626784.2019.1664254

22. 'The crisis is creating a growing need for financial and human resources to address this serious problem. Counselling centres in post-secondary educational institutions have difficulty meeting the growing needs of students as they are underfunded and understaffed. Resources are required to increase staffing, improve training, and increase physical space on campus for counselling centres.' Alicia Kruisselbrink, 'A Suffering Generation: Six Factors Contributing to the Mental Health Crisis in North American Higher Education' *College Quarterly* 16 (2013). Available online at: https://files.eric.ed.gov/fulltext/EJ1016492.pdf. See also James E. Côté, 'The Enduring Usefulness of Erikson's Concept of the Identity Crisis in the 21st Century: An Analysis of Student Mental Health Concern' *Identity* 18(4) (2018), 1–13. Available online at: https://www. researchgate.net/publication/328124487_The_Enduring_Usefulness_ of_Erikson's_Concept_of_the_Identity_Crisis_in_the_21st_Century_ An_Analysis_of_Student_Mental_Health_Concerns/citation/download.

23. https://www.universitiesuk.ac.uk/stepchange

24. https://www.universitiesuk.ac.uk/policy-and-analysis/stepchange/ Pages/case-for-action.aspx

25. Jade Boyd and Thomas Kerr, 'Policing 'Vancouver's mental health crisis': a critical discourse analysis' *Critical Public Health* 26:4, (2016) 418–433. Available online at: https://doi.org/https://doi.org/10.108 0/09581596.2015.1007923

26. Transitions (into university, and going from one year to another) or doing professional placements or years abroad have been identified as particular stressors. See Meredith L. Terry, Mark R. Leary and Sneha Mehta, 'Self-compassion as a Buffer against Homesickness, Depression, and Dissatisfaction in the Transition to College' *Self and Identity* (2012). Available online at: https://doi.org/10.1080/15298868.2012.667913

27. Margaret Price, *Mad at School: Rhetorics of Mental Disability and Academic Life* (Michigan: University of Michigan Press, 2011).

28. Kristiina Brunila, 'The Rise of the Survival Discourse in an Era of Therapisation and Neoliberalism' *Education Inquiry* 5:1 (2014). Available online at https://doi.org/10.3402/edui.v5.24044

29. Jennifer M. Poole, Tania Jivraj, Araxi Arslanian, Kristen Bellows, Sheila Chiasson, Husnia Hakimy, Jessica Pasini, Jenna Reid, 'Sanism, Mental Health, and Social Work/Education: A Review and Call to Action' *Intersectionalities* Vol 1 (2012), no pages. Available online at: https:// journals.library.mun.ca/ojs/index.php/ij/article/view/348

30. Poole et al 'Sanism', no pages.

31. Akemi Nishida, 'Neoliberal Academia and a critique from Disability Studies' in Pamela Block, Devva Kasnitz, Akemi Nishida, Nick Pollard, *Occupying Disability: Critical Approaches to Community, Justice, and Decolonizing Disability* (Springer, 2016), 145–157.
32. Carole Leathwood and Valerie Hey, 'Gender/ed. discourses and emotional sub-texts: theorising emotion in UK higher education' *Teaching in Higher Education*, 14:4 (2009), 429–440. Available online at: https://doi.org/ https://doi.org/10.1080/13562510903050194
33. Leathwood and Hey, 'Gender/ed'.
34. Leathwood & Hey, 'Gender/ed'.
35. See K. Ecclestone and C. Rawdin, 'Reinforcing the 'diminished' subject? The implications of the 'vulnerability zeitgeist' for well-being in educational settings' *Cambridge Journal of Education* 46:3 (2016), 377–393. Available online at: https://doi.org/10.1080/0305764X.2015.1120707
36. Rhiannon Firth, 'Somatic Pedagogies: Critiquing and Resisting the Affective Discourse of the Neoliberal State from an Embodied Anarchist Perspective' *Ephemera: Theory and Politics in Organization* Vol 16 (2016), 121–142, 125.
37. Firth, 'Somatic', 125.
38. Firth, 'Somatic', 125.
39. Luigi Esposito, Fernando M. Perez, 'Neoliberalism and the Commodification of Mental Health' *Humanity and Society* 38/4 (2014), 414–442. Available online at: https://doi.org/10.1177/0160597614544958
40. Esposito et al, 'Neoliberalism'. See also J. Sugarman, 'Neoliberalism and psychological ethics' *Journal of Theoretical and Philosophical Psychology* 35(2), (2015) 103–116. Available online at: https://doi.org/10.1037/a0038960
41. Margaret Thornton, 'Law Student Wellbeing: A Neoliberal Conundrum' *Australian Universities' Review* 58 (2) (2016), 42–50. Available online at: https://ssrn.com/abstract=2887812
42. Citing Simon Wessely, Nick Bennett, 'The crisis in student wellbeing is about emotional fitness, not mental illness' WONKHE (11th November 2019). Available online at: https://wonkhe.com/blogs/the-crisis-in-student-wellbeing-is-about-emotional-fitness-not-mental-illness/. On the danger of medicalising normal emotions, grief is another example. Grief can of course include grieving all sorts of things: loss of loved ones, relationship break-ups, not getting into the university your parents wanted you to go to, and all other sorts of disappointments. We need to show compassion for all these griefs, whilst also communicating that these emotions in themselves are normal.
43. Leathwood and Hey, 'Gender/ed', 429–440.

44. 'Ideas rooted in a mental health/illness binary abound in higher learning, as both curriculum content and through institutional procedures that reinforce structures of normalcy.' Sarah Snyder et al, 'Unlearning through Mad Studies: Disruptive pedagogical praxis' *in Curriculum Inquiry* 49(4) (2019), 485–502. Available online at: https://doi.org/10.108 0/03626784.2019.1664254

45. Snyder et al, 'Unlearning'.

46. Gill and Donaghue, 'Resilience', 91. In Northern Europe, the focus on hyper-productivity, increasing auditing and rankings, and 'a space of economic efficiency and intensifying competition', for example, leads to an 'internalized desire to measure one's own value' as a student or academic. Lawrence D. Berg, Edward H. Huijbens and Henrik Gutzon Larsen 'Producing anxiety in the neoliberal university' *Canadian Geographer* 60 (2016), 168–180. Available online at: https://doi.org/10.1111/cag.12261

47. Békés cited and discussed in David Webster and Nicola Rivers, 'Resisting resilience: disrupting discourses of self-efficacy' *Pedagogy, Culture & Society* 27:4, (2019) 523–535. Available online at: DOI: https://doi.org/10.1080/14681366.2018.1534261

48. Webster and Rivers, 'Resisting'.

49. Kristiina Brunila, 'The Rise of the Survival Discourse in an Era of Therapisation and Neoliberalism' *Education Inquiry*, 5:1, (2014), 7–23, 19. Available online at: DOI: https://doi.org/10.3402/edui.v5.24044

50. Salman Türken, Hilde Eileen Nafstad, Rolv Mikkel Blakar & Katrina Roen, 'Making Sense of Neoliberal Subjectivity: A Discourse Analysis of Media Language on Self-development', *Globalizations* 13:1 (2016) 32–46. Available online at: https://doi.org/10.1080/14747731.2015.1033247

51. https://www.universitiesuk.ac.uk/policy-and-analysis/stepchange/Pages/case-for-action.aspx

52. Brunila, 'The Rise', 9.

53. Brunila, 'The Rise', 9.

54. Brunila, 'The Rise', 13.

55. Vik Loveday Goldsmiths, 'Embodying Deficiency Through 'Affective Practice': Shame, Relationality, and the Lived Experience of Social Class and Gender in Higher Education' *Sociology* 50/6 (2016), 1140–1155.

56. 'Although many social work students suffer from mental health symptoms, the majority of them do not seek help, because of shame … social work students consider that their community perceives mental health problems negatively and that their self-criticism, self-compassion and role identity relate to their poor mental health.' Yasuhiro Kotera, Pauline Green, David Sheffield, 'Mental Health Attitudes, Self-Criticism,

Compassion and Role Identity among UK Social Work Students' *The British Journal of Social Work*, Volume 49, Issue 2 (2019), 351–370, 351.

57. 'In response to a strong need to evade the stigma and to retain family honour some international students develop a tendency to somaticize their psychological problems and express them though physiological disorders.' Sakurako Mori, 'Addressing the Mental Health Concerns of International Students' *Counseling and Development* 78 (2000), 137–144.

58. Webster and Rivers, 'Resisting', 523–535.

59. Webster and Rivers, 'Resisting', 523–535.

60. Webster and Rivers, 'Resisting', 523–535.

61. Webster and Rivers, 'Resisting', 523–535.

62. Emily Hutcheon and Bonnie Lashewicz, 'Theorizing resilience: critiquing and unbounding a marginalizing concept', *Disability & Society* 29:9 (2014), 1383–1397. Available online at: https://doi.org/ https://doi.org/10.1080/09687599.2014.934954

63. Kathleen Lynch 'Carelessness: A hidden doxa of higher education' *Arts and Humanities in Higher Education* 9 (2010), 54–67.

64. Lynch, 'Carelessness', 63.

65. Caroline Walker and Alan Gleaves 'Constructing the Caring Higher Education Teacher: A Theoretical Framework' *Teaching and Teacher Education* 54 (2016), 65–76, 66.

66. Lynch, 'Carelessness', 58.

67. Lynch, 'Carelessness', 58.

68. Lynch, 'Carelessness', 58.

69. Lynch, 'Carelessness', 58.

70. Valerie Hey, 'Affective asymmetries: academics, austerity and the mis/recognition of emotion' *Contemporary Social Science* 6 (2011), 207–22.

71. Sandra Wilde, *Care in Education: Teaching with Understanding and Compassion* (London: Routledge, 2013), 1.

72. Wilde, *Care*, 5.

73. Leathwood and Hey, 'Gender/ed', 429–440.

74. R. Gill, 'Beyond individualism: the psychosocial life of the neoliberal university' in M. Spooner (ed.), *A Critical Guide to Higher Education & the Politics of Evidence: Resisting Colonialism, Neoliberalism, & Audit Culture* (Regina, Canada: University of Regina Press, 2017), 1–21.

75. Gill, 'Beyond', 1–21.

76. Charlotte Bloch, *Passion and Paranoia: Emotions and the Culture of Emotion in Academia* (Farnham: Ashgate, 2012), 2.

77. Mountz, Alison, Anne Bonds, Becky Mansfield, Jenna Loyd, Jennifer Hyndman, Margaret Walton-Roberts, Ranu Basu, Risa Whitson, Roberta Hawkins, Trina Hamilton, and Winifred Curran, 'For Slow Scholarship:

A Feminist Politics of Resistance through Collective Action in the Neoliberal University' *ACME: An International Journal for Critical Geographies* 14 (4) (2015), 1235–59, 1245. Available online at: https://www.acme-journal.org/index.php/acme/article/view/1058

78. Jeffrey R. Di Leo, *Higher Education under Late Capitalism: Identity, Conduct, and the Neoliberal Condition* (London: Palgrave Macmillan, 2017), x.

79. Joan C. Tronto, 'Creating Caring Institutions: Politics, Plurality, and Purpose', *Ethics and Social Welfare* 4:2 (2010), 158–171. Available online at: DOI: https://doi.org/10.1080/17496535.2010.484259

80. https://www.mentalhealth.org.uk/campaigns/mental-health-awareness-week/why-kindness-theme.

81. https://www.mentalhealth.org.uk/campaigns/mental-health-awareness-week/why-kindness-theme.

82. Sharon Salzberg, *The Force of Kindness: Change Your Life with Love and Compassion* (Colorado: Sounds True Inc., 2010), 5.

83. Of course, all this can be exploited by someone who feels they are attuned to emotion and either cannot see where appropriate boundaries are or who deceives themselves as to where they are. The more 'emotionally-distanced' educational practices are, the easier it might be to police those boundaries. I am therefore advocating for more emotional engagement *and* clearer boundaries.

84. Sara C. Motta and Anna Bennett, 'Pedagogies of care, care-full epistemological practice and 'other' caring subjectivities in enabling education' *Teaching in Higher Education* 23:5 (2018), 631–646. Available online at: https://doi.org/10.1080/13562517.2018.1465911

85. Sue Clegg and Stephen Rowland, 'Kindness in pedagogical practice and academic life' *British Journal of Sociology of Education* 31:6 (2010), 719–735. Available online at: https://doi.org/10.1080/0142569 2.2010.515102

86. Clegg and Rowland, 'Kindness', 719–735.

87. Clegg and Rowland, 'Kindness', 719–735.

88. Clegg and Rowland, 'Kindness', 719–735.

89. Clegg and Rowland, 'Kindness', 719–735.

90. Isaac Prilleltensky and Ora Prilleltensky, *Promoting Well-Being: Linking Personal, Organizational, and Community Change* (New Jersey: Wiley, 2006), 1.

91. Áine Mahon, 'Towards a higher education: Contemplation, compassion, and the ethics of slowing down' *Educational Philosophy and Theory*, (2019). Available online at: https://doi.org/10.1080/00131857.201 9.1683826. See also Andy Cramp and Catherine Lamond, 'Engagement and kindness in digitally mediated learning with teachers' *Teaching in*

Higher Education 21:1 (2016), 1–12. Available online at: https://doi.org/10.1080/13562517.2015.1101681

92. Mahon, 'Towards'.
93. Riyad A. Shahjahan, 'Being 'Lazy' and Slowing Down: Toward decolonizing time, our body, and pedagogy' *Educational Philosophy and Theory* 47:5 (2015), 488–501. Available online at: https://doi.org/10.1080/00131857.2014.880645
94. Shahjahan, 'Being', 488–501.
95. 'Further, the increasingly normative role of virtual and online educational communities and communication can exacerbate stress and create a perceived "time crunch".' Shahjahan, 'Being', 488–501. Available online at: https://doi.org/10.1080/00131857.2014.880645
96. Shahjahan, 'Being', 488–501.
97. Mayuzumi cited in Shahjahan, 'Being', 488–501.
98. Mahon, 'Towards', 3–4.
99. Chrissie Rogers, '"I'm complicit and I'm ambivalent and that's crazy": Care-less spaces for women in the academy' *Women's Studies International Forum* 61 (2017), 115–122. Available online at: https://doi.org/10.1016/j.wsif.2016.07.002
100. Suanne Gibson and Delia Baskerville, 'Editorial' *Pastoral Care in Education*, 35:3 (2017), 149–151. Available online at: https://doi.org/10.1080/02643944.2017.1364534
101. Citing Ahmed, Mountz et al, 'For Slow', 1239.
102. Gill, 'Beyond'.
103. https://www.advance-he.ac.uk/consultancy-and-enhancement/collaborative-projects/embedding-mental-wellbeing-curriculum, 2019–2020.
104. 'Madness most often meets university curricula through the framework of mental illness and mental health. As such, while we acknowledge madness has been a persistent presence in curricula across the university, its inclusion has overwhelmingly reinforced madness as always only mental illness.' Snyder et al, 'Unlearning'.
105. University of Exeter Education Strategy. Available online at: https://www.exeter.ac.uk/about/vision/educationstrategy/
106. https://www.advance-he.ac.uk/knowledge-hub/embedding-mental-wellbeing-curriculum-maximising-success-higher-education
107. https://www.advance-he.ac.uk/knowledge-hub/embedding-mental-wellbeing-curriculum-maximising-success-higher-education. See also Joan Riley and Mindy McWilliams, 'Engaged Learning through Curriculum Infusion' *Peer Review* Vol. 9, Iss. 3, (2007), 14–17.
108. https://engelhard.georgetown.edu/impact/
109. Inna Michaeli, 'Self-Care: An Act of Political Warfare or a Neoliberal Trap?' *Development* 60 (2017), 50–56.

110. Gibbs, 2017.
111. Katz, 2012.
112. Tracy Payle, 'A Planning Model for your Content which Plays to Needs and Emotions', *Picklejar Communications* (2017). Available online at: http://www.picklejarcommunications.com/2017/07/04/planning-model-content-strategy-plays-needs-emotions/
113. The Compassionate Frome project sought to improve health of the community by overcoming social isolation via a network of community connectors who enabled isolated individuals to access community groups/ resources.   See   https://www.compassionate-communitiesuk.co.uk/ projects

    For helpful tips on building community in blended/hybrid learning environments, see the following: 'Building Community' *Centre for Learning and Teaching Western University* https://teaching.uwo.ca/ teaching/engaging/building-community.html; Melissa Wehler, 'Five Ways to Build Community in Online Classrooms' *Faculty Focus Higher Ed Teaching Strategies*: https://www.facultyfocus.com/articles/online-education/five-ways-to-build-community-in-online-classrooms/'Blended'; 'Blended Learning Design Planner' *Stanford Teaching Commons*: https://teachingcommons.stanford.edu/gallery/ blended; 'Planner Resource Pack', *University of Birmingham*: https:// www.birmingham.ac.uk/Documents/college-social-sciences/social-policy/CEIMH/DiBLPlannerResourcePack.pdf
114. https://digitalcapability.jiscinvolve.org/wp/2019/09/03/defining-digital-wellbeing/.
115. Kristi Kaeppel, 'Let's Get Physical: Improving Learning Through Movement':   https://gcci.uconn.edu/2018/05/10/lets-get-physical-improving-learning-through-movement/Forging Links between learning and a student's own experiences enhances self-compassion and wellbeing.
116. Tips on design of contemplative pedagogical practice can be found below: 'Contemplative Pedagogy', *Columbia Centre for Teaching and Learning*: https://ctl.columbia.edu/resources-and-technology/resources/ contemplative-pedagogy/; Nancy Chick, 'Mindfulness in the Classroom' Vanderbilt   University: https://cft.vanderbilt.edu/guides-sub-pages/ contemplative-pedagogy; 'Exploring the Role of Contemplative Teaching and Learning in Higher Education' *Contemplative Pedagogy Network*: https://contemplativepedagogynetwork.com/what-is-contemplative-pedagogy/. For contemplative modes of pedagogy with regard to Asian students, see C. C. Wong and W. Mak, 'Writing can heal: Effects of self-compassion writing among Hong Kong Chinese college students' *Asian*

American Journal of Psychology 7 (1) (2016), 74–82. Available online at: https://doi.org/10.1037/aap0000041

117. 'Gratitude helps people feel more positive emotions, relish good experiences, improve their health, deal with adversity and build strong relationships' *Harvard Health Beat*. Available online at: https://www.health. harvard.edu/healthbeat/giving-thanks-can-make-you-happier

118. Positioning places of higher education 'working with a richer conception of students as affective, embodied selves based on an understanding of agency which avoids the twin perils of the logocentrism of "modernity's man", a metaphysics of modernity which reduces everything to rationality, or the flattened, de-centred linguistic self of postmodernism'. Colin Beard, Sue Clegg and Karen Smith, 'Acknowledging the affective in higher education' *British Educational Research Journal* 33 (2007), 235–252.

119. Beard et al, 'Acknowledging', 235–252.

120. Beard et al, 'Acknowledging', 235–252.

121. Matthew Wayne Seeger, Timothy Lester Sellnow, Robert R. Ulmer, *Communication and Organizational Crisis* (Greenwood Publishing Group, 2003), 4.

122. James E. Côté, 'The Enduring Usefulness of Erikson's Concept of the Identity Crisis in the 21st Century: An Analysis of Student Mental Health Concerns' *Identity* 18(4) (2018), 1–13.

123. Seeger et al, *Communication*, 7.

124. Mohamed Buheji and Dunya Ahmed, 'Foresight of Coronavirus (COVID-19) Opportunities for a Better World' *American Journal of Economics* 10(2) (2020), 97–108, 9. Available online at: https://doi.org/10.5923/j.economics.20201002.05

125. Buheji and Ahmed, 'Foresight', 97.

126. Buheji and Ahmed, 'Foresight', 101.

127. Buheji and Ahmed, 'Foresight', 102.

128. Buheji and Ahmed, 'Foresight', 102.

129. Vaneeta D'Andrea and David Gosling, *Improving Teaching And Learning In Higher Education: A Whole Institute Approach* (McGraw-Hill Education, 2005), 2.

130. D'Andrea and David Gosling, *Improving*, 2.

131. David Forbes, 'Accommodation or Transformation?' in Małgorzata Powietrzyńska and Kenneth Tobin, *Weaving Complementary Knowledge Systems and Mindfulness to Educate a Literate Citizenry for Sustainable and Healthy Lives* (Leiden: Brill, 2017), 145–158.

CHAPTER 7

[Mis-]Directed Compassion? Power, Sexual Violence, and Misconduct in the Neoliberal Academy

In June 2020, it was reported that a prominent academic in the biblical studies field, Jan Joosten (at the time the holder of the Regius Professorship of Hebrew at the University of Oxford), had been sentenced to imprisonment and listed on the sex offender's register by a French court for procurement and possession of over 27,000 child abuse images and videos.[1] Stephen Young in a revealing online response to the case entitled 'Love the Scholarship but Hate the Scholar's Sin: "Himpathy" for an Academic Paedophile Enables a Culture of Abuse' employs 'himpathy', a concept coined by Kate Manne in her work on the logic of misogyny,[2] to define 'the excessive sympathy sometimes shown towards male perpetrators of sexual violence'.[3] Young, drawing on Manne's work, calls out those academic cultures which 'eras[e] the voices of those who suffer at the hands of men whil[st] also reinforce[ing] the power of men ... A vortex of violence [rooted in] patriarchy.'[4] Young details and plots various social media postings in the immediate wake of the news of Joosten's crimes which rehearse 'dominant paths of sympathy flow[ing] to Joosten, not to his thousands of victims'.[5] The Society of Biblical Literature's (SBL) immediate reaction to the case was seen in part designed to protect Joosten's dignity, whilst completely ignoring his child victims. A pithy statement in the corner of the SBL website noted: 'On June 23, 2020, at the request of the Society of Biblical Literature, Prof Jan Joosten resigned from all positions, associations, and pending publications of the Society he is no longer

L. J. Lawrence, *Refiguring Universities in an Age of Neoliberalism*, Palgrave Critical University Studies, https://doi.org/10.1007/978-3-030-73371-1_7

a member of SBL.'[6] Sarah Schectman circulated a letter to members petitioning for a stronger response to the crime and on her twitter feed wrote: 'This is it? Name his crime. Take a position on it. Express your disgust. Your members are looking to you for an expression of your values, and this tells them you have none.'[7] In responses like the SBL statement, the bodies and voices of victims and survivors are obscured from view by 'himpathetic' focus on 'him': their abuser. Young further notes that for some respondents Joosten himself is almost recast as victim—'prey to the exploitation of pornographers'—and as a result retains and secures his identity as 'one of the finest Hebraists of our time'.[8] Young accordingly cites Anette Yoshiko Reed's tweet which vehemently contests the 'rhetoric of separating a person from their scholarship' as this trope inevitably is 'applied unevenly to different sorts of people' more often than not 'protecting prestigious white men from responsibility for their own deeds'.[9] To separate a person from their work is in her view untenable: for 'whether intended or not to promote a person's work by engaging it is to amplify their prestige and to route legitimacy to them'.[10] This in turn profits and secures their powerful reputations and enables further exploitation, whilst at the same time devaluing and disregarding the bodies of those they have injured or harmed. As such, Young forcefully concludes:

> Forget tinkering with 'love scholarship and hate the scholar's sin'. Let's try something different: 'love the victims and hate anything that exploits them'.[11]

In the wake of the #Metoo movement (a now well-known form of feminist hashtag activism),[12] many academics (past and present, largely male though some female)[13] have been outed as perpetrators of sexual violence and/or misconduct,[14] yet there still remains a dominant trend within the academy to focus on the 'accomplishments of the harasser' and in so doing corroborate the imaginary that the powerful academic stores more worth than others' rights to safety. Such responses perpetuate complicity and silence within disciplines and institutions and risk naively focusing on the neoliberal individual's accomplishments, rather than corporate and social responsibility in systems which injure and damage others. In short, they misdirect compassion to the perpetrator, instead of the wounded.

This chapter will first seek to review some of the (mis-)directions of compassion surfaced within high-profile cases of sexual violence within the fields of biblical studies and theology. This poses fundamental questions regarding the guild's identity, professional values, and practices: for example should the legacy of those convicted perpetrators of sexual violence be ensured through future citation, or featuring their work as required reading on curricula? Or should we actively and intentionally promote anti-violence methodologies and initiate what could be termed a 'detoxifying' of the curriculum? Second, an allied institutional example to think with, the Church of England, and its recent work centred on safeguarding and communal restoration in the wake of sexual violence and clergy misconduct which has sought to direct compassion not just to those individuals that suffer but also the wider community and organisation will be introduced. Reading these church contexts, alongside recent work in this area in higher education, including the important contributions of the 1752 UK based-research group on sexual harassment in higher education, some pointers for appropriately directed compassionate responses within universities in this area will be considered. Such work is demanding and costly. Anna Hush in her work on feminist resistance to sexual violence in university communities notes that there is still a certain resistance to feminist interventions, on the basis of 'a certain nostalgia for times when sexuality was "free" (that is, unscrutinized)'.[15] She also notes that neoliberal dynamics within education tend to 'sugge[st] that sexual politics lie squarely outside the realm of university life',[16] or worse still 'passively normalize cultures of abuse and harassment'.[17] She believes, however, that the academy can be re-imagined as a site for 'transforming unjust sexual norms, given the intimate relationships between institutions, bodies, and desires',[18] which inevitably provide the social and symbolic networks of those spaces. Interventions are needed which will direct compassion appropriately so that the academy is 'ultimately more equal for women and [all] other marginalized people'.[19]

[Mis-]Directed Compassion?

Paul Bloom in his influential book, *Against Empathy: The Case for Rational Compassion*, notes that 'empathy biases us in favour of individuals we know while numbing us to the plight of thousands'.[20] The SBL committee's initial handling of Joosten's case, and their immediate reaction to seemingly seek to protect his dignity over and against his victims, is illustrative in this regard. Bloom accordingly notes that consciously limiting propensities of empathy to the known is in reality the most compassionate decision (an authentic noticing of distress of the 'other' and taking action to reduce it) that can be made.

Within particular discipline cultures, and the neoliberal academy more broadly, there are of course dominant forces at play which often incubate empathy for the celebrated and distinguished, and negate compassion for 'others'. The so-called neoliberal rock-star scholar[21] often garners, procures, and is guaranteed certain goods and affective reactions from others:

> The godlike position of some academics has been reflected in a number of high profile cases … When sexual harassment and violence are reckoned up institutionally, the patriarchal impulse to shield privileged men is intensified by the fact that the reputation of the perpetrator operates as a proxy for that of the university [discipline and/or field].[22]

Where such individuals comment on their own actions (a privilege in itself), there is also often deliberate recasting designed to elicit empathy within colleagues. Joosten, for example, is quoted as labelling his child pornography compulsion as 'a secret garden, in contradiction with myself'.[23] Adam Ferner and Darren Chetty would liken such tactics to the deployment of tears which the ancient Romans called '*commiseratio*' evident 'when powerful men ask others to sympathize with what they construe as powerlessness'.[24] These are effective diversionary tactics and tools of power, constituting what Sara Ahmed labels '"recentring"'.[25] Johanna Stiebert, however, rightly labels Joosten's responses as 'jarring and repugnant'. She sees his *commiseratio* tactics specifically engineered for the consumption of his professional audience: 'conjur[ing] up images from [the biblical book of the] Song of Songs of eroticism and lovemaking ("You are a garden locked up, my sister, my bride," Song of Songs 4:12)' but this is no innocuous secret garden, as Stiebert piercingly and justifiably retorts: 'this is brutal child pornography … and watching [it] is not a victimless crime.'[26] The discursive move to separate the intellectual from their so-called private actions (such as sexual violence) also plays into long-held binaries between mind and body within the academy. Anna Hush reveals that:

> These twin dichotomies uphold the imaginary of the university as a disembodied, public domain of reason, intimately linked with the masculine symbolic order … The image of the university as a purified realm of rationality, and the symbolic disavowal of the body, leaves little room for the consideration of how sexual imaginaries operate in and through universities.[27]

There is also a sense in which memories are often deliberately (and empathetically) airbrushed around certain academic figures (and their intellectual legacies) who are perpetrators of sexual violence or misconduct.[28] Richard Pervo, another prominent biblical scholar who was convicted of downloading child pornography in 2001, was re-admitted and continued to attend SBL after serving his sentence, was given the honour of a festschrift in 2017,[29] and, on the occasion of his death, afforded an SBL member's obituary which celebrated his work on 'shifting scholarly consensus on the date of [the biblical book of] Acts', but failed to mention anything of his sexual crimes and convictions.[30] What could be termed 'moral luminaries' in the field are also still celebrated (and reputations in part protected) even in light of devastating testimonies of their sexual violence. John Howard Yoder, for example, a world-renowned Mennonite ethicist and pacifist,[31] worked at the Anabaptist Mennonite Biblical Seminary where he abused over 100 women under the guise of ethical experimentation and research in 'familial touching'. When he landed a job at the University of Notre Dame, whilst concealing reasons for his departure from his previous institution, he was nevertheless shielded and protected once the university became aware of his past history, before victims publically voiced their stories in 1992.[32] Stanley Hauerwas, whose intellectual contribution to the field and own theological formation was in part built upon Yoder's work, belies a typical misplaced empathetic tendency to recover Yoder's character, enshrine his 'intellect and renown'[33] (with a mind somehow disconnected from his body), and exonerate his actions by re-categorising him as a victim. Hauerwas writes:

> One of the aspects of this whole sad story that saddens me is that I have had to recognize how much energy John put into this aspect of his life. His attempt to maintain these multiple relationships would have exhausted any normal person. But John was not normal – intellectually or physically. When I think about the time he dedicated to developing justifications for his experimentation, I feel depressed. Of course, John gave us the great gift of the clarity of his mind, but that same analytic ability betrayed him just to the extent that he used it to make unjustified distinctions, such as those about the significance of different ways of touching that could only result in self-deception.[34]

Hilary Scarsella in her article 'Not Making Sense: Why Stanley Hauerwas' Response to Yoder's Sexual Abuse Misses the Mark'[35] makes clear the sort of himpathetic optics which structure Hauerwas' account. She also incisively identifies how Hauerwas' defence testifies to the ongoing influence and protection of perpetrators of sexual violence (even after their death) through the propagation of their ideas and writings which serve to silence victims over again. She writes:

> While Hauerwas' article makes certain explicit claims in support of sexual violence survivors and in condemnation of Yoder's abusive behaviour, and while these doubtless have some value, it simultaneously reproduces logics and rhetoric that silence and dismiss those same survivors in order to preserve modes of thought and relationship dear to the writer, that are threatened by the figure of the sexually abused. In so doing, what might be read as Hauerwas's attempt to move himself into alliance with sexual violence survivors is, at the very least, compromised.

Amy Chilton too notes the costs involved in the dangerous elision of Yoder's victims, by continuing to cite his ideas without acknowledgement of their suffering. Movingly she writes:

> I may stand on the shoulders of theological giants, but Yoder's egregious actions have forced my gaze downward only to see that I also stand on the hunched backs of Yoder's victims. If I make it in this increasingly uncertain world of the theological academy, my rise will be due in part because of their fall. That is a burden passed on to me that I do not wish to bear. The price paid to extract Yoder's thoughts is simply too high.[36]

Mark Tooley urges subsequent generations to acknowledge the survivors and to call out Yoder and others who perpetrate sexual violence:

> Hauerwas has built a career on Yoder's theological malpractice, so his reluctance late in life to reconsider is humanly understandable. But others who are younger and less invested should watch and learn from Yoder's imbroglio.[37]

Another recent high-profile case of sexual violence in the discipline is L'Arche founder, Jean Vanier, a figure who garnered almost saint-like status in disability activism and theology (Nobel Peace Prize nominee and recipient of the Archbishop of Canterbury's Templeton Prize in 2015). L'Arche, a religious organisation which focused on living in community with those with intellectual disabilities and was founded on values of respect and integrity for all, was rocked by the revelations published in a posthumous internal report released in February 2020, that their founder, in the 'context of giving spiritual guidance', had between 1975 and 1990 sexually abused a number of women.[38] To their credit, L'Arche and others fore-fronted the bravery and pain of the victims in all their communications following the release of the report, but now wrestle with the ongoing status of their founder in light of his manipulative sexual acts. Morgan Lowrie plots the uncomfortable process of disassociation from him which they now have to navigate: 'the last few days have been difficult, given that many in the organization knew Vanier personally and considered him an inspiration. But now … L'Arche will find inspiration from his victims instead.'[39]

Post #Metoo there is perhaps a sense that landscapes are shifting, and more voices internal to the academy are both naming abuse and abusers, and campaigning for cultural change. One notable voice in my own discipline has been Elaine Pagels' in her scholarly memoir, *Why Religion? A Personal Story*.[40] Pagels, a world authority on the Gnostic Gospels, opens up about her own experience of being sexually assaulted by her doctoral supervisor at Harvard, Helmut Koester, decades beforehand. In an interview following the publication of her memoir, Pagels, in response to the question of what led her to voice this experience so many years after it happened, admits:

> I almost didn't. I thought about it carefully, yet wrote about it before the #MeToo movement started. Drew Faust, the first woman president of Harvard, had just given me an honorary degree at Harvard, and when I heard that she had set up a committee on sexual harassment, I thought about confronting Koester at that time. I didn't have the opportunity before he died, but I did talk to the dean in charge of depositions and discovered that there were many people to whom it had happened with the same professor and others. This was part of the story about being a woman graduate student almost anywhere in that time. I didn't feel that I owed him any protection, since he didn't protect any of his students.[41]

The doctoral supervisory relationship is of course potentially one of the more close connections within the academy; it is also one of the most hierarchical and can enable exploitation on account of the innate dependencies of the weaker member on the stronger (in relation to research funding, references, and professional opportunities). Pagels' moving account testifies though to the problematic cultures of silence which were (and still are) often maintained by individuals and institutions around such cases. As a result, Karen Guth insists that we must all bravely 'name tainted legacies that harm' and call out disciplinary and institutional frameworks which are complicit (and therefore) enabling of sexual violence.[42] Ahmed too in her work on sexual violence in higher education notes that these actions and responses frequently work like bullying: 'increasing the costs of fighting against something, making it easier to accept something than to struggle against something'.[43] Judith Herman, likewise, in her moving and powerful work on trauma and recovery, underscores this sort of complicit 'covering up' which is both less painful and less demanding than directing compassion to the victim:

> It is very tempting to take the side of the perpetrator. All the perpetrator asks is that the bystander do nothing. He appeals to the universal desire to see, hear, and speak no evil. The victim on the contrary, asks the bystander to share the burden of pain. The victim demands action, engagement, and remembering.[44]

A rightly directed 'compassionate' response to these issues would consciously not value a perpetrator's intellectual contributions, over the bodies, minds, and experiences of their victims. Our curricula and our citations need to bear witness, and voice, to the suffering of others: in short, they need conscious (and compassionate) 'detoxifying'.[45] Brian Leiter in his article 'Academic Ethics: Should Scholars Avoid Citing the Work of Awful People?'[46] raises the issue of citational legacy of perpetrators of hate and violence, and argues that academics should cite work, regardless of the identity and actions of the scholar, as this involves acknowledgement of prior work on which you depend, and 'an epistemic authority in your own contribution to knowledge'.[47] The Nazi era provides allied material for reflection here, even if the crimes are not specifically sexual. Lukas Bormann, for example, audited archival research piece on the early members of the *Society of New Testament Studies* (SNTS), for example, showing how sympathetically (himpathetically?) the UK and non-German members of SNTS committee wrote to Gerhard Kittel after he was removed from his position after the war for forwarding Nazi ideology.[48] Underlying, it was in part an attempt to keep 'politics' and 'study of the New Testament' separate, but one can see in hindsight how immoral that was (Kittel's name remained on the SNTS committee headed paper even after this).

Another example would be the *Theological Dictionary of the New Testament* (TDNT). Most historical commentators use and cite this monumental work, but it was edited by people deeply implicated in the Nazi regime.[49] Not citing TDNT may not be an option in all cases, and if one were going to comment on the stance of each entry, you'd have to know and research the scholars' biography in each case, but at the very least it means using TDNT cautiously and critically, and signalling where appropriate the problematic nature of the context and scholars from which it comes. In those instances where appearances on reading lists or citations are unavoidable, then they should always be accompanied by the stories of those they hurt. A footnote in Daniel Oudshoorn's work is perhaps one model of such an approach. Citing Koester, he writes:

> It was only after I was in the final stages of editing this manuscript for publication that I learned about Elaine Pagels' report about the ways in which Helmut Koester sexually abused her and other students … I would have preferred to have scrubbed him from my manuscript [as I have done in the past with John Howard Yoder and Stanley Hauerwas after Hauerwas published his rape apologist letter on behalf of his eternally unapologetic rapist friend in 2017] given that I think that men who exploited their power to get away with serially abusing women should be remembered for what they did and not for what they said, but instead of re-working my manuscript at this late stage, I have chosen to note the matter here.[50]

'Detoxifying' citations and curricula, however, in relation to high-profile cases of sexual violence can only be part of the solution. Broader cultural change within institutions particularly with regard to staff sexual misconduct, which is often dealt with and shrouded in confidentiality internally, is also needed if the academy is going to direct compassion appropriately to all those that suffer on account of such incidents and more importantly work towards futures where such incidents are prevented. Another institutional context which has reflected deeply on this issue, the Church of England, is perhaps instructive here.

DIRECTING INSTITUTIONAL COMPASSION IN CONTEXTS
OF SEXUAL VIOLENCE AND STAFF MISCONDUCT

The Church of England (and Anglican Communion more broadly) is an organisational context which has had to humbly acknowledge its own failures in appropriately preventing and responding to sexual violence, and clergy misconduct, within its organisational life. It has also in recent times considered the nature of just and compassionate responses to all victims and survivors affected by sexual violence and clergy misconduct. Cultural safeguarding and routes to restoration on which to base new futures have accordingly been tentatively plotted. In this sense the church has faced a parallel task to that which higher education now faces in this area: it too has had to 'attend to the complex ways in which the erotic enters and flows through [spiritual and] educational spaces';[51] how 'sexuality has been a constitutive aspect of institutional imaginaries';[52] and how dependencies formed within relationships marked by power inevitably are vulnerable to exploitation. Moreover, higher education, akin to a church community of spiritual formation, is increasingly recognised to 'have an ethical responsibility to undertake preventative work to address sexual violence [and misconduct] in their communities'.[53] This stands in marked contrast to a neoliberal vision which posits the university as mere 'service provider' or 'corporation'.

The Church of England 'Faith and Order Commission' released a report in 2017 entitled 'Forgiveness and Reconciliation in the Aftermath of Abuse'.[54] Interpreting the biblical tradition of Tamar's harrowing rape by her half-brother Amnon in 2 Samuel 13.1–39.16,[55] the report lists four dimensions of sexual violence and abuse: (a) 'serious harm on the part of the victim'; which is facilitated by (b) 'an imbalance of power between victim and perpetrator'; connected to (c) 'the perpetrator's position of trust'; assisted by (d) 'deceit on the perpetrator's behalf, denying what has happened and making others more or less witting accomplices'.[56] The latter dimension in particular underscores the uncomfortable truth that institutions (albeit unintentionally) often act as accomplices of sexual violence and misconduct: 'on account of naivety, negligence, and complicity that have let [them become] arena[s] of abuse'.[57] Just as a priest holds influence over a congregation, so too academics hold influence over their students and research subjects: they are wielders of what one author evocatively terms 'Ivory Power'.[58] Billie Wright Dziech and Linda Weiner underscore the staff/student encounter as one which needs to be seen (in spite of legal age markers or assumed consent) as one of inevitable vulnerability of the weaker member in relation to the stronger. They attest that:

> Few students are ever, in the strictest sense, consenting adults. A student can never be a genuine equal of a professor insofar as his professional position gives him power over her … Whether the student consents to the involvement or whether the professor ever intends to use his power against her is not the point. The issue is that the power and the role disparity always exist.[59]

More fundamentally, Amia Srinivasan, reviewing US university regulation of staff/student sexual relationships, identifies such encounters as 'a pedagogical failure', that is, 'a failure to satisfy the duties that arise from the practice of teaching':

> Implicit in that relationship is the promise that the teacher will work to equalize the asymmetry in knowledge between him and his student. When the teacher takes the student's longing for epistemic power as an occasion for his own gratification, allowing himself to be—or, worse, making himself—the object of her desire, he has failed her as a teacher.[60]

Srinivasan also investigates the ways in which the identities of those involved (particularly the student) are often injuriously transformed by the scenario:

> The student is not only, in the eyes of her professor-boyfriend, transformed from a student, whose needs he is meant to serve, into someone who is meant to serve his needs (his errands, his ego). She is also transformed in the eyes of her academic community as a whole. She is unable to relate any longer to her other professors as her teachers; they are now her boyfriend's (judgmental) colleagues. She may stay enrolled, but is she any longer a student? If she leaves, are we surprised?[61]

Allied process is also detectable in church contexts where clergy sexual misconduct frequently leads to anger, scapegoating, and victim blaming, within communities. In recognising both church and academy as contexts of inequitable power, the need to cultivate trust, responsibility, and moral authority is (or should be) central to both. The Faith and Order Commission report notes that 'Trust depends on truthfulness: that people act in accordance with their promises'. And in those instances where this fails, there must be 'a strong culture of accountability and transparency which will make it more difficult for deceit to be sustained and pass undetected'.[62] In this respect, cultural change cannot be solely based on institutional policy documents. Fredrik Bondestam and Maja Lundqvist attest to this in their systematic review of sexual harassment policies in higher education. They note that bureaucratic policy documents often have a focus on individuals, or particular case management, rather than theoretical contextualisation of sexual harassment or broader cultural patterns which often play a part in legitimating, normalising, or neutralising such actions within institutions[63]:

> Sexual harassment is in fact made possible through precarious working conditions, higher education being organized hierarchically, a lack of active leadership, the ongoing favorization of toxic academic masculinities, biased and unjust competition for research funding, and a societal normalization of gender-based violence. Therefore, the solutions to sexual harassment in higher education is not more of the same; it rather implies restructuring working conditions in higher education, challenging toxic academic masculine cultures, deciding on bold economic and social reforms counteracting intersectional inequalities, and not the least strong incentives in all parts of society combatting men's violence against women.[64]

Emma Chapman, Anna Bull, and Tiffany Page, under the auspices of the 1752 group, likewise note the lack of inclination by universities to accept they are part of the ongoing problem: their policies frequently serving to 'protect perpetrators and impose confidentiality on complainants'.[65] They propose more explicit codes of conduct within organisational life around this issue, which are signed, and drawn upon in those instances where behaviours fall short of expected professional standards. On the basis of such insights, many institutions (including Yale, Harvard, Pennsylvania, Northwestern, Stanford, MIT, Duke, and University College London) have prohibited sexual relationships of staff entirely with any current student.[66] Such moves signal more clear and transparent institutional positions.

Compassionate response to victims and survivors also needs careful curation. The Faith and Order Commission report underscores that the church's primary task must always be to 'listen with care and sensitivity to those who have been abused, supporting them on the road towards healing and in taking steps towards the achievement of temporal justice'.[67] Beyond external or internal legal and review processes, it notes that the church also has a duty to pursue some form of restorative practice in the aftermath of sexual violence and abuse. Restorative justice, a concept which gained traction in Desmond Tutu's Truth and Reconciliation project in South Africa, could be employed in this respect. This is not just focused on isolated victims and perpetrators, but also the wider circles of responsibility: 'those who knew what was happening at the time, those who have come to know about it and those affected by it'.[68] Restorative practice in relation to sexual violence or staff misconduct is a contentious issue. Many cite the possible revictimisation of the victim/survivor, and their compromised safety; however, others note that it could offer wider opportunities for raising voices and crafting justice in this area.[69] Crucial in this respect is the key distinction made between confidentiality ('designed to protect the victim') and secrecy ('which protects and enables the abuser'). Whilst openness and transparency are important components in giving the wounded voice actually institutionally, there is often 'very little transparency ... into [institutional] record or responses to incidents, both historic and recent'.[70] Chapman, Bull, and Page similarly note that in this vein confidentiality processes can be perceived as tools of 'extra discrimination' towards the complainant.[71] The church too has recognised that it should not cultivate processes of 'secrecy' or 'retraumatization' for those involved.[72] As such, the development and dissemination of leadership programmes, based on trauma, and trauma-informed care and also periodic congregational meetings (including knowledge of both institutional and interpersonal re-traumatisation) have been seen as critical.[73] 'Victim-focused Compassionate Care' has also been important in providing 'assurance that victim/survivors who report will not face institutional traumatization'. Recommendations have included the formation of institutional 'Compassionate Care Teams' which would serve as hubs, and have as their ongoing goal to 'develop and socialize best practices, steering towards the ultimate goal of ending all retraumatization'. There is also attestation within church thinking, to the collateral damage that the congregational community frequently endures, something which is not often replicated within university oversight of such cases, where colleagues, students, or departmental communities can become sucked into negative cycles, and vortexes of violence. Not to mention the enormous burdens on both individuals and institutions—time, energy, and bandwidth spent trying to deal with an abuser and the fallout from what has happened, which are burdensome on colleagues as well as on students. It is noted that little energy has been devoted to the complex work of re-growing community in the wake of sexual violence or sexual misconduct. Yet, a community cannot heal which 'is not openly and properly guided through the recovery process in a healthy manner'.[74] As such, the church report from an Episcopal Church in the US pays witness to:

> The very difficult work of understanding, accepting, and growing in community after the betrayal that clergy sexual misconduct represents. This is a serious, sacred, time-consuming, long-term undertaking. The responsibility for congregational healing appears to be left entirely to the resident clergy who may be at a loss as to how to deal with denial and consequently just want the problem to disappear as quickly and quietly as possible. This is antithetical to trauma-informed care; it is detrimental to the short- and long-term health and vitality of the congregation; and it results in the creation of a hostile environment for the primary victim.[75]

In the higher education sector, the 1752 group recommend an 'undisciplining' workshop in this regard. Undisciplining workshops challenge givens within disciplines or institutions. They are normally problem- or issue-driven and involve interactivity, emergence, collaboration between involved parties, and partnership. The 1752 workshop invites participants (staff, students, support services, etc.) to reflect together on a specifically commissioned play—'The Girls Get Younger Every Year' by Phil Crockett Thomas[76]—as an example of restorative communal practice. The author of the play writes:

> It's loosely structured on the form of Augusto Boal's Forum Theatre – which necessitates a depressing ending that acts as a springboard for a discussion of the issues it raises, and how to tackle them. My hope is that in supplying an audience with characters to use as proxies, they can then talk about related experiences without having to "out" themselves or others.[77]

Such exercises demand the construction of what Jilly Boce Kay and Sarah Banet-Weiser call 'feminist respair' within the academy and attunement to the knotty and complex issues of power frequently involved.[78] The concept of 'respair' denotes 'the need for mutual support' and 'collectivity'. Respair cannot isolated to individuals or cases, but rather is always premised on a 'collective subject':

> We might think of respair as the feminist rejoinder to the sEXIT; respair is about staying with the trouble, sticking with the mess, and committing to

the hard work of repair collectively, not individually. Respair recognises the intrinsic vulnerability and interdependency of humans; it recognises that we need to carry each other, in order to not shoulder the harms of affective injustice alone. Respair might also help us to keep hoping even when all the odds seem stacked against us, because it is only by seeing those odds and just how big they are that we will have any chance of beating them.[79]

Alison Phipps, too, in her work within the Changing University Cultures initiative (UUK Changing Cultures, 2016), notes how Grounded Action Inquiry can be adopted as a restorative practice which acts as 'a potential alternative tool which to name and interrupt power relations, and encourage institutions into more honest modes of operation'[80]: or what she terms 'speaking into' institutions. She proposes experiential activities based on 'first (self), second (relations with others) and third-personal (systemic or organisational)' dynamics. She sees such processes as evoking parrhesia, a Foucauldian form of 'truth telling', which acknowledges the complexities and webs of power which both truth, emotion, privilege, power, and institutional discourses coalesce to create.[81] Furthermore, Phipps notes that:

> 'Speaking in' also means that as well as demanding accountability from perpetrators and institutions, we examine our own roles in protecting colleagues and friends and/or looking the other way. This makes use of the intersectional injunction to 'ask the other question' (Matsuda 1991), which usually means considering multiple forms of discrimination, but can also help us to understand our lives as complex mixtures of victimhood and perpetration. It is difficult territory, but if we are to explore what Lorde (1984, 131) calls 'the contradictions of self', it must be acknowledged that we can occupy several positions at once.[82]

She sees these restorative practices as guarding against an outrage economy, which 'tends to reward outspokenness for its own sake, due to its revenue-generating potential'[83] and ultimately inflict even deeper and long-lasting wounds and scars on communal life. On a wider sector scale, the 1752 group has petitioned for staff-to-student misconduct to be considered more explicitly in relation to health and safety, wellbeing, and equality, diversity and inclusion strategies within institutions. Why doesn't, for example, Athena SWAN include reflection on compassionate handling and prevention of these encounters?[84] Such indicators would send a strong message to the sector on the shifted institutional landscape on the issue.

Conclusion

This chapter has attempted to deal with the disturbing reality of sexual violence and staff sexual misconduct within the academy. It has traced economies of empathy which often misdirect attention to a perpetrator (so-called 'himpathy') and their academic contributions, over and against the wounded bodies, minds, and lives of those they injure. In those instances where these scholars' works and ideas are cited or taught, they must be accompanied by a conscious 'detoxifying' of the curricula which openly frames their work through the experiences of their victims. Notions of scholarly inheritance, that underpin expressions of himpathy, also frequently enable certain academics to cultivate their own role as the 'patriarch' of a 'family' or household group of students who are prime for abuse, whether that abuse is mental, spiritual, and/or sexual, and exert power in damaging ways as a result.

In relation to staff sexual misconduct, it has been proposed that institutions need to initiate more thoroughgoing culture change in this area. Policies so often fail to culturally contextualise or admit collective dimensions of these encounters, instead focusing solely on individuals involved and their specific case management. The University has a 'duty of care' both to students and to staff, but frequently the duty of care is much more carefully defined in relation to staff—because it's defined in employment law—whereas the duty of care to students is much more vague: when one is dealing with processes that are quite obscure, this is quite difficult to fight against.[85] Universities also need to more carefully consider, as the Church of England has started to try to do, compassionate and restorative practices for the whole community involved. Departments, disciplines, and institutions can be torn apart by these situations and the cultures of silence (often intended as confidential 'protection') which can breed mistrust, suspicion, and scepticism within them. Rightly directed compassion must always be situated in the discernment of suffering and proactive moves to alleviate it. In areas of sexual violence, and staff sexual misconduct, this can never be dealt with via policies or single case management alone, focused purely on a single victim and their perpetrator, but rather broader restorative reflection and practice that facilitates discernment of institutional constructions, collective and cultural, which enabled, but can also prevent, such incidents and ultimately serve to make the academy a safer space for all.

NOTES

1. Archie Bland and Jon Henley 'Oxford professor sentenced to jail in France over child abuse images' *The Guardian* (22nd June 2020). Available online at: https://www.theguardian.com/world/2020/jun/22/oxford-university-professor-jan-joosten-jailed-france-child-abuse-images
2. Kate Manne, *Down Girl: The Logic of Misogyny* (Oxford: Oxford University Press, 2017).
3. Kate Manne cited in Stephen Young, 'Love the Scholarship but Hate the Scholar's Sin: 'Himpathy' for an Academic Paedophile Enables a Culture of Abuse' *Religion Dispatches* (24th June 2020). Available online at: https://religiondispatches.org/love-the-scholarship-but-hate-the-scholars-sin-himpathy-for-an-academic-pedophile-enables-a-culture-of-abuse/.
4. Young, 'Religion', no pages.
5. Young, 'Religion', no pages.
6. Within hours of the reaction, the SBL added, 'As part of SBL's commitment to human rights—especially the protection of children from exploitation—the SBL Council has directed a contribution to Thorn, an organization that works to eliminate child sexual abuse from the internet and across all international boundaries.' Society of Biblical Literature, https://www.sbl-site.org/. This hopefully is a genuine compassionate response, not a monetising of sexual violence apart from an authentic acceptance of the victims' suffering.
7. Dr. Black Lives Matter Schectman, (@sschectman) *Twitter* (24th June 2020).
8. Young, 'Religion', no pages.
9. Young, 'Religion', no pages.
10. Young, 'Religion', no pages.
11. Young, 'Religion', no pages.
12. 'The #Metoo tweets challenge the discourse around sexual violence and coercion in several ways. First of all, whereas references to sexual violence in everyday discourse usually entail a rather abstract notion of violence, the #Metoo tweets these notions with details about the experience of violence from survivors' perspectives. . . . Secondly, the similarities and commonalities among very different experiences make the structural and societal aspects of fill intimate violations visible … thirdly, already the phrase MeToo implies a form of political dissent. Its testimonial character, saying this happened to me, is already a challenge to the idea that one must rise above pain and suffering in order to acquire political agency. Proclaiming MeToo points to the role of vulnerability for political activism. At the core of the movement lies a challenge to the idea that activism must be borne out through a conquering of suffering, to an overcoming of the past.'

Laura Moisi, 'Collective Reckonings: Re-Writing Trauma, Memory and Violence on Social Media'. Available online at: https://www.academia.edu/39742504/Collective_Reckonings_ReWriting_Trauma_Memory_and_Violence_on_Social_Media

13. See the widely publicised case of Avitall Ronnell and Nimrod Reitman. Colleen Falherty, 'Harassment and Power' *Inside Higher Ed* (20th August 2018). Available online at: https://www.insidehighered.com/news/2018/08/20/some-say-particulars-ronell-harassment-case-are-moot-it-all-comes-down-power

14. Laura A. Gray-Rosendale (ed), *Me Too, Feminist Theory, and Surviving Sexual Violence in the Academy* (Lanham: Lexington Books/Fortress Academic, 2020).

15. Anna Hush, 'The Imaginary Institution of the University' *Angelaki* 24:4 (2019), 136–150. Available online at: https://doi.org/10.1080/0969725X.2019.1635833, 136.

16. Hush, 'Imaginary', 136.

17. Hush, 'Imaginary', 137.

18. Hush, 'Imaginary', 137.

19. Amia Srinivasan, 'Sex as a Pedagogical Failure' *Yale Law Journal* 129 (2020), 924–1275, 924.

20. Paul Bloom, *Against Empathy: The Case for Rational Compassion* (New York: Ecco Press, 2018), 1.

21. John Smyth, *The Toxic University: Zombie Leadership, Academic Rock Stars and Neoliberal Ideology* (London: Palgrave, 2017).

22. Alison Phipps, 'Reckoning up: sexual harassment and violence in the neo-liberal university' *Gender and Education* 32:2 (2020), 227–243. Available online at: https://doi.org/10.1080/09540253.2018.1482413, 234.

23. Bland and Henley, 'Oxford', no pages.

24. Adam Ferner and Darren Chetty, *How to Disagree: Negotiate Difference in a Divided World* (London: White Lion Publishing, 2019), 11.

25. Ahmed cited in Ferner and Chetty, *How to Disagree*, 11.

26. Johanna Stiebert, 'Privilege Beyond Bounds: A Response to the Conviction of Jan Joosten' *The Shiloh Project Group Blog* (26th June 2020). Available online at: Shiloh-project.group.shef.ac.uk

27. Hush, 'Imaginary', 137.

28. 'We use the term sexual misconduct to describe forms of power enacted by academic, professional, contracted, and temporary staff in their relations with students (this can also occur in relations with other staff members) in higher education. Sexual misconduct can include harassment, assault, grooming, coercion, bullying, sexual invitations and demands, comments, non-verbal communication, creation of atmospheres of discomfort, and promised resources in exchange for sexual access. The term "sexual harass-

ment" captures only some of the possible abuses of power that may occur within a higher education institution. Sexual misconduct impacts students of all gender identities and sexualities. It raises issues of unequal relationships, consent, and the prevention of equal access to education for all.' Emma Chapman, Anna Bull and Tiffany Page, 'Solutions for Sexual Misconduct in Higher Education' 1752 Group. Available online at: https://1752group.com/solutions-for-sexual-misconduct-in-higher-education/

29. Harold Attridge, Dennis MacDonald and Clare Rothschild (eds), *Delightful Acts: New Essays on Canonical and Non-Canonical Acts* (Tübingen: Mohr Siebeck, 2017). The title of the volume 'Delightful Acts' is itself bizarrely troubling, in terms of either ignoring or (worse) deliberately endorsing (surely not?), his sexual offences and perversions. It is such a bizarrely double entendre title which seems hard to imagine anyone would choose once they knew of his record.

30. This obituary seems to have been taken down from the SBL website in the week following the Joosten case.

31. John Howard Yoder, *The Politics of Jesus* (Grand Rapids: William B. Eerdmans Publishing Company, 1972).

32. Soli Salgado, 'Allegations of sexual harassment against John Howard Yoder extend to Notre Dame' (June 25th, 2015). Available online at: https://www.ncronline.org/news/accountability/allegations-sexual-harassment-against-john-howard-yoderextend-notre-dame. See also Rachel Goossen 'Defanging the Beast: Mennonite Responses to John Howard Yoder's Sexual Abuse' Available online at: http://www.bishop-accountability.org/news5/2015_01_Goossen_Defanging_the_Beast.pdf

33. Rachel Goossen 'Historical Justice in an Era of #MeToo: Legacies of John Howard Yoder' (7th December 2017). Available online at: https://divinity.uchicago.edu/sightings/articles/historical-justice-era-metoo-legacies-john-howard-yoder

34. Stanley Hauerwas, 'In defence of "our respectable culture": Trying to make sense of John Howard Yoder's sexual abuse' (18th October, 2017). Available online at: https://www.abc.net.au/religion/in-defence-of-our-respectable-culture-trying-to-make-sense-of-jo/10095302

35. Hilary Scarsella 'Not Making Sense: Why Stanley Hauerwas's Response to Yoder's Sexual Abuse Misses the Mark' (30th November 2017). Available online at: https://www.abc.net.au/religion/not-making-sense-why-stanley-hauerwass-response-to-yoders-sexual/10095168

36. Amy Chilton, 'My rise, their fall: A theologian's burden in response to the reality of sexual abuse' (27th October 2017). Available online at: https://baptistnews.com/article/rise-fall-theologians-burden-response-reality-sexual-abuse/#.XvsFtG5FxPY

37. Mark Tooley, 'Yoder, Sex Abuse, and War' (8th June 2018). Available online at: https://providencemag.com/2018/06/yoder-sex-abuse-war/

38. BBC, 'L'Arche founder Jean Vanier sexually abused women – internal report' (22nd February, 2020). Available online at: https://www.bbc.co.uk/news/world-51596516

39. Morgan Lowrie, 'Canadian Organizations Grapple with Jean Vanier's Legacy After Sex Abuse Report' *The Canadian Press* (24th February 2020). Available online at: https://www.theglobeandmail.com/canada/article-canadian-organizations-grapple-with-jean-vaniers-legacy-after-sex-2/

40. Elaine Pagels, *Why Religion? A Personal Story* (New York: Harper Collins, 2018).

41. Jana Riess, 'Elaine Pagels on grief, her #MeToo story, and why we find meaning in religion' *Religion News Service* (26th October 2018). Available online at: https://religionnews.com/2018/10/26/elaine-pagels-on-grief-her-metoo-story-and-why-we-find-meaning-in-religion/

42. Karen V. Guth, 'Moral Injury, Feminist and Womanist Ethics, and Tainted Legacies' *Journal of the Society of Christian Ethics* 38, Issue 1 (2018), 167–186. Available online at: https://doi.org/10.1353/sce.2018.0010

43. Sara Ahmed, *Living a Feminist Life* (Durham: Duke University Press, 2017), 141.

44. Judith Herman, *Trauma and Recovery: The Aftermath of Violence–From Domestic Abuse to Political Terror* (New York: Basic Books, 1997), 7–8.

45. Dr. Nerdlove, 'On Finding Out Your Heroes are Monsters (Or: Detoxifying a Culture)' (19th June 2020). Available online at: https://www.doctornerdlove.com/on-finding-out-your-heroes-are-monsters-or-detoxifying-comic-culture/

46. Brian Leiter, 'Academic Ethics: Should Scholars Avoid Citing the Work of Awful People?' *Chronicle* (25th October 2018). Available online at: https://www.chronicle.com/article/Academic-Ethics-Should/244882

47. 'In each case, citation has its purpose—ensuring the integrity of the scholarly discipline in question. Failure to cite because of a scholar's misconduct—whether for being a Nazi or a sexual harasser—betrays the entire scholarly enterprise that justifies the existence of universities and the protection of academic freedom.' Leiter 'Academic Ethics', no pages.

48. Lukas Bormann, 'Auch unter politischen Gesichtspunkten sehr sorgfältig ausgewählt: Die ersten deutschen Mitglieder der Studiorum Novi Testamenti Societas (SNTS) 1937–1946', *New Testament Studies* 58.3 (2012), 416–452. Available online at: http://journals.cambridge.org/action/displayAbstract?fromPage=online&aid=8601450

49. Maurice Casey, 'Some Anti-Semitic Assumptions in the Theological Dictionary of the New Testament' *Novum Testamentum* 41 (1999), 280–291.

50. Daniel Oudshoorn, *Pauline Eschatology: The Apocalyptic Rupture of Eternal Imperialism* (Eugene: Cascade Books, Wipf and Stock, 2020), 12.
51. Hush, 'Imaginary', 141.
52. Hush, 'Imaginary', 142.
53. Hush, 'Imaginary', 142.
54. Faith and Order Commission 'Forgiveness and Reconciliation in the Aftermath of Abuse' Church House Publishing, (2017). Available online at: https://www.churchofengland.org/sites/default/files/2017-10/forgivenessandreconciliation_0.pdf
55. Faith and Order Commission 'Forgiveness', 11.
56. Faith and Order Commission 'Forgiveness', 11.
57. Faith and Order Commission 'Forgiveness', 11.
58. Michele Antoinette Paludi (ed), *Ivory Power: Sexual Harassment on Campus* (New York: State University of New York Press, 1990).
59. Billie Wright Dziech and Linda Weiner, *The Lecherous Professor: Sexual Harassment on Campus* (Illinois: University of Illinois Press, 1990), 74.
60. Amia Srinivasan, 'Sex as a Pedagogical Failure' *Yale Law Journal* 129 (Feb 2020), 924–1275, 1103. The language of 'vulnerable adults' and possible safe-guarding implications is contested. Emma Percy outlines possible infantalising or victimhood tropes endemic in language of safeguarding, and particularly striking a lack of emphasis on students' agency. Better she suggests is focus and language centred on power structures and the inevitable 'risks' such structures pose, rather than just 'safeguarding': 'We need to continue to take safeguarding seriously. But we also need a much clearer understanding of who falls under the safeguarding legislation for adults, and I suggest we should be in better step with the definitions used by caring organisations that are beyond the church. We also need better harassment and bullying policies, and properly trained harassment advisers, who know how to help people make appropriate decisions for themselves; and how and when to call out bad behaviour.' Emma Percy, 'Safeguarding Vulnerable Adults, or Adults at Risk? What's in a Word?' blog post, *Modern Church* (8th July 2020). Available online at: https://modernchurch.org.uk/revd-canon-dr-emma-percy-safeguarding-vulnerable-adults-or-adults-at-risk-whats-in-a-word
61. Srinivasan, 'Sex', 1125.
62. Faith and Order Commission 'Forgiveness', 39. Rachel Hall and David Batty "Abuse of power': should universities ban staff-student relationships? UCL has become the third UK university to ban relationships between lecturers and their students' *The Guardian* (26th Feb 2020). Available online at: https://www.theguardian.com/education/2020/feb/26/abuse-of-power-should-universities-ban-staff-student-relationships

63. Fredrik Bondestam and Maja Lundqvist, 'Sexual harassment in higher education – a systematic review' *European Journal of Higher Education* (2020), 1–23, 10. Available online at: https://doi.org/10.1080/2156823 5.2020.1729833

64. Bondestam and Lundqvist, 'Sexual', 16.

65. Emma Chapman, Anna Bull, Tiffany Page, 'Solutions for Sexual Misconduct in Higher Education' 1752 Group. Available online at: https://1752group. com/solutions-for-sexual-misconduct-in-higher-education

66. Srinivasan, 'Sex ', 924.

67. Faith and Order Commission 'Forgiveness', 13.

68. Faith and Order Commission 'Forgiveness', 13.

69. Clare McGlynn, Nicole Westmarland, Nikki Godden, '"I Just Wanted Him to Hear Me" Sexual Violence and the Possibilities of Restorative Justice' *Journal for Law and Society* 39 (2012), 213–240. Available online at: https://doi.org/10.1111/j.1467-6478.2012.00579.x

70. Episcopal Diocese of San Diego, 'Report of the Task Force on Compassionate Care for Victims of Clergy Sexual Misconduct' (2018), 7. Available online at: https://edsd.org/wp-content/uploads/2018/11/ Report-of-CCTF-Final.pdf

71. Chapman, Bull and Page, 'Solutions', no pages.

72. Episcopal Diocese of San Diego, 'Report', 8.

73. Episcopal Diocese of San Diego, 'Report', 2.

74. Episcopal Diocese of San Diego, 'Report', 5.

75. Episcopal Diocese of San Diego, 'Report', 5.

76. Phil Crockett Thomas, 'The Girls Get Younger Every Year' (2017). Available online at: https://crowdedmouth.wordpress. com/2017/04/27/tggyeyplay/

77. Thomas, 'The Girls', no pages.

78. Jilly Boyce Kay and Sarah Banet-Weiser, 'Feminist Anger and Feminist Respair' *Feminist Media Studies* 19 (2019), 603–609. Available online at: https://doi.org/10.1080/14680777.2019.1609231

79. Kay and Banet-Weiser, 'Feminist' 603.

80. Phipps, 'Reckoning', 227.

81. 'Parrhesia is generally understood as coming from below and directed upward, whether it is the philosopher's criticism of the tyrant or the citizen's criticism of the majority of the assembly … The most famous example, which Foucault also analyzes in great detail is the figure of Diogenes, who commands Alexander from the precariousness of his barrel to move out of his light. Dio Chrysostom's description of this meeting is followed by a long *parrhesiastic* dialogue, in which Diogenes probes the boundaries of the *parrhesiastic* contract between the sovereign and the philosopher, constantly seeking to shift the boundaries of this contract in a game of

provocation and retreat. Like the citizen expressing a minority opinion in the democratic setting of the agora, the Cynic philosopher also practices a form of *parrhesia* with respect to the monarch in public.' Gerald Raunig 'The Double Criticism of Parrhesia. Answering the Question "What is a Progressive (Art) Institution?"' *Transversal* (2004). Translated by Aileen Derieg. Available online at: https://transversal.at/transversal/0504/raunig/en

82. Phipps, 'Reckoning', 238.
83. Phipps, 'Reckoning', 238.
84. Chapman, Bull and Page, 'Solutions', no pages.
85. Similarly, whilst the Church of England's processes are more robust, many people would say it is also still failing in terms of its care of and compassion towards complainants. Again, processes are tugging against complainants in favour of caution with regard to the institution's role as employee of those complained against; which is why, many people advocate a completely independent investigation process for the church.

CHAPTER 8

Conclusion

Henry Giroux, in his ambitious project to rethink higher education as a democratic public sphere, berates the ways in which 'in its drive to become a primary accomplice to corporate values and power [higher education has increasingly rendered] social problems [as] both irrelevant and invisible'.[1] Furthermore, the sector (albeit often unconsciously) 'mimics the inequalities and hierarchies of power … that produce a vast range of hardships and suffering in the larger social order'.[2] He urges critical pedagogies to be employed which challenge neoliberal conceptions and stem complicity of higher education organisations in what he evocatively terms the 'production of violence':

> Only through such a supportive and critical educational culture can students learn how to become individual and social agents, rather than merely disengaged spectators, able both to think otherwise and to act upon civic commitments fundamental to promoting the common good and producing a meaningful democracy. … Higher education has no legitimate or ethical reason for engaging in practices that are organized largely for the production of violence. It is important to reclaim higher education as a site of moral and political practice whose purpose is not only to introduce students to the great reservoir of diverse intellectual ideas and traditions, but also to engage those inherited bodies of knowledge thorough critical dialogue, analysis, and comprehension.[3]

© The Author(s), under exclusive license to Springer Nature Switzerland AG 2021
L. J. Lawrence, *Refiguring Universities in an Age of Neoliberalism*, Palgrave Critical University Studies,
https://doi.org/10.1007/978-3-030-73371-1_8

Attention in this book (illustrated in part by reference to the subject disciplines in which I research and the particular institution in which I work) has been drawn to selected ways in which neoliberal discourses, dynamics, and tendencies (including competitive individualism, marketisation of higher education, institutional brand preservation, cultures of hyper-productivity, frenetic time, auditing and performance cultures, eliding of inequalities based on historical injustices and structural hierarchies, pathologisation of (social) distress) have and continue to shape higher education, and the experiences of those who work and study within it.[4] Compassion has been proposed here as an important primary focus and objective in refiguring the sector along more affiliative lines. William Carter, too, in his reparative invitation to discover 'compassion in higher education' accordingly notes:

> Our society needs not just employable, credentialed workers, but people who can, regardless of their economic roles or status, stand against fear with a compulsion for redemptive action – people who embody compassion. If we expect such characteristics of our students, we must model them ourselves.[5]

As such, Chap. 2, 'A Prolegomenon to Refiguring the Neoliberal University: Reading with Early Christian Traditions of Compassion in the Throes of a Pandemic', proposed the present pandemic moment as a time of awakening in which inequalities are not reversed but rather magnified: 'the stakes are higher. The question of what is right or good to do – of what compassion … looks like at a time like this – suddenly has fresh urgency and potency.'[6] Through reflection on spiritual archaeologies of compassion in biblical traditions, so-called catastrophe compassion in stimulating recalibration and re-imagination of systems of human interconnectedness, obligations, and responsibilities, and the proverbial 'ditches en route to Jericho' have brought the vistas of more affiliative futures into sharper view.[7]

Chapter 3, 'Envisioning Compassionate Campuses: Critically Probing Organisational Values, Mission Statements and Cultures', plotted some of the uses of compassion, as a value propounded by selected religious, spiritual, and social-justice organisations and movements. It also traced those higher education institutions which have championed compassion in their cultures and identities—'who they are and not just what they do'[8]—and the ways in which these institutions deployed compassionate mission statements and values audaciously for utilitarian, rather than normative objectives.

Chapter 4, 'Compassionate Curricula? Northern and Southern Epistemologies and Cognitive [In-]Justice', traced, through a lens of southern theory, inequalities between knowledge economies based on northern hegemony and southern extroversion. It also outlined some dimensions of models of epistemic disobedience and justice, which need to be instilled through critical pedagogies within curricula and programmes, to make students aware of how the webs of power (and their own positionality within these) are constructed, perpetuated, and could be conceived 'other-wise' more equitably.

Chapter 5, 'Compassionate Campus Climates: Confronting Privilege and Prejudice with Compassionate Citizenship', looked at some of the dynamics (most particularly whiteness and laddism) which lay behind hate speech incidents at the University of Exeter. It also traced reparative institutional responses, which focused on changing culture (including around rituals of induction and anti-racist pedagogies) which have endeavoured to promote more compassionate, pro-social, and intercultural competencies within educational programmes.

Chapter 6, 'Compassion and Kindness: Refiguring Discourses of Student Mental Health and Wellbeing', set out to challenge the neoliberal discourses of crisis, resilience, and therapeutisation frequently associated with those seen as 'other' ('at risk', 'vulnerable') to a rational/sanist norm. Institutional reproduction of pathologising and individualising models in relation to student mental (ill) health and wellbeing, to the neglect of social models and consideration of broader cultural discourses, were challenged. In modelling alternative discourses, compassion and kindness (which aim for all students to 'thrive' not just 'survive') were proposed as alternatives in which stigma and stereotypes could be challenged and whole institutional approaches could refigure notions of time, affect, and community responsibility, in more associative directions.

Chapter 7, '[Mis-]Directed Compassion? Power, Sexual Violence and Misconduct in the Neoliberal Academy', reviewed reactions to and questions posed (regarding identity, values, and practices) by high-profile cases of sexual violence and misconduct committed by academics. Anti-violence methodologies should be employed and detoxifying curricula projects pursued. Only in this light can misdirected dynamics of empathy be mitigated and appropriate compassionate responses targeted to those damaged and injured by these actions. Work in this area recently carried out by the Church of England, in particular communal restoration (within the community and organisation), was reflected on. This offers important pointers for the higher education sector which also needs transformation from a sole focus on policy (individuals or case management) to a recognition of its own practices and cultures which have at times been complicit in silencing and eliding communal and collective damage of these actions.

Throughout this project, the power of collective action to transform discourses, ideologies, and identities, and put compassion at the heart of higher education cultures (where people not only take notice but also take concrete action to address the suffering or inequalities of others), has not been underestimated. In garnering voices of experience (including those marginalised, minoritised, and/or 'othered' in some way in institutional visions, climates, and curricula), I have attempted to show how these have the poignant and potent power to shift institutional gaze, challenge normative ideologies, and not only facilitate the recognition of suffering/inequality and distress but also stimulate commitment to take action to alleviate this (act compassionately). In all instances, the sector needs to be brutally honest, transparent, and conscious of its own participation in the sustaining of wounding neoliberal discourses, dynamics, scenarios, and stories. The very sociality and 'community' of university and scholarly cultures can both lift up some and diminish 'other' social groups. Academics work in nested family groups of knowledge and power from the 'inheritance' and 'legacy' bestowed by the professors and universities who trained us, to the ways in which we pass on that inheritance to recurring generations of students, both undergraduate and postgraduate. Students become professors, they pass it on again to their students, and so the cycle continues. This may be one of the reasons why it is perceived as being so hard to change university cultures because that legacy endorses individual promotion within competitive groups.

To conclude, I am cautiously encouraged that global events, stimulated by Covid-19, Black Lives Matter movements, and pro-democracy campaigns, hail this moment (like never before) as demanding a critical mass of compassion. Pro-social behaviours and affiliative values within and across communities globally has been recognised as critical for the future and will no doubt foster and stimulate further reflection in higher education in this regard. For compassion to be instilled as a primary objective, and viable and meaningful operational mode within the sector, then institutions urgently require 'compassionate leadership' to facilitate and support the sorts of transformations demanded. For cultural change will not be achieved by mere words or token gestures,[9] 'tool kits' which may or may not be engaged and implemented, but rather, honest interactions and actual interventions in which we all are made aware of our own position and complicity in dynamics and discourses which oppress. Only these can energise the more fundamental changes needed to construct 'compassionate campuses' and refigure the identities, values, and experiences of human beings, which exist within, and emerge from them.

Notes

1. Henry A. Giroux 'Bare Pedagogy and the Scourge of Neoliberalism: Rethinking Higher Education as a Democratic Public Sphere' *The Educational Forum*, 74:3 (2010), 184–196, 184. Available online at: https://doi.org/10.1080/00131725.2010.483897
2. Giroux, 'Bare' 184.
3. Giroux, 'Bare' 184–187.
4. As I complete this book, which has attempted to cut to the heart of the ways in which cultures of academic institutions, knowledge, and practice are produced, perpetuated, and valued, I face questions about whether this book will be 'REFable', suitable for submission to the Research Excellence Framework, used to 'assess the quality of research at UK Higher Education Institutions'. The Research Excellence Framework's stated purpose is outlined as follows: 'The funding bodies' shared policy aim for research assessment is to secure the continuation of a world-class, dynamic and responsive research base across the full academic spectrum within UK higher education. We expect that this will be achieved through the threefold purpose of the REF: 1. To provide accountability for public investment in research and produce evidence of the benefits of this investment. 2. To provide benchmarking information and establish reputational yardsticks, for use within the HE sector and for public information. 3. To inform the selective allocation of funding for research.' See https://www.ref.ac.uk/. The REF structure (despite frequent protestations otherwise) is largely nested in discipline silos, and privileges (at least in the humanities) 'weighty' research monographs, over others sorts of (transdisciplinary or co-written) texts. This system frequently functions as a disincentive for academics (in my own discipline at least) to write collaboratively, 'outside of their lane' or comfort zone, and/or transcend boundaries to comment on institutional values or cultures in which they operate. It is another example of a neoliberal structure which has the power to exclude, silence, and disempower. It also inevitably breeds individualistic competition among colleagues and institutions.

5. William Carpenter, 'Finding Compassion in Higher Education: A Provocation' *Bringing Theory to Practice* (Winter 2018). Available online at: https://www.bttop.org/news-events/feature-finding-compassion-higher-education-provocation

6. Kitty Wheater, 'What is Compassion in the Time of COVID-19?' *Edinburgh University Chaplaincy.* Available online at: https://www.ed.ac.uk/chaplaincy/compassion-for-our-times/what-is-compassion-in-the-time-of-covid-19

7. 'Seeing compassion as interpersonal work highlights the competence or skilful action involved in doing compassion. It requires not only skilful action but also emotional attunement' (Frost et al., 2006 p. 850). Cited in Andre L. Delbecq, 'Organizational compassion: a litmus test for a spiritually centred university culture' *Journal of Management, Spirituality & Religion* 7:3 (2010), 241–249. Available online at: http://doi/org/10.1080/1476608 6.2010.499998. Also see Byron Greenberg and David Bejou, 'A Call to Corporate Compassion' *Journal of Relationship Marketing* 11:1 (2012) 1–6. Available online at: DOI: https://doi.org/10.1080/1533266 7.2012.653602

8. Greenberg and Bejou, 'A Call', no pages.

9. 'Collaborative culture' not 'contrived collegiality' is key. See Andy Hargreaves and Ruth Dawe, 'Paths of professional development: Contrived collegiality, collaborative culture, and the case of peer coaching' *Teaching and Teacher Education* Volume 6 (1990), 227–241. Available online at: https://doi.org/10.1016/0742-051X(90)90015-W

Bibliography

Aaltola, Mika, *Western Spectacle of Governance and the Emergence of Humanitarian World Politics* (London: Palgrave Macmillan, 2009).

Aaltola, Mika, *Understanding the Politics of Pandemic Scares: An Introduction to Global Politicosomatics* (Oxford: Routledge, 2012).

Abelman, Robert, and Atkin, David et al., 'The Trickle-Down Effect of Institutional Vision: Vision Statements and Academic Advising' *NACADA Journal* 27 (2007), 4–21.

Aberth, John, *Plagues in World History* (Lanham: Rowman & Littlefield Publishers, 2011).

Adésínà, Jìmí O., 'Realising the Vision: The Discursive and Institutional Challenges of Becoming an African University' *African Sociological Review* 9 (2005), 23–39.

Ahmed, Sara, *On Being Included: Race and Diversity in Institutional Life* (Durham: Duke University Press, 2012).

Ahmed, Sara, *Living a Feminist Life* (Durham: Duke University Press, 2017).

Anderson, Sharon K. and Middleton, Valerie A., *Explorations in Diversity: Examining Privilege and Oppression in a Multicultural Society* (Brooks/Cole Cengage Learning, 2011).

Anderson, Sharon and Middleton, Valerie, 'An Awakening to Privilege, Oppression and Discrimination' chapter 1 in Sharon Anderson and Valerie Middleton (eds), *Explorations in Diversity: Examining the Complexities of Privilege, Discrimination and Oppression* (Oxford: Oxford University Press, 3ed. 2018), 3–8.

Andersson, Johan, Sadgrove, Joanna, and Valentine, Gill, 'Consuming campus: geographies of encounter at a British university' *Social & Cultural Geography*, 13:5 (2012), 501–515. Available online at: doi:https://doi.org/10.108 0/14649365.2012.700725.

Anstiss, Tim, Passmore, Jonathan, and Gilbert, Paul, 'Compassion the Essential Orientation' *The Psychologist* 33 (2020), 38–42. Available online at: https://thepsychologist.bps.org.uk/volume-33/may-2020/compassion-essential-orientation.

Armstrong, Karen, *The Battle for God: Fundamentalism in Judaism, Christianity and Islam (Alfred Knopf,* 2000).

Armstrong, Karen, *The Great Transformation The Beginning of Our Religious Traditions* (London: Atlantic Books, 2006).

Armstrong, Karen, 'Charter for Compassion' (2008). Available online at: https://charterforcompassion.org/charter.

Armstrong, Karen, *Twelve Steps to a Compassionate Life* (London: Bodley Head, 2011).

Armstrong, Karen, *The Lost Art of Scripture* (London: Bodley Head, 2019).

Arndt, Susan, 'Blinded by Privilege: The West and the Rest Under Lockdown', *De Gruyter Conversations* Spring 2020. Available online at: https://blog. degruyter.com/white-privilege-in-the-time-of-covid-19/

Attridge, Harold, MacDonald, Dennis, and Rothschild, Clare (eds), *Delightful Acts: New Essays on Canonical and Non-Canonical Acts* (Tübingen: Mohr Siebeck, 2017).

Austin, A. E., 'Faculty cultures, faculty values' *New Directions for Institutional Research* 68 (1990), 61–74.

Bailey, Randall, 'Whatever happened to Good Old White Boys? A Review of the Global Bible Commentary' (2004). Available online at: https://www.vanderbilt.edu/AnS/religious_studies/GBC/proscons.htm.

Balslev, Anindita Niyogi and Dirk Evers (eds), Compassion in the World's Religions: Envisioning Human Solidarity (New Brunswick: Transaction Publishers, 2010).

Barer, David, 'The NHS: National Religion or National Football' *British Medical Journal* 352 (2016). Available online at: doi:https://doi.org/10.1136/bmj.i1023.

Barnd, Natchee, 'Constructing a Social Justice Tour: Pedagogy, Race, and Student Learning through Geography', *Journal of Geography* 115:5 (2016), 212–223. Available online at: doi:https://doi.org/10.1080/00221341.2016.1153132.

Barnett, Ronald, 'Knowing and becoming in the higher education curriculum' *Studies in Higher Education* 34:4 (2009), 429–440. Available online at: https://www.tandfonline.com/doi/abs/10.1080/03075070902771978.

Barr, Sabrina, 'Almost Half of Students have Experienced a Serious Psychological Issue', *The Independent* (10th March 2020). Available online at: https://www.

universitiesuk.ac.uk/policy-and-analysis/reports/Documents/2020/uuk-stepchange-mhu.pdf.

Bates, Stephen, 'Stephen Bates learns to be a better person with the help of Karen Armstrong' *The Guardian* (12th Feb 2011). Available online at: https://www.theguardian.com/books/2011/feb/12/twelve-stepscompassionate-life-karen-armstrong.

BBC, 'L'Arche founder Jean Vanier sexually abused women – internal report' (22nd February, 2020). Available online at: https://www.bbc.co.uk/news/world-51596516.

Beard, Colin, Clegg, Sue, and Smith, Karen, 'Acknowledging the affective in higher education' *British Educational Research Journal* 33 (2007), 235–252.

Beaty, Michael D. and Henry, Douglas V., 'Introduction: Retrieving the Tradition, Remembering the End' in Michael D. Beaty and Douglas V. Henry (eds), *The Schooled Heart: Moral Formation in American Higher Education* (Waco: Baylor University Press, 2007), 1–28.

Beavis, Mary and Michael Gilmour (eds), *Dictionary of the Bible and Western Culture* (Sheffield: Sheffield Phoenix Press, 2012).

Beckford, Robert, 'Better Must Come: Black Pentecostals, the Pandemic and the Future of Christianity' *Vimeo* (2020). Available online at: https://vimeo.com/414095431.

Begum, Neema and Saini, Rima, 'Decolonising the Curriculum' *Political Studies Review* Volume 17:2 (2019), 196–201. Available online at: doi:10.1177/1478929918808459.

Benhabib, Seyla, *The Claims of Culture: Equality and Diversity in the Global Era* (Princeton, New Jersey: Princeton University Press, 2002).

Bennett, Nick, 'The crisis in student wellbeing is about emotional fitness, not mental illness.' *WONKHE* (11th November 2019). Available online at: https://wonkhe.com/blogs/the-crisis-in-student-wellbeing-is-about-emotional-fitness-not-mental-illness/.

Bennett, Nick, 'Mental Fitness Helps us All to Thrive: It Should be in the Curriculum' *WONKHE* (7th September 2020). Available online at: https://wonkhe.com/blogs/mental-fitness-helps-us-all-to-thrive-it-should-be-in-the-curriculum/.

Berg, Lawrence D., Huijbens, Edward H. and Larsen, Henrik Gutzon, 'Producing anxiety in the neoliberal university' *Canadian Geographer* 60 (2016), 168–180. Available online at: doi:https://doi.org/10.1111/cag.12261.

Berlant, Lauren, 'Introduction: Compassion (and Withholding)' in Lauren Berlant (ed), *Compassion: The Culture and Politics of an Emotion* (New York: Routledge, 2004), 1–13.

Bloom, Paul, *Against Empathy: The Case for Rational Compassion* (New York: Ecco Press, 2018).

Bhusal, Manoj, 'The World After COVID-19: An Opportunity for a New Beginning' *International Journal of Scientific and Research Publications*, Volume 10, Issue 5 (May 2020) 735–741. Available online at: https://tuhat. helsinki.fi/ws/portalfiles/portal/137399898/manoj_bhusal_the_world_ after_COVID_19.pdf.

Bird, K. Schucan and Pitman, L., 'How diverse is your reading list? Exploring issues of representation and decolonisation in the UK' *Higher Education* 79 (2019). Available online at: doi: https://doi.org/10.1007/s10734-019-00446-9. See also https://www.ucl.ac.uk/news/2019/nov/university-reading-lists-dominated-white-european-men.

Bjarnason, Davíð, Stefánsdóttir, Valgerður and Beukes, Lizette 'Signs speak as loud as words: deaf empowerment in Namibia' *Development in Practice* 22 (2012), 190–201. Available online at: doi:https://doi.org/10.1080/0961452 4.2012.640986.

Bland, Archie and Henley, Jon, 'Oxford professor sentenced to jail in France over child abuse images' *The Guardian* (22nd June 2020). Available online at: https://www.theguardian.com/world/2020/jun/22/oxford-university-professor-jan-joosten-jailed-france-child-abuse-images.

Bloch, Charlotte, *Passion and Paranoia: Emotions and the Culture of Emotion in Academia* (Farnham: Ashgate, 2012).

Bondestam, Fredrik, and Lundqvist, Maja, 'Sexual harassment in higher education – a systematic review' *European Journal of Higher Education* (2020), 1–23. Available online at: doi: https://doi.org/10.1080/2156823 5.2020.1729833.

Borg, Marcus, *Meeting Jesus Again for the First Time* (New York: HarperOne, 2006).

Bormann, Lukas, 'Auch unter politischen Gesichtspunkten sehr sorgfältig ausgewählt: Die ersten deutschen Mitglieder der Studiorum Novi Testamenti Societas (SNTS) 1937–1946', *New Testament Studies* 58.3 (2012), 416–452. Available online at: http://journals.cambridge.org/action/displayAbstract?fro mPage=online&aid=8601450.

Boyd, Jade and Kerr, Thomas, 'Policing 'Vancouver's mental health crisis': a critical discourse analysis' *Critical Public Health* 26:4 (2016), 418–433. Available online at: doi: https://doi.org/10.1080/09581596.2015.1007923.

Brabazon, Honor, 'The academy's neoliberal response to COVID-19: Why faculty should be wary and how we can push back' *Academic Matters OCUFA's Journal of Higher Education* (2020). Available online at: https://academic-matters.ca/neoliberal-response-to-Covid-19/.

Branch, Carole and Klinkenberg, Dean, 'Compassion Fatigue Among Paediatric Healthcare Providers' *The American Journal of Maternal/Child Nursing* (2015), Available online at: doi: 10.1097/NMC.0000000000000133.

Breidlid, Anders, *Education, Indigenous Knowledges, and Development in the Global South* (Oxford/New York: Routledge, 2012).

Brown, Darryl, 'Racism and Race Relations in the University' *Virginia Law Review* 76 (1990), 295–335.

Brown, Lorraine and Jones, Ian, 'Encounters with racism and the international student experience', *Studies in Higher Education* 38 (2013), 1004–1019. Available online at doi:https://doi.org/10.1080/03075079.2011.614940.

Brown, Roger, Pratt, Chris and Curnow, Trevor, 'The abject failure of marketization in higher education' *The Guardian* (5th April 2019). Available online at: https://www.theguardian.com/education/2019/apr/05/the-abject-failure-of-marketisation-in-higher-education.

Brunila, Kristiina, 'The Rise of the Survival Discourse in an Era of Therapeutisation and Neoliberalism' *Education Inquiry* 5:1 (2014). Available online at: doi: https://doi.org/10.3402/edui.v5.24044.

Brunsma, David L., Brown, Eric S. and Placier, Peggy, 'Teaching Race at Historically White Colleges and Universities: Identifying and Dismantling the Walls of Whiteness' *Critical Sociology* 39 (2012), 717–738.

Buheji, Mohamed, and Ahmed, Dunya, 'Foresight of Coronavirus (COVID-19) Opportunities for a Better World' *American Journal of Economics* 10(2) (2020), 97–108. Available online at: doi: https://doi.org/10.5923/j.economics.20201002.05.

Byrom, Nicola and Ecclestone, Kathryn, 'Are universities encouraging students to believe hard study is bad for their mental health?' *Times Higher Education* (2nd April 2020). Available online at: https://www.timeshighereducation.com/features/are-universities-encouraging-students-believe-hard-study-bad-their-mental-health.

Cabrera, Nolan L., 'Beyond Black and White: How White, Male, College Students See Their Asian American Peers, Equity & Excellence in Education' *Equity and Excellence in Education* 47 (2014), 133–151. Available online at: doi:https://doi.org/10.1080/10665684.2014.900427.

Calder, William B., 'Achieving an Institution's Values, Vision, and Mission' *College Quarterly* 17 (2014). Available online at: https://www.jisc.ac.uk/full-guide/vision-mission-and-values.

Callister, Erin and Thomas Plante, 'Does Faith That Does Justice Education Improve Compassion?' in Thomas Plante (ed), *The Psychology of Compassion and Cruelty, Understanding the Emotional, Spiritual, and Religious Influences* (Santa Barbara: Praeger, 2015), 109–124.

Campbell, J., Gilmore L., and Cuskelly, M., 'Changing Student Teachers' Attitudes Towards Disability and Inclusion' *Journal of Intellectual & Developmental Disability* Volume 28 (2003), 369–379.

Candappa, Mano, Arnot, Madeleine and Pinson, Halleli, 'Compassion, Justice and Sanctuary: Can Asylum-Seeking and Refugee Students "Belong" in British Schools?' Paper presented at the British Educational Research Association Annual Conference, University of Manchester, 2–5 September 2009. Available online at: http://www.leeds.ac.uk/educol/documents/192216.pdf.

Cardenel, Ernesto, *The Gospel in Solentiname*, vol. 4, trans. D. Walsh (Maryknoll: Orbis Books, 1982).

Carpenter, William, 'Finding Compassion in Higher Education: A Provocation' *Bringing Theory to Practice* (Winter 2018). Available online at: https://www.bttop.org/news-events/feature-finding-compassion-higher-education-provocation.

Carson, Susan, Hawkes, Lesley, Gislason, Kari, and Cantrell, Kate, 'Literature, tourism and the city: writing and cultural change', *Journal of Tourism and Cultural Change* 15:4 (2017), 380–392. Available online at: doi:https://doi.org/10.1080/14766825.2016.1165237.

Case, Kim A., 'Raising White Privilege Awareness and Reducing Racial Prejudice: Assessing Diversity Course Effectiveness' *Teaching of Psychology* 34 (2007), 231–235. Available online at: doi:https://doi.org/10.1080/00986280701700250.

Casey, Maurice, 'Some Anti-Semitic Assumptions in the Theological Dictionary of the New Testament' *Novum Testamentum* 41 (1999), 280–291.

Cassell, E. J., 'Compassion' in C. R. Snyder & S. J. Lopez (eds), *Handbook of Positive Psychology* (Oxford: Oxford University Press, 2002), 434–445.

Casella, Eleanor, 'Lockdown: On the Materiality of Confinement' in Adrian Myers and Gabriel Moshenska (eds), *Archaeologies of Internment* (New York: Springer, 2011), 285–95.

Chapman, Emma, Bull, Anna and Page, Tiffany, 'Solutions for Sexual Misconduct in Higher Education'. 1752 Group. Available online at: https://1752group.com/solutions-for-sexual-misconduct-in-higher-education/.

Chick, Nancy, 'Mindfulness in the Classroom' Vanderbilt University. Available online at: https://cft.vanderbilt.edu/guides-sub-pages/contemplative-pedagogy.

Chilton, Amy, 'My rise, their fall: A theologian's burden in response to the reality of sexual abuse' (27th October 2017). Available online at: https://baptist-news.com/article/rise-fall-theologians-burden-response-reality-sexual-abuse/#.XvsFtG5FxPY.

Choudhery, Tahmina, 'We Can't Separate the Issues of Race and Reopening Universities' WONKHE (3rd June 2020). Available online at: https://wonkhe.com/blogs/we-cant-separate-the-issues-of-race-and-reopening-in-universities/.

Clegg, Sue, and Rowland, Stephen, 'Kindness in pedagogical practice and academic life' *British Journal of Sociology of Education* 31:6 (2010), 719–735. Available online at: doi:https://doi.org/10.1080/01425692.2010.515102.

Clifford, Valerie and Montgomery, Catherine, 'Designing an internationalised curriculum for higher education: embracing the local and the global citizen' *Higher Education Research and Development* 36(6) (2017), 1138–1151. Available online at: doi:10.1080/07294360.2017.1296413.

Clough, David, 'Should Christians eat less meat?' *Church Times* (22nd May 2020). Available online at: https://www.churchtimes.co.uk/articles/2020/22-may/features/features/should-christians-eat-less-meat.

Clouston, Teena J., 'Transforming learning: teaching compassion and caring values in higher education' *Journal of Further and Higher Education* Vol 42 (2018), 1015–1024.

Cohn, Samuel K. Jr, *Epidemics: Hate and Compassion from the Plague of Athens to AIDS* (Oxford: Oxford University Press, 2018).

Connell, Raewyn, *Southern Theory* (Cambridge: Polity, 2007).

Connell, Raewyn, 'Southern Bodies and Disability: Rethinking Concepts' *Third World Quarterly* 32 (2011) Available online at: doi:10.1080/0143659 7.2011.614799.

Connell, Raewyn, 'Using Southern Theory: Decolonizing Social Thought in Theory, Research and Application' *Planning Theory* (2013) 12 (2), 210–223.

Connell, Raewyn, 'Masculinities in global perspective: hegemony, contestation, and changing structures of power' *Theory and Society* 45/4 (2016), 303–318. Available online at: doi:https://doi.org/10.1007/s11186-016-9275-x.

Connell, Raewyn, 'Southern theory and World Universities' *Higher Education Research & Development* 36:1 (2017), 4–15. Available online at: https://www.tandfonline.com/doi/abs/10.1080/07294360.2017.1252311.

Connell, Raewyn, *The Good University: What Universities Actually Do and Why it's Time for Radical Change* (London: Zed Books, 2019).

Corcoran, Carole and Thompson, Aisha, 'What's Race Got to Do, Got to Do with It?' Denial of Racism on Predominantly White College Campuses' in Jean Lau Chin (ed), *The Psychology of Prejudice and Discrimination: Racisms in America* (Westport: Praegar, 2004), 137–176.

Côté, James E., 'The Enduring Usefulness of Erikson's Concept of the Identity Crisis in the 21st Century: An Analysis of Student Mental Health Concern' *Identity* 18(4) (2018), 1 –13. Available online at: https://www.researchgate.net/publication/328124487_The_Enduring_Usefulness_of_Erikson's_Concept_of_the_Identity_Crisis_in_the_21st_Century_An_Analysis_of_Student_Mental_Health_Concerns/citation/download.

Cramp, Andy and Lamond, Catherine, 'Engagement and kindness in digitally mediated learning with teachers' *Teaching in Higher Education* 21:1 (2016), 1–12. Available online at: doi:10.1080/13562517.2015.1101681.

Crawford, Joseph, Butler-Henderson, Kerryn, Rudolph, Jürgen, Glowatz, Matthias et al., 'COVID-19: 20 Countries' Higher Education Intra-Period Digital Pedagogy Responses' *Journal of Applied Teaching and Learning* 3 (1) (2020), 1–20.

Crossley, James, 'By What Authority Are You Doing These Things?: A Brief History of the Bible in English Political Discourse from Margaret Thatcher to Jeremy Corbyn' *Biblical Theology Bulletin* 46 (2016), 144–153. Available online at: doi:https://doi.org/10.1177/0146107916655291.

Crossley, James, *Harnessing Chaos: The Bible in English Political Discourse Since 1968* (London: T&T Clark/Bloomsbury, 2014).

Crumpton, Stephanie, 'Trigger warnings, covenants of presence, and more: Cultivating safe space for theological discussions about sexual trauma' *Teaching Theology and Religion* 20 (2017), 137–147. Available online at: https://onlinelibrary.wiley.com/doi/abs/10.1111/teth.12376.

Curtis, Katherine, Gallagher, Ann, Ramage, Charlotte, et al, 'Using Appreciative Inquiry to develop, implement and evaluate a multi-organisation 'Cultivating Compassion' programme for health professionals and support staff' *Journal of Research in Nursing* 22 (2017), 150–165.

D'Andrea, Vaneeta and Gosling, David, *Improving Teaching And Learning In Higher Education: A Whole Institute Approach* (New York: McGraw-Hill Education, 2005).

Darley, J. M. and Batson, C. Daniel, '"From Jerusalem to Jericho": A Study of Situational and Dispositional Variables in Helping Behavior' *Journal of Personality and Social Psychology* 27 (1973), 100–108.

Davids, Nuraan and Waghid, Yusef, 'Higher education as a pedagogical site for citizenship education' *Education, Citizenship and Social Justice* 11 (2016), 34–43.

Davis, Leonard, *Enforcing Normalcy: Disability, Deafness and the Body* (London: Verso, 1995).

de Wit, H., 'Intercultural bible reading and hermeneutics' In H. de Wit, L. Jonker, M. Kool, & D. Schipani (eds), *Through the Eyes of Another: Intercultural Reading of the Bible* (Elkhart: Institute of Mennonite Studies – Vrije Universiteit, 2004), 477–492.

Delbecq, Andre L., 'Organizational compassion: a litmus test for a spiritually centred university culture' *Journal of Management, Spirituality and Religion*, 7 (2010) 241–249. Available online at: doi: https://doi.org/10.1080/14766608 6.2010.499998.

Dennis, Marguerite, 'Higher education opportunities after COVID-19' *University World News* (9th May 2020). Available online at: https://www.university-worldnews.com/post.php?story=20200507152524762.

Dessel, A. B., Goodman, K. D., Woodford, M. R., 'LGBT discrimination on campus and heterosexual bystanders: Understanding intentions to intervene' *Journal of Diversity in Higher Education*, 10(2) (2017), 101–116. Available online at: doi:https://doi.org/10.1037/dhe0000015.

Di Leo, *Jeffrey, Higher Education under Late Capitalism: Identity, Conduct, and the Neoliberal Condition* (London: Palgrave Macmillan, 2017).

Dietrich, Walter, and Luz, Ulrich (eds), *The Bible in a World Context: An Experiment in Contextual Hermeneutics: An Experiment in Contextual Hermeneutics* (Grand Rapids: Eerdmans, 2002).

Dowers, Paul, 'Pity, Empathy, and the Tragic Spectacle of Human Suffering: Exploring the Emotional Culture of Compassion in Late Ancient Christianity' *Journal of Early Christian Studies* 18 (2010), 1–27. Available online at: https://muse.jhu.edu/article/377440/pdf.

Downey, John and Stage, Frances, 'Hate Crimes and Violence on College and University Campuses' Journal of College Student Development 40 (1999), 3–9.

du Plooy, Belinda, 'Ubuntu and the recent phenomenon of the Charter for Compassion' *South African Review of Sociology* 45 (2014), 83–100. Available online at: doi: https://doi.org/10.1080/21528586.2014.887916.

Dutton, Jane E. and Worline, Monica C., 'Educators, It's Time to Put on Your Compassion Hats' *Harvard Business Publishing* (3rd April, 2020). Available online at: https://hbsp.harvard.edu/inspiring-minds/educators-its-time-to-put-on-your-compassion-hats?itemFindingMethod=Editorial.

Dziech, Billie Wright and Weiner, Linda, *The Lecherous Professor: Sexual Harassment on Campus* (Illinois: University of Illinois Press, 1990).

Ecclestone, K. and Rawdin, C., 'Reinforcing the 'diminished' subject? The implications of the 'vulnerability zeitgeist' for well-being in educational settings', *Cambridge Journal of Education* 46:3 (2016), 377–393. Available online at: doi: https://doi.org/10.1080/0305764X.2015.1120707.

Episcopal Diocese of San Diego, 'Report of the Task Force on Compassionate Care for Victims of Clergy Sexual Misconduct' (2018). Available online at: https://edsd.org/wp-content/uploads/2018/11/Report-of-CCTF-Final.pdf.

Epstein, Debbie, and Morrell, Robert, 'Approaching Southern Theory: Explorations of Gender in South African Education' *Gender and Education* 24 (2012), 469–482.

Erevelles, Nirmala, 'Understanding curriculum as normalizing text: disability studies meet curriculum theory' *Journal of Curriculum Studies* 37:4 (2005), 421–439. Available online at: doi: https://doi.org/10.1080/002202703 2000276970.

Esposito, Luigi, Perez, Fernando M., 'Neoliberalism and the Commodification of Mental Health' *Humanity and Society* 38/4 (2014), 414–442. Available online at: doi:https://doi.org/10.1177/0160597614544958.

Faith and Order Commission 'Forgiveness and Reconciliation in the Aftermath of Abuse' Church House Publishing (2017). Available online at: https://www.churchofengland.org/sites/default/files/2017-10/forgivenessandreconciliation_0.pdf.

Falherty, Colleen, 'Harassment and Power' *Inside Higher Ed* (20th August 2018). Available online at: https://www.insidehighered.com/news/2018/08/20/some-say-particulars-ronell-harassment-case-are-moot-it-all-comes-down-power.

Fenton, R. A., Mott, H. L., McCartan, K. and Rumney, P., *The Intervention Initiative*. Bristol: UWE and Public Health England (2014). Available online at: https://uwe-repository.worktribe.com/output/824075/the-intervention-initiative.

Ferner, Adam and Chetty, Darren, *How to Disagree: Negotiate Difference in a Divided World* (London: White Lion Publishing, 2019).

Finn, Mike, *British Universities in the Brexit Moment: Political, Economic and Cultural Implications* (Bingley: Emerald Publishing, 2018).

Fiorenza, Elisabeth Schüssler, *Democratizing Biblical Studies: Toward an Emancipatory Educational Space* (Louisville: Westminster John Knox, 2009).

Firth, Rhiannon, 'Somatic Pedagogies: Critiquing and Resisting the Affective Discourse of the Neoliberal State from an Embodied Anarchist Perspective' *Ephemera: Theory and Politics in Organization* Vol 16 (2016), 121–142.

Flowers, Jonathan Charles, 'The Coming Campus Protests: College leaders will be judged by their actions—not their words' *Chronicle of Higher Education* (10th June 2020). Available online at: https://www.chronicle.com/article/The-Coming-Campus-Protests/248967.

Flynn, M. and Mercer, D., 'Is compassion possible in a market-led NHS?' *Nursing Times* 109 (2013) 12–14.

Foege, William, 'Plagues: Perceptions of Risk and Social Responses' in Arien Mack (ed), *In Time of Plague: The History and Consequences of Lethal Epidemic Disease* (New York: New York University Press, 1991), 9–20.

Forester, John, 'Kindness, Planners' Response to Vulnerability, and an Ethics of Care in the Time of COVID-19', *Planning Theory & Practice* (2020) 1–4. Available online at: doi:https://doi.org/10.1080/14649357.2020.1757886.

Foubert, John D., Brosi, Matthew W., and Bannon, R. Sean, 'Pornography Viewing among Fraternity Men: Effects on Bystander Intervention, Rape Myth Acceptance and Behavioral Intent to Commit Sexual Assault' *Sexual Addiction & Compulsivity* 18:4 (2011), 212–231. Available online at: doi: https://doi.org/10.1080/10720162.2011.625552.

Francois, Myriam, 'It's not just Cambridge University – all of Britain benefited from slavery' *The Guardian* (7th May 2019). Available online at: https://www.theguardian.com/commentisfree/2019/may/07/cambridge-university-britain-slavery.

Freire, Paulo, *Pedagogy of the Oppressed* (30th anniversary ed.) (New York: Bloomsbury, 2000).

Frost, Peter et al, 'Narratives of Compassion in Organizations' in Stephen Fineman (ed), *Emotion in Organizations* (London: Sage, 2000), 25–45.

Furey, Sheila, Springer, Paul, and Parsons, Christine, 'Positioning university as a brand: distinctions between the brand promise of Russell Group, 1994 Group, University Alliance, and Million+ universities' *Journal of Marketing for Higher Education* (2014), 24:1, 99–121. Available online at: doi: https://doi.org/10.1080/08841241.2014.919980.

Gaffikin, Frank and Perry, David C., 'Discourses and Strategic Visions: The U.S. Research University as an Institutional Manifestation of Neoliberalism in a Global Era' *American Educational Research Journal* 46 (2009), 115–144. Available online at: doi:https://doi.org/10.3102/0002831208322180.

Gonsalves Maria Goretti, 'The Confluence of Creeds' *ACADEMICIA: An International Multidisciplinary Research Journal* 8 (2018), 41–45.

Gibbs, P., (ed), *Pedagogy of Compassion* (Switzerland: Springer, 2017a).

Gibbs, P., 'Higher Education: A Compassion Business or Edifying Experience?' in Paul Gibson, Suanne and Baskerville, Delia, 'Editorial' *Pastoral Care in Education*, 35:3 (2017b), 149–151. Available online at: doi:https://doi.org/10.1080/02643944.2017.1364534.

Gilbert, Paul, *The Compassionate Mind* (London: Constable & Robinson Ltd., 2010).

Gilbert, Paul (ed), *Compassion: Concepts, Research and Applications* (London; New York: Routledge, 2017a)

Gilbert, Theo, 'When Looking Is Allowed: What Compassionate Group Work Looks Like in a UK University' in P. Gibbs (ed), *The Pedagogy of Compassion at the Heart of Higher Education* (Switzerland: Springer, 2017b), 189–202.

Gill, R., 'Beyond individualism: the psychosocial life of the neoliberal university' in M. Spooner (ed.), *A Critical Guide to Higher Education & the Politics of Evidence: Resisting Colonialism, Neoliberalism, & Audit Culture* (Regina, Canada: University of Regina Press, 2017), 1–21.

Gill, Rosalind and Donaghue, Ngaire, 'Resilience, apps and reluctant individualism: Technologies of self in the neoliberal academy' *Women's Studies International Forum* 54 (2016), 91 –99.

Gin, Kevin J., Martínez-Alemán, Ana M., Rowan-Kenyon, Heather T., and Hottell, Derek, 'Racialized Aggressions and Social Media on Campus' *Journal of College Student Development* 58 (2017), 159–174. Available online at: https://muse.jhu.edu/article/650712/pdf.

Giroux, Henry, 'Neoliberalism, Corporate Culture, and the Promise of Higher Education: The University as a Democratic Public Sphere' *Harvard Educational Review* Vol. 72, No. 4, (2002) 425–464. Available online at: https://doi.org/10.17763/haer.72.4.0515nr62324n71p1.

Giroux, Henry, 'Bare Pedagogy and the Scourge of Neoliberalism: Rethinking Higher Education as a Democratic Public Sphere' *The Educational Forum*, 74:3 (2010), 184–196, 184. Available online at: doi:https://doi.org/10.1080/00131725.2010.483897.

Goetz, J.L. and Keltner, D. Simon-Thomas, E., 'Compassion: An evolutionary analysis and empirical review' *Psychological Bulletin*, 136 (3) (2010), 351–374.

Goldsmiths, Vik Loveday, 'Embodying Deficiency Through 'Affective Practice': Shame, Relationality, and the Lived Experience of Social Class and Gender in Higher Education' *Sociology* 50/6 (2016), 1140–1155.

Goossen, Rachel, '"Defanging the Beast": Mennonite Responses to John Howard Yoder's Sexual Abuse' (2015). Available online at: http://www.bishop-accountability.org/news5/2015_01_Goossen_Defanging_the_Beast.pdf.

Goossen, Rachel, 'Historical Justice in an Era of #MeToo: Legacies of John Howard Yoder' (7th December 2017). Available online at: https://divinity.uchicago.edu/sightings/articles/historical-justice-era-metoo-legacies-john-howard-yoder.

Grandin, Temple, with Scariano, M., *Emergence: Labelled Autistic* (Florida: Costello, 1986).

Grange, L. Le, 'Decolonising the University Curriculum' *South African Journal of Higher Education* 30/2 (2016), 1–12.

Gray-Rosendale, Laura A. (ed), *Me Too, Feminist Theory, and Surviving Sexual Violence in the Academy* (Maryland: Lexington Books/Fortress Academic, 2020).

Greaves, Paul, 'Exeter is Better Than This' *Devon Life* (6th March 2020). Available online at: https://www.devonlive.com/news/devon-news/exeter-better-this-racist-coronavirus-3923885.

Grech, Shaun, and Soldatic, Karen, *Disability in the Global South: The Critical Handbook* (Switzerland: Springer, 2016).

Greenberg, Byron, and Bejou, David, 'A Call to Corporate Compassion' *Journal of Relationship Marketing* 11:1 (2012) 1–6. Available online at: doi: https://doi.org/10.1080/15332667.2012.653602

Gregory, James, 'Engineering Compassion: The Institutional Structure of Virtue' *Journal of Social Policy* 44 (2015), 339–356.

Gryboski, Michael, 'President Obama Cites the Bible in Immigration Speech' *The Christian Post* (21st November, 2014). Available online at: https://www.christianpost.com/news/president-obama-cites-the-bible-in-immigration-speech.html.

Guinier, Lani, 'Admission Rituals as Political Acts: Guardians at the Gates of our Democratic Ideals' *Harvard Law Review* 117 (2003–2004). Available online at: https://heinonline.org/HOL/Page?collection=journals&handle=hein.journals/hlr117&id=141&men_tab=srchresults.

Gunnell, David, Kidger, Judi, and Elvidge, Hamish, 'Adolescent mental health in crisis' *British Medical Journal* 361 (2018). Available online at: doi:https://doi.org/10.1136/bmj.k2608.

Gusa, Diane, 'White Institutional Presence: The Impact of Whiteness on Campus Climate' *Harvard Educational Review* 80 (2010), 464–490.

Guth, Karen V., 'Moral Injury, Feminist and Womanist Ethics, and Tainted Legacies' *Journal of the Society of Christian Ethics* Volume 38, Issue 1 (2018), 167–186. Available online at: doi:https://doi.org/10.1353/sce.2018.0010.

Guzmán, Nadyne, 'The Leadership Covenant: Essential Factors for Developing Co-creative Relationships Within a Learning Community' *Journal of Leadership Studies* Volume 2 (1995), 151–160. Available online at: doi:https://doi.org/10.1177/107179199500200412.

Haang'andu, Privilege, 'Transnationalizing Disability in Embedded Cultural-Cognitive Worldviews: The Case of Sub-Saharan Africa' *Disability and the Global South* 5/1 (2018), 1292–1314. Available online at: https://disability-globalsouth.files.wordpress.com/2018/02/dgs-05-01-06.pdf.

Hadebe, Nontando M., 'Commodification, decolonisation and theological education in Africa: Renewed challenges for African theologians' *HTS Theological Studies* 73/3 (2017), no pages. Available online at: http://www.scielo.org.za/scielo.php?script=sci_arttext&pid=S0259-94222017000300050.

Haihambo, Cynthy, and Lightfoot, Elizabeth, 'Cultural Beliefs Regarding People with Disabilities in Namibia: Implications for the Inclusion of People with Disabilities' *International Journal of Special Education* 25/3 (2010), 76–87. Available online at: University of Minnesota Digital Conservancy, http://hdl.handle.net/11299/171770.

Hall, Edith, *Greek Tragedy: Suffering Under the Sun* (Oxford: Oxford University Press, 2010).

Hall, Peter A., and Lamont, Michèle, *Successful Societies: How Institutions and Culture Affect Health* (Cambridge: Cambridge University Press, 2009).

Hall, Rachel, and Batty, David, "Abuse of power': should universities ban staff-student relationships? UCL has become the third UK university to ban relationships between lecturers and their students' *The Guardian* (26th Feb 2020). Available online at: https://www.theguardian.com/education/2020/feb/26/abuse-of-power-should-universities-ban-staff-student-relationships.

Hao, R. N., 'Critical compassionate pedagogy and the teacher's role in first-generation student success' *New Directions for Teaching and Learning* 127 (2011), 91–98.

Hargreaves, Andy and Dawe, Ruth, 'Paths of professional development: Contrived collegiality, collaborative culture, and the case of peer coaching' *Teaching and Teacher Education* Volume 6 (1990), 227–241. Available online at: doi:https://doi.org/10.1016/0742-051X(90)90015-W.

Hauerwas, Stanley, 'In defence of "our respectable culture": Trying to make sense of John Howard Yoder's sexual abuse' (18th October, 2017). Available online at: https://www.abc.net.au/religion/in-defence-of-our-respectable-culture-trying-to-make-sense-of-jo/10095302.

Hayden, Dolores, *The Power of Place: Urban Landscapes as Public History* (Cambridge, Mass.: MIT Press, 1997). Pages 380–392 Received 08 Oct 2015 Accepted 04 Mar 2016 Published online: 04 Apr 2016

Heinze, Eric, *Hate Speech and Democratic Citizenship* (Oxford: Oxford University Press, 2016).

Heller, Monica and McElhinny, Bonnie, *Language, Capitalism, Colonialism: Toward a Critical History* (Toronto: University of Toronto Press, 2017).

Hem, Marit Helene and Heggen, Kristin, 'Is compassion essential to nursing practice?' *Contemporary Nurse* 17:1–2 (2004), 19–31. Available online at: doi:https://doi.org/10.5172/conu.17.1-2.19.

Henkel, M., 'Academic values and the university as corporate enterprise' *Higher Education Quarterly* 51 (1997), 134–143.

Henry, Frances and Tator, Carol, 'Introduction: Racism in the Canadian University' Frances Henry and Carol Tator (eds), *Racism in the Canadian University: Demanding Social Justice, Inclusion, and Equity* (Toronto: University of Toronto Press, 2009), 3–21.

Herman, Judith, *Trauma and Recovery: The Aftermath of Violence–From Domestic Abuse to Political Terror* (New York: Basic Books, 1997).

Hewerdine, M., 'Studying the New Testament using a Disability Hermeneutic: Notes for Contextual Bible Studies' MA Dissertation, Queens Foundation for Ecumenical Theological Education, Birmingham, UK (2011). Available online at: https://www.academia.edu/2252176/_Studying_the_New_Testament_using_a_Disability_Hermeneutic_Notes_for_Contextual_Bible_Studies_

Hewison, A., Sawbridge Y. et al., 'Leading with compassion in health care organisations: The development of a compassion recognition scheme-evaluation and analysis' *Journal of Health Organization and Management* 32 (2018), 338–354. Available online at: doi:https://doi.org/10.1108/JHOM-10-2017-0266.

Hey, Valerie, 'Affective asymmetries: academics, austerity and the mis/recognition of emotion' *Contemporary Social Science* 6 (2011), 207–22.

Higton, Mike, *A Theology of Higher Education* (Oxford: Oxford University Press, 2012).

Hitching, P., *The Church and Deaf People* (Milton Keynes: Paternoster Press, 2003).

Holtzman, Richard, 'George W. Bush's Rhetoric of Compassionate Conservatism and Its Value as a Tool of Presidential Politics' Bryant University Dissertation (2010). Available online at: https://digitalcommons.bryant.edu/cgi/viewcontent.cgi?article=1018&context=histss_jou.

Howell, Colleen, Lorenzo, Theresa, and Sompeta-Gcaza, Siphokazi, 'Reimagining personal and collective experiences of disability in Africa' *Disability & the Global South* 6/2 (2019), 1719–1735.

Hunter, M., 'Decentering the White and Male Standpoints in Race and Ethnicity Courses' in A. A. Macdonald and S. Sánchez-Casal (eds), *Twenty-First-Century Feminist Classrooms. Comparative Feminist Studies Series* (New York: Palgrave Macmillan, 2002).

Hurley, Zoe, 'Postdigital Feminism and Cultural Visual Regimes: COVID-19 at Women's Only University in the Gulf', *Postdigital Science and Education* (19th May 2020). Available online at: doi:https://doi.org/10.1007/s42438-020-00134-3.

Hush, Anna, 'The Imaginary Institution of the University' *Angelaki* 24:4 (2019), 136–150. Available online at: DOI: 10.1080/0969725X.2019.1635833, 136.

Hutcheon, Emily and Lashewicz, Bonnie, 'Theorizing resilience: critiquing and unbounding a marginalizing concept', *Disability & Society* 29:9 (2014), 1383–1397. Available online at: DOI: 10.1080/09687599.2014.934954.

Jain, Andrea, 'An Update on Journal Publishing and a Plea for Our Discipline in the Time of Pandemic' (March 2020). Available online at: https://www.aarweb.org/AARMBR/Publications-and-News-/Newsroom-/News-/An-Update-on-Journal-Publishing-and-a-Plea-for-our-Discipline-in-the-Time-of-Pandemic.aspx.

Jayakumar, Uma, 'Can Higher Education Meet the Needs of an Increasingly Diverse and Global Society? Campus Diversity and Cross-Cultural Workforce Competencies' *Harvard Educational Review* 78 (2008), 615–651. Available online at: doi: https://doi.org/10.17763/haer.78.4.b60031p350276699.

John, Helen C., *Biblical Interpretation and African Traditional Religion: Cross-Cultural and Community Readings in Owamboland Namibia*, Biblical Interpretation Series Vol 176 (Leiden: Brill, 2019a).

John, Helen, C., 'Conversations in Context: Cross-Cultural (Grassroots) Biblical Interpretation Groups Challenging Western-centric (Professional) Biblical Interpretation.' *Biblical Interpretation* 27.1 (2019b), 36–68.

Jones, Alexandra, 'The Pandemic of Kindness: Will We Be More Compassionate After Coronavirus' *Independent* (24th April 2020). Available online at: https://www.independent.co.uk/life-style/coronavirus-response-change-society-acts-of-kindness-politics-homeless-volunteers-a9482531.html.

Jones, June and Pattison, Stephen, 'Compassion as a Philosophical and Theological Concept' in Alistair Hewison and Yvonne Sawbridge (eds), *Compassion in Nursing* (London: Palgrave, 2016), 43–56.

Juntrasook, Adisorn and Burford, James, 'Animating Southern Theory in the Context of Thai Higher Education' *Higher Education Research and Development* 36 (1) (2017), 21–27. Available online at: https://www.tandfonline.com/doi/full/10.1080/07294360.2017.1249069.

Kaeppel, Kristi, 'Let's Get Physical: Improving Learning Through Movement', University of Connecticut, School of Education (2018). Available online at: https://gcci.uconn.edu/2018/05/10/lets-get-physical-improving-learning-through-movement/

Kahn, William A., 'Caring for the Caregivers: Patterns of Organizational Caregiving' *Administrative Science Quarterly* Vol. 38, No. 4 (1993), 539–563.

Kain, Ruth, 'How Neoliberalism is Damaging your Mental Health' *The Conversation* (30th January 2018). Available online at: http://theconversation.com/how-neoliberalism-is-damaging-your-mental-health-90565.

Kalwant, Bhopal, *White Privilege: The Myth of a Post-Racial Society* (Bristol: Policy Press, 2018).

Kanov, Jason et al, 'Compassion in Organizational Life' *American Behavioral Scientist* 47 (2004), 808–827.

Kaufman, Peter and Schipper, Janine, *Teaching with Compassion: An Educator's Oath to Teach from the Heart* (Maryland: Rowman & Littlefield Publishers, 2018).

Kay School of Media, Communication and Sociology, University of Leicester, Leicester, UK, Jilly Boyce and Banet-Weiser Department of Media and Communications, The London School of Economics and Political Science, London, UK, Sarah, 'Feminist Anger and Feminist Respair' *Feminist Media Studies* 19 (2019), 603–609. Available online at: doi: https://doi.org/10.108 0/14680777.2019.1609231.I

Kirmayer, Laurence, J., 'Rethinking cultural competence' *Transcultural Psychology* 49 (2012), 149–164. Available online at: doi:https://doi.org/10.1177/ 1363461512444673.

Kishimoto, Kyoko, 'Anti-racist pedagogy: from faculty's self-reflection to organizing within and beyond the classroom', *Race Ethnicity and Education*, 21:4 (2018), 540–554. Available online at: doi:https://doi.org/10.1080/1361332 4.2016.1248824.

Kleinsasser, Anne, Jouriles, Ernest, McDonald, Renee N, and Rosenfield, David, 'An online bystander intervention program for the prevention of sexual violence' *Psychology of Violence* Vol 5(3) (2015), 227–235.

Kohler, Kaufmann and Hirsch, Emil G., 'COMPASSION' in Online Jewish Encyclopedia. Available at: http://www.jewishencyclopedia.com/articles/ 4576-compassion.

Kotera, Yasuhiro, Green, Pauline, Sheffield, David, 'Mental Health Attitudes, Self-Criticism, Compassion and Role Identity among UK Social Work Students', *The British Journal of Social Work*, Volume 49, Issue 2 (2019), 351–370.

Kruisselbrink, Alicia, 'A Suffering Generation: Six Factors Contributing to the Mental Health Crisis in North American Higher Education' *College Quarterly*, 16 (2013), no pages. Available online at: https://files.eric.ed.gov/fulltext/ EJ1016492.pdf.

Kuenssberg, Sally, 'The discourse of self-presentation in Scottish university mission statements' *Quality in Higher Education* 17 (2011) 279–298. Available online at: doi: https://doi.org/10.1080/13538322.2011.625205.

Lampert, Khen, *Traditions of Compassion: From Religious Duty to Social Activism* (London: Palgrave Macmillan, 2005).

Lange, Frits de and Claassens, L. Juliana, *Considering Compassion: Global Ethics, Human Dignity and the Compassionate God* (Pickwick Publications, 2018).

Langstraat Lisa and Bowdon, Melody, 'Service-Learning and Critical Emotion Studies: On the Perils of Empathy and the Politics of Compassion' *Michigan Journal of Community Service Learning* (2011) 5–14.

Lawrence, Louise J., 'Scribes Trained for the Kingdom of Heaven: Reflections on Reading the Bible for Politics in Community, Secondary and Higher Education Contexts in Scotland' *Discourse* Vol 5 (2006), 99–122.

Lawrence, Louise J., *Sense and Stigma in the Gospels: Depictions of Sensory-Disabled Characters* (Oxford: Oxford University Press, 2013).

Lawrence, Louise J., *Bible and Bedlam: Madness, Sanism, and New Testament Interpretation* (London: Bloomsbury, 2018).

Leathwood, Carole and Hey, Valerie, 'Gender/ed discourses and emotional sub-texts: theorising emotion in UK higher education' *Teaching in Higher Education*, 14:4 (2009), 429–440. Available online at: doi: 10.1080/13562510903050194.

Leeuwen, Luuk van, Winkel, Kees, and Dijkstra, Hans, *Vision, Mission, Compassion: Why People Matter in Organisations* (Assen: van Gorcum, 2007).

Leibowitz, Brenda, 'Cognitive justice and the higher education curriculum', *Journal of Education* (University of KwaZulu-Natal) 68 (2017). Available online at: http://www.scielo.org.za/scielo.php?script=sci_arttext&pid=S2520-98682017000100006.

Leiter, Brian, 'Academic Ethics: Should Scholars Avoid Citing the Work of Awful People?' *Chronicle* (25th October 2018). Available online at: https://www.chronicle.com/article/Academic-Ethics-Should/244882.

Leonardo, Zeus, 'The Color of Supremacy: Beyond the discourse of 'white privilege''' *Educational Philosophy and Theory* 36 (2004), 137–152.

Lewis, Alan, Webley Paul, Winnett Adrian, and Craig Mackenzie, 'Morals and Markets: Some Theoretical and Policy Implications of Ethical Investing' in Peter Taylor-Gooby (ed) *Choice and Public Policy* (London: Palgrave Macmillan, 1998), 164–182.

Lewis, Hannah, *Deaf Liberation Theology* (Aldershot: Ashgate, 2007).

Lewis, Ruth, Marine, Susan, and Kenney, Kathryn, 'I get together with my friends and try to change it' Young feminist students resist 'laddism', 'rape culture' and 'everyday sexism'' *Journal of Gender Studies* 27 (2018), 56–72. Available online at: doi:https://doi.org/10.1080/09589236.2016.1175925.

Lillius, Jacoba et al 'The Contours and Consequences of Compassion at Work' *Journal of Organizational Behaviour* 29 (2008), 193–218.

Lin, Jing and Oxford, Rebecca L., 'Introduction: Expanding the Roles of Higher Education and Contemplative Pedagogies for Wisdom and Innovation' in Jing Lin, Rebecca L. Oxford and Edward J. Brantmeier (eds), *Re-Envisioning Higher Education: Embodied Pathways to Wisdom and Social Transformation* (Charlotte: Information Age Publishing, 2013), xi–xv.

Linley, Jodi, 'Racism Here, Racism There, Racism Everywhere: The Racial Realities of Minoritized Peer Socialization Agents at a Historically White Institution' *Journal of College Student Development* 59 (2018), 21–36.

Lips-Wiersma, Marjolein, and Nilakant, Venkataraman, 'Practical Compassion: Toward a Critical Spiritual Foundation for Corporate Responsibility' in Jerry Biberman and Len Tischler (eds), *Spirituality in Business: Theory, Practice and Future Directions* (New York: Palgrave Macmillan, 2008), 51–72.

Lissovoy, Noah De, 'Pedagogy in Common: Democratic education in the global era' *Educational Philosophy and Theory*, 43:10 (2011), 1119–1134. Available online at: doi: https://doi.org/10.1111/j.1469-5812.2009.00630.x.

Loosley, Emma, *Architecture and Asceticism: Cultural Interaction between Syria and Georgia in Late Antiquity* (Leiden: Brill, 2018).

Lowrie, Morgan, 'Canadian Organizations Grapple with Jean Vanier's Legacy After Sex Abuse Report' *The Canadian Press* (24th February, 2020). Available online at: https://www.theglobeandmail.com/canada/article-canadian-organizations-grapple-with-jean-vaniers-legacy-after-sex-2/.

Lynch, Kathleen, 'Carelessness: A hidden doxa of higher education' *Arts and Humanities in Higher Education* 9 (2010), 54–67.

Maginess, T. & MacKenzie, A., 'Achieving moralised compassion in Higher Education' *Journal of Perspectives in Applied Academic Practice*, 6 (2018), 42–48. Available online at: https://doi.org/10.14297/jpaap.v6i3.370.

Mahon, Áine, 'Towards a higher education: Contemplation, compassion, and the ethics of slowing down' *Educational Philosophy and Theory*, (2019). Available online at: doi:https://doi.org/10.1080/00131857.2019.1683826.

Manathunga, Catherine and Grant, Barbara, 'Editorial: Southern Theories and Higher Education' *Higher Education Research and Development* Vol 36 (2017) 1–3.

Mangalwaldi, Vishal, *The Book that Made Your World: How the Bible Created the Soul of Western Civilization* (Nashville: Thomas Nelson, 2011).

Mani, B. Venkat, 'Fighting the Shadow Pandemic' *Inside Higher Ed* (14th May, 2020). Available online at: https://www.insidehighered.com/views/2020/05/14/inclusive-teaching-needed-help-combat-xenophobia-racism-and-discrimination-brought.

Mann, Rachel, 'Where do we go from here?' (6th May 2020). Available online at: https://therachelmannblogspot.blogspot.com/2020/05/where-do-we-go-from-here-towards.html?spref=tw.

Manne, Kate, *Down Girl: The Logic of Misogyny* (Oxford: Oxford University Press, 2017).

Marshall, Christopher D., *Compassionate Justice: An Interdisciplinary Dialogue with Two Gospel Parables On Law, Crime, and Restorative Justice* (Cascade Books, 2012).

Mawdsley, Emma, Fourie, Elsje, Nauta, Wiebe (eds) *Researching South-South Development Cooperation: The Politics of Knowledge Production* (London: Routledge, 2019).

Maxwell, Bruce, 'Pursuing the Aim of Compassionate Empathy in Higher Education' in P. Gibbs (ed), *The Pedagogy of Compassion at the Heart of Higher Education* (Switzerland: Springer, 2017), 33–48.

McGlynn, Clare, Westmarland, Nicole, Godden, Nikki, '"I Just Wanted Him to Hear Me" Sexual Violence and the Possibilities of Restorative Justice' *Journal for Law and Society* 39 (2012), 213–240. Available online at: doi:https://doi.org/10.1111/j.1467-6478.2012.00579.x.

McGregor, Rafe and Sang-Ah Park, Miriam, 'Towards a deconstructed curriculum: Rethinking higher education in the Global North' *Teaching in Higher Education* 24:3 (2019), 332–345. Available online at: doi:https://doi.org/10.1080/13562517.2019.1566221.

Meekosha, Helen, 'Decolonising disability: thinking and acting globally' *Disability and Society* 26 (2011), 667–682. Available online at: doi:https://doi.org/10.1080/09687599.2011.602860.

Merali, Faruk, 'NHS managers' commitment to a socially responsible role: the NHS managers' views of their core values and their public image' *Social Responsibility Journal* (2005) Available online at: https://pdfs.semanticscholar.org/ed54/f65a1c377fcdb503e054a6ed081cca346849.pdf.

Mercer, Dave 'Imagined in Policy, Inscribed on Bodies: Defending an Ethic of Compassion in a Political Context Comment on 'Why and How Is Compassion Necessary to Provide Good Quality Healthcare?'' *International Journal of Health Policy Management* 4 (10) (2015), 681–683. Available online at: https://doi.org/10.15171/ijhpm.2015.125.

Mendes, Kaitlynn, Ringrose, Jessica, Keller, Jessalynn, '#MeToo and the promise and pitfalls of challenging rape culture through digital feminist activism' *European Journal of Women's Studies* 25 (2018), 236–246.

Merz, Annette, 'Ways of Teaching Compassion in the Synoptic Gospels' in Frits de Lange and L. Juliana Claassens (eds), *Considering Compassion: Global Ethics, Human Dignity, and the Compassionate God* (Eugene: Wipf and Stock, 2018), 66–86.

Michaeli, Inna, 'Self-Care: An Act of Political Warfare or a Neoliberal Trap?' *Development* 60 (2017), 50–56.

Midgett, Aida, Doumas, Diana M., Trull, Rhiannon, and Johnson, Jamie, 'Training Students Who Occasionally Bully to Be Peer Advocates: Is a Bystander Intervention Effective in Reducing Bullying Behavior?' *Journal of Child and Adolescent Counseling*, 3:1 (2017) 1–13. Available online at: doi: https://doi.org/10.1080/23727810.2016.1277116.

Mirguet, Françoise, *An Early History of Compassion: Emotion and Imagination in Hellenistic Judaism* (Cambridge: Cambridge University Press, 2017).

Monroe, Kristen Renwick, *The Hand of Compassion: Portraits of Moral Choice during the Holocaust*, (Princeton: Princeton University Press, 2004).

Moisi, Laura, 'Collective Reckonings: Re-Writing Trauma, Memory and Violence on Social Media' Available online at: https://www.academia.edu/39742504/Collective_Reckonings_Re-Writing_Trauma_Memory_and_Violence_on_Social_Media.

Moore, Suzanne, 'Jacinda Ardern is showing the world what real leadership is: sympathy, love, and integrity' (18th March 2019). Available online at: https://

www.theguardian.com/commentisfree/2019/mar/18/
jacinda-ardern-is-showing-the-world-what-real-leadership-is-sympathy-love-
and-integrity.

Moore, S. L. Ellsworth, J. B. and Kaufman, R., 'Visions and missions: Are they
useful? A quick assessment' *Performance Improvement* 50 (2011), 15–24.

Mori, Sakurako, 'Addressing the Mental Health Concerns of International
Students' *Counseling and Development* 78 (2000), 137–144.

Morphew, C. C. and Hartley, M., 'Mission statements: A thematic analysis of rhetoric across institutional type' *The Journal of Higher Education* 77
(2006), 456–471.

Motsa, Zodwa, 'When the Lion Tell the Story: A Response from South Africa' *Higher
Education Research and Development* 26 (2017), 28–35. Available online at:
https://www.researchgate.net/publication/311565769_When_the_
lion_tells_the_story_a_response_from_South_Africa.

Mott, Carrie and Cockayne, Daniel, 'Citation matters: mobilizing the politics of
citation toward a practice of 'conscientious engagement'' *Gender, Place &
Culture* 24:7 (2017), 954–973. Available online at: doi:https://doi.org/1
0.1080/0966369X.2017.1339022.

Motta, Sara C. and Bennett, Anna, 'Pedagogies of care, care-full epistemological
practice and 'other' caring subjectivities in enabling education' *Teaching in
Higher Education* 23:5 (2018), 631–646. Available online at: doi:https://doi.
org/10.1080/13562517.2018.1465911.

Mountz, Alison, Bonds, Anne, Mansfield, Becky, Loyd, Jenna, Hyndman, Jennifer,
Walton-Roberts, Margaret, Basu, Ranu, Whitson, Risa, Hawkins, Roberta,
Hamilton, Trina, and Curran, Winifred, "For Slow Scholarship: A Feminist
Politics of Resistance through Collective Action in the Neoliberal University".
ACME: An International Journal for Critical Geographies 14 (4), (2015)
1235–59. Available online at: https://www.acme-journal.org/index.php/
acme/article/view/1058.

Mukhopadhyay, Tito, *The Mind Tree* (New York: Arcade Publishing, 2003).

Murphy, Michael P. A., 'COVID-19 and emergency eLearning: Consequences of
the securitization of higher education for post-pandemic pedagogy'
Contemporary Security Policy (2020), 1–14. Available online at: doi:https://
doi.org/10.1080/13523260.2020.1761749.

Mutch, Carol, and Tatebe, Jennifer, 'From collusion to collective compassion:
putting heart back into the neoliberal university', *Pastoral Care in Education*
35:3 (2017), 221–234. Available online at: doi:https://doi.org/10.108
0/02643944.2017.1363814.

Mutua, Kagendo and Swadener, Beth Blue, *Decolonizing Research in Cross-
Cultural Contexts: Critical Personal Narratives* (New York: State University of
New York Press, 2011).

Myers, Carrie-Anne, and Cowie, Helen, 'Bullying at University: The Social and Legal Contexts of Cyberbullying Among University Students' *Journal of Cross-Cultural Psychology* 48 (2017), 1172–1182.

Nadar, Sarojini, 'Beyond the "ordinary reader" and the "invisible intellectual": Shifting contextual bible study from liberation discourse to liberation pedagogy' *Old Testament Essays* 22/2 (2009), 384–403. Available online at: http://www.scielo.org.za/scielo.php?script=sci_arttext&pid=S1010-99192009000200009.

Nakata, N. Martin, Nakata, Victoria, Keech, Sarah, and Bolt Reuben, Gili, Nura, 'Decolonial goals and pedagogies for Indigenous studies' Decolonization: Indigeneity, *Education and Society* Vol 1 no 1 (2012), 120–140.

Nerdlove, Dr. 'On Finding Out Your Heroes are Monsters (Or: Detoxifying a Culture)' (19th June 2020). Available online at: https://www.doctornerdlove.com/on-finding-out-your-heroes-are-monsters-or-detoxifying-comic-culture/.

Neuberger, Julia, 'The NHS as a Theological Institution' *British Medical Journal* 319 (1999), 1588. Available online at: doi:https://doi.org/10.1136/bmj.319.7225.1588

Nguyen, Xuan Thuy, 'Critical Disability Studies at the Edge of Global Development: Why Do We Need to Engage with Southern Theory?' *Canadian Journal of Disability Studies* 7 (2018), no pages. Available online at: https://doi.org/10.15353/cjds.v7i1.400.

Nishida, Akemi, 'Neoliberal Academia and a critique from Disability Studies' in Pamela Block, Devva Kasnitz, Akemi Nishida, Nick Pollard, *Occupying Disability: Critical Approaches to Community, Justice, and Decolonizing Disability* (Switzerland: Springer, 2016), 145–157.

Nørgård, Rikke Toft, Smedegaard, Søren and Bengtsen, Ernst, 'Academic citizenship beyond the campus: a call for the peaceful university' *Higher Education Research & Development* 35:1 (2016), 4–16. Available online at: https://www.tandfonline.com/doi/abs/10.1080/07294360.2015.1131669.

Nussbaum, Martha, *Cultivating Humanity: A Classical Defense of Reform in Liberal Education* (Cambridge/London: Harvard University Press, 1997).

Nussbaum, Martha, *Upheavals of Thought: The Intelligence of Emotions* (Cambridge: Cambridge University Press, 2001).

Nussbaum, Martha, *Not for Profit: Why Democracy Needs the Humanities* (Princeton: Princeton University Press, 2010).

NS, 'This is what unpalatable student activism costs'. Available online at: https://medium.com/@ns1997/this-is-what-unpalatable-student-activism-costs-5d06f653a84f

NUS, 'That's What She Said: Women Student's Experiences of 'Lad Culture' at Universities' (2013). Available online at: https://www.nus.org.uk/PageFiles/12238/Thats%20What%20She%20Said%20-%20Full%20Report%20(1).pdf.

O'Donnell, Karen, 'Theology from the place where it hurts' #TheologyinIsolation 3 (23rd March 2020). Available online at: https://scmpress.hymnsam.co.uk/blog/theologyinisolation-3-karen-odonnell-theology-from-the-place-where-it-hurts.

O'Connell, Maureen H., *Compassion: Loving Our Neighbor in an Age of Globalization* (New York: Orbis Books, 2009).

Oliveira, Ines B., 'Itinerant Curriculum Theory Against Epistemicides: A Dialogue Between the Thinking of Santos and Paraskeva' *Journal of the American Association for the Advancement of Curriculum Studies* 12/1 (2017). Available online at: https://doi.org/10.14288/jaaacs.v12i1.189708.

Oltermann, Philip, 'Mama Merkel: The 'Compassionate Mother' of Syrian Refugees' *The Guardian* (1st September 2015). Available online at: https://www.theguardian.com/world/shortcuts/2015/sep/01/mama-merkel-the-compassionate-mother-of-syrian-refugees.

Opdebeeck, H. and Habisch, A., 'Compassion: Chinese and western perspectives on practical wisdom in management' *Journal of Management Development* Vol. 30 (2011), 778–788. Available online at: doi:https://doi.org/10.1108/02621711111150272.

Oudshoorn, Daniel, *Pauline Eschatology: The Apocalyptic Rupture of Eternal Imperialism* (Cascade Books, Wipf and Stock, 2020).

Ozdem, Guven, 'An Analysis of the Mission and Vision Statements on the Strategic Plans of Higher Education Institutions' *Educational Sciences: Theory and Practice* 11 (2011), 1887–1894.

Paludi, Michele Antoinette (ed), *Ivory Power: Sexual Harassment on Campus* (New York: State University of New York Press, 1990).

Pagels, Elaine, *Why Religion? A Personal Story* (New York: Harper Collins, 2018).

Papadopoulos, Irena, Shea, Sue, Taylor, Georgina, Pezzella, Alfonso and Foley, Laura, 'Developing tools to promote culturally competent compassion, courage, and intercultural communication in healthcare' *Journal of Compassionate Health Care* 3 (2016). Available online at: doi:https://doi.org/10.1186/s40639-016-0019-6.

Paraskeva, João M., *Curriculum Epistemicide: Towards an Itinerant Curriculum Theory* (New York: Routledge, 2015).

Parliamentary and Health Service Ombudsman, 'Care and Compassion?: Report of the Health Service Ombudsman Great Britain' (2016) Available online at: https://www.ombudsman.org.uk/sites/default/files/201610/Care%20and%20Compassion.pdf.

Payle, Tracy, 'A Planning Model for your Content which Plays to Needs and Emotions', *Picklejar Communications* (2017). Available online at: http://www.picklejarcommunications.com/2017/07/04/planning-model-content-strategy-plays-needs-emotions/.

Percy, Emma, 'Safeguarding Vulnerable Adults, or Adults at Risk? What's in a Word?' Blog Post, *Modern Church* (8th July 2020). Available online at: https://modernchurch.org.uk/revd-canon-dr-emma-percy-safeguarding-vulnerable-adults-or-adults-at-risk-whats-in-a-word

Perera, Sanjee, 'Waking in Gethsemane' #TheologyinIsolation 12 (10th April 2020). Available online at: https://scmpress.hymnsam.co.uk/blog/theologyinisolation-12-waking-in-gethsemane.

Perry, Kristen, "'I Want the World to Know': The Ethics of Anonymity in Ethnographic Literacy Research", in G. Walford (ed), *Methodological Developments in Ethnography* (Studies in Educational Ethnography, Vol. 12) (Bingley: Emerald Group Publishing Limited, 2007), 137–154.

Perry, Barbara "No biggie': The denial of oppression on campus' *Education, Citizenship and Social Justice* 5 (2010), 265–279. Available online at: doi:https://doi.org/10.1177/1746197910387543.

Peters, Michael A., 'Love and social distancing in the time of COVID-19: The philosophy and literature of pandemics', *Educational Philosophy and Theory* (April 2020) 1–5. Available online at: doi:https://doi.org/10.1080/0013185 7.2020.1750091.

Peters, Timothy D., 'Corporations, Sovereignty and the Religion of Neoliberalism' *Law and Critique* 29 (2018), 271–292.

Phipps, Alison, '(Re)theorising laddish masculinities in higher education' *Gender and Education* 29 (2017), 815–830. Available online at doi:https://doi.org/1 0.1080/09540253.2016.1171298.

Phipps, Alison, 'Reckoning up: sexual harassment and violence in the neoliberal university' *Gender and Education* 32 (2020), 227–243. Available online at: doi:https://doi.org/10.1080/09540253.2018.1482413.

Phipps, Alison, Ringrose, Jessica, Renold, Emma and Jackson, Carolyn, 'Rape culture, lad culture and everyday sexism: researching, conceptualizing and politicizing new mediations of gender and sexual violence' *Journal of Gender Studies* 27 (2018), 1–8. Available online at doi:https://doi.org/10.1080/0958923 6.2016.1266792.

Phipps, Alison and Young, Isabel, "'Lad culture" in higher education: Agency in the sexualization debates' *Sexualities* 18 (2015), 459–479.

Phull, Kiran, Ciflikli, Gokhan, Meibauer, Gustav, 'Gender and bias in the International Relations curriculum: Insights from reading lists' *European Journal of International Relations* 25:2 (2019), 383–407. Available online at: doi:https://doi.org/10.1177/1354066118791690.

Pitcher, Sorrel, 'Students' Constructions of Mental Illness: Using Discourse Analysis to Develop Critical Language Awareness' Thesis, Department of Psychology University of Cape Town, (2013). Available online at: http://www.careers.uct.ac.za/sites/default/files/image_tool/images/117/Sorrel.Pitcher.pdf.

Poole, Jennifer M., Jivraj, Tania, Arslanian, Araxi, Bellows, Kristen, Chiasson, Sheila, Hakimy, Husnia, Pasini, Jessica, Reid, Jenna, 'Sanism, Mental Health, and Social Work/Education: A Review and Call to Action' *Intersectionalities* Vol 1 (2012). Available online at: https://journals.library.mun.ca/ojs/index.php/ij/article/view/348.

Powietrzyńska, Małgorzata and Tobin, Kenneth, *Weaving Complementary Knowledge Systems and Mindfulness to Educate a Literate Citizenry for Sustainable and Healthy Lives* (Leiden: Brill, 2017).

Price, Margaret, *Mad at School: Rhetorics of Mental Disability and Academic Life* (Michigan: University of Michigan Press, 2011).

Prilleltensky, Isaac and Prilleltensky, Ora, *Promoting Well-Being: Linking Personal, Organizational, and Community Change* (New Jersey: Wiley, 2006).

Punt, Jeremy, 'Postcolonial biblical criticism in South Africa: some mind and road mapping' *Neotestimentica* 37 (2003), 59–85.

Rashedi, Roxanne, and Plante, Thomas G, and Callister, Erin S., 'Compassion Development in Higher Education' *Journal of Psychology and Theology* 43/2 (2015), 131–139.

Raunig, Gerald, 'The Double Criticism of Parrhesia. Answering the Question "What is a Progressive (Art) Institution?" *Transversal* (2004). Translated by Aileen Derieg. Available online at: https://transversal.at/transversal/0504/raunig/en.

Reason, Robert D. and Rankin, Susan R., 'Differing Perceptions: How Students of Color and White Students Perceive Campus Climate for Underrepresented Groups' *Journal of College Student Development* 46 (2005a), 43–61. Available online at: https://muse.jhu.edu/article/177605

Reason, Robert, and Rankin, Susan, 'Differing' Perceptions: How Students of Color and White Students Perceive Campus Climate for Underrepresented Groups' *Journal of College Student Development* 46 (2005b), 43–61. Available online at: https://muse.jhu.edu/article/177605.

Reason, Robert, and Rankin, Susan, 'College Students' Experiences and Perceptions of Harassment on Campus: An Exploration of Gender Differences' *College Student Affairs Journal* 26 (2006), 7–29. Available online at: https://files.eric.ed.gov/fulltext/EJ902800.pdf.

Richard, Pablo, 'Jesus: A Latin American Perspective' in Daniel Patte (ed), *The Global Bible Commentary* (Nashville: Abingdon Press, 2004), 337–341.

Riess, Jana, 'Elaine Pagels on grief, her #MeToo story, and why we find meaning in religion' *Religion News Service* (26th October 2018). Available online at: https://religionnews.com/2018/10/26/elaine-pagels-on-grief-her-metoo-story-and-why-we-find-meaning-in-religion/.

Riley, Joan and McWilliams, Mindy, 'Engaged Learning through Curriculum Infusion' *Peer Review* Vol. 9, Iss. 3, (2007), 14–17.

Rogers, Chrissie, "I'm complicit and I'm ambivalent and that's crazy": Care-less spaces for women in the academy' *Women's Studies International Forum* 61 (2017), 115–122. Available online at: doi:https://doi.org/10.1016/j. wsif.2016.07.002.

Rosenberg, Charles, 'The Definition and Control of Diseases: An Introduction' *Social Research* Vol. 55, No. 3, (1988), 327–330.

Rozycki, E. G., 'Mission and vision in education' *Educational Horizons* 82 (2004), 94–98.

Ruiz, Pedro Ortega and Vallejos, Ramon Minguez, 'The Role of Compassion in Moral Education', *Journal of Moral Education* 28:1 (1999), 5–17. Available online at: doi:10.1080/030572499103278.

Salzberg, Sharon, *The Force of Kindness: Change Your Life with Love and Compassion* (Colorado: Sounds True Inc., 2010).

Salgado, Soli, 'Allegations of sexual harassment against John Howard Yoder extend to Notre Dame' (25th June 2015). Available online at: https://www.ncron-line.org/news/accountability/allegations-sexual-harassment-against-john-howard-yoder.

Saltmarsh, Sue, 'No, I'm Not OK': Disrupting 'Psy' Discourses of University Mental Health Awareness Campaigns' in Eva Petersen and Zsuzsa Millei, *Interrupting the Psy-Disciplines in Education* (Palgrave Macmillan, 2016), 167–183.

Saunders, Daniel B., 'Neoliberal Ideology and Public Higher Education in the United States' *Journal for Critical Education Policy Studies*, vol.8. no.1 (2014). Available online at: http://www.jceps.com/wp-content/uploads/PDFs/ 08-1-02.pdf.

Sauntson H. and Morrish, L., 'Vision, values and international excellence: the 'products' that university mission statements sell to students' in M. Molesworth, R. Scullion, and E. Nixon (eds.), *The Marketisation of Higher Education and the Student as Consumer* (London and New York, Routledge: 2010), 73–85.

Scarsella, Hilary, 'Not Making Sense: Why Stanley Hauerwas's Response to Yoder's Sexual Abuse Misses the Mark' (30th November 2017). Available online at: https://www.abc.net.au/religion/not-making-sense-why-stanley-hauerwass-response-to-yoders-sexual/10095168.

Schlosser, Lewis Z. and Sedlacek, William E., 'Hate on Campus: A Model for Evaluating, Understanding, and Handling Critical Incidents' *About Campus: Enriching the Student Learning Experience* 6 (2001), 25–27.

Schüssler Fiorenza, E., *Democratizing Biblical Studies: Toward an Emancipatory Educational Space* (Louisville: Westminster John Knox, 2009).

Seeger, Matthew Wayne, Sellnow, Timothy Lester, and Ulmer, Robert R., *Communication and Organizational Crisis* (Westport: Greenwood Publishing Group, 2003).

Seggie, Fatma Nevra and Sanford, Gretchen, 'Perceptions of female Muslim students who veil: campus religious climate' *Race, Ethnicity and Education* 13 (2010), 59–82.

Segovia, Fernando and Stephen Moore, *Postcolonial Biblical Criticism: Interdisciplinary Intersections* (London: T&T Clark, 2005).

Shackle, Samira, 'The way universities are run is making us ill': inside the student mental health crisis' *The Guardian* (27th September 2019). Available online at: https://www.theguardian.com/society/2019/sep/27/anxiety-mental-breakdowns-depression-uk-students.

Shahjahan, Riyad A., 'Being 'Lazy' and Slowing Down: Toward decolonizing time, our body, and pedagogy' *Educational Philosophy and Theory* 47:5 (2015), 488–501. Available online at: doi: https://doi.org/10.1080/0013185 7.2014.880645.

Shepherd, Andrew, 'COVID-19 an invitation to ecological repentance?' *Stimulus: The New Zealand Journal of Christian Thought and Practice* Volume 27 Issue 2 (May 2020). Available online at: https://hail.to/laidlaw-college/publication/1tI5uq8/article/DbwFVdI.

SHRE, 'Degrees of Laddishness: Laddism in Higher Education' SRHE Feb 2014 – DRAFT. Available online at: https://eprints.lancs.ac.uk/id/eprint/68650/2/Dempster_and_Jackson_srhe_for_press.pdf/

Simoni, Jane M., and Walters, Karina L., 'Heterosexual Identity and Heterosexism Recognizing Privilege to Reduce Prejudice' *Journal of Homosexuality* Vol 41 (2008), 157–172. Available online at: doi:https://doi.org/10.1300/J082v41n01_06.

Simpson, A.V., Clegg, S.R. and Freeder, D., 'Compassion, Power and Organization' (2013) Available online at: https://opus.lib.uts.edu.au/bitstream/10453/27945/4/Organization_and_Compassion_8.4.pdf.

Slavin, Stuart J., Schindler, Debra L., and Chibnall, John T., 'Medical Student Mental Health: Improving Student Wellness Through Curricular Changes' *Acad Med* 89(4) (2014), 573–577.

Smith, Steve, 'Message from the Vice-Chancellor to staff and students' (5th June 2020). Available online at: https://www.exeter.ac.uk/coronavirus/communications/vc5june/.

Smyth, John, *The Toxic University: Zombie Leadership, Academic Rock Stars and Neoliberal Ideology* (London: Palgrave, 2017).

Snyder, Sarah N., Pitt, Kendra-Ann, Shanouda, Fady, Voronka, Jijian, Reid, Jenna and Landry, Danielle, 'Unlearning through Mad Studies: Disruptive pedagogical praxis' *Curriculum Inquiry* 49:4 (2019a) 485–502. Available online at: DOI: https://doi.org/10.1080/03626784.2019.1664254.

Snyder, Sarah, et al, 'Unlearning through Mad Studies: Disruptive pedagogical praxis' in *Curriculum Inquiry* 49(4) (2019b), 485–502. Available online at: doi:https://doi.org/10.1080/03626784.2019.1664254.

Solnit, Rebecca, *A Paradise Built in Hell: The Extraordinary Communities That Arise in Disaster* (New York: Penguin/Random House, 2010).

Spencer, Nick, *The Political Samaritan: How Power Hijacked a Parable* (London: Bloomsbury, 2017).

Srinivasan, Amia, 'Sex as a Pedagogical Failure' *Yale Law Journal* 129 (2020), 924–1275.

Stiebert, Johanna, 'Privilege Beyond Bounds: A Response to the Conviction of Jan Joosten' *The Shiloh Project Group Blog* (26th June 2020). Available online at: Shiloh-project.group.shef.ac.uk.

Stöckl, Andrea, 'Ethnography, Travel Writing and the Self: Reflections on Socially Robust Knowledge and the Authorial Ego' *Forum: Qualitative Social Research* 7 (2006). Available online at: https://doi.org/10.17169/fqs-7.2.113.

Stotzer, Rebecca L. and Hossellman, Emily 'Hate Crimes on Campus: Racial/Ethnic Diversity and Campus Safety' *Journal of Interpersonal Violence* 27 (2011), 644–661.

Strauss, Clara et al, 'What is compassion and how can we measure it? A review of definitions and measures' *Clinical Psychology Review* Volume 47 (2016), 15–27.

Sugarman, J., 'Neoliberalism and psychological ethics' *Journal of Theoretical and Philosophical Psychology* 35(2), (2015) 103–116. Available online at: doi:https://doi.org/10.1037/a0038960.

Sugirtharajah, R.S., 'A Brief Memorandum on Postcolonialism and Biblical Studies' *Journal for the Study of the New Testament* 21 (1999), 3–5. Available online at: doi:https://doi.org/10.1177/0142064X9902107301.

Sundari, Anitha, and Lewis, Ruth, *Gender based violence in university communities: policy, prevention and educational interventions in Britain* (Bristol: Policy Press, 2018).

Sussex Student Union, 'Hate Crime and Coronavirus' (11th February, 2020). Available online at: https://www.sussexstudent.com/news/article/ussu/Students-Union-statement-regarding-hate-crime-and-coronavirus/.

Swadener, Beth Blue and Mutua, Kagendo, 'Decolonizing Performances: Deconstructing the Global Postcolonial' in Norman K. Denzin, Yvonna S. Lincoln, Linda Tuhiwai Smith (eds) *Handbook of Critical and Indigenous Methodologies* (New York: Sage Publishing, 2008), 31–44.

Swinton, John, *Raging with Compassion: Pastoral Responses to the Problem of Evil* (Grand Rapids: William B Eerdmans Publishing Co, 2007).

Terry, Meredith L., Leary, Mark R. and Mehta, Sneha, 'Self-compassion as a Buffer against Homesickness, Depression, and Dissatisfaction in the Transition to College' *Self and Identity* (2012). Available online at: doi: https://doi.org/10.1080/15298868.2012.667913.

Thelin, John R., *A History of American Higher Education* (Baltimore: John Hopkins University Press, 2001).

Thomas, Phil Crockett, 'The Girls Get Younger Every Year' (2017). Available online at: https://crowdedmouth.wordpress.com/2017/04/27/tggyeyplay/.

Thornton, Margaret, 'Law Student Wellbeing: A Neoliberal Conundrum' *Australian Universities' Review* 58(2) 42–50. Available online at: https://ssrn.com/abstract=2887812.

Timothy Leadership Training Institute (TLTI), "Loving Your Neighbor in the COVID-19 Epidemic." Available online at: https://www.crcna.org/news-and-views/good-samaritan-and-COVID-19.

Tooley, Mark, 'Yoder, Sex Abuse, and War' *Providence Mag* (8th June 2018). Available online at: https://providencemag.com/2018/06/yoder-sex-abuse-war/.

Torres, Carlos A. and Schugurensky, Daniel, 'The political economy of higher education in the era of neoliberal globalization: Latin America in comparative perspective' *Higher Education* 43 (2002), 429–455.

Trahar, Sheila, Juntrasook, Adisorn, Burford, James, von Kotze, Astrid, and Wildemeersch, Danny, 'Hovering on the periphery? 'Decolonising' writing for academic journals' *Compare: A Journal of Comparative and International Education* 49:1 (2019), 149–167. Available online at: doi: https://doi.org/10.1080/03057925.2018.1545817.

Trail, Juliet and Cunningham, Tim, 'The Compassionate University: How University of Virginia is Changing the Culture of Compassion at a Large American Public University' *Journal of Perspectives in Applied Academic Practice* 6 (2018). Available online at: https://jpaap.napier.ac.uk/index.php/JPAAP/article/view/358/511.

Trelstad, M., 'The Ethics of Effective Teaching: Challenges from the Religious Right and Critical Pedagogy' *Teaching Theology and Religion* 11 (2008), 191–202.

Tronto, Joan C., 'Creating Caring Institutions: Politics, Plurality, and Purpose', *Ethics and Social Welfare* 4:2 (2010), 158–171. Available online at: doi:https://doi.org/10.1080/17496535.2010.484259.

Tufts, Steven and Thomas, Mark, 'The University in the Populist Age' Academic Matters – OCUFA's *Journal of Higher Education* (2017). Available online at: https://academicmatters.ca/the-university-in-the-populist-age/.

Türken, Salman, Nafstad, Hilde Eileen, Blakar, Rolv Mikkel and Roen, Katrina, 'Making Sense of Neoliberal Subjectivity: A Discourse Analysis of Media Language on Self-development', *Globalizations*, 13:1 (2016) 32–46. Available online at: doi:https://doi.org/10.1080/14747731.2015.1033247.

Ujamaa Centre, 'Contextual Bible Study Manual'. Available online at: http://ujamaa.ukzn.ac.za/Libraries/manuals/Ujamaa_CBS_bible_study_Manual_part_1_2.sflb.ashx.

University and College Union, 'UCU announces 14 strike days at 74 UK universities in February and March' UCU (3rd February 2020). Available online at: https://www.ucu.org.uk/article/10621/UCU-announces-14-sJtrike-days-at-74-UK-universities-in-February-and-March.

University of Edinburgh, 'Compassion in the time of coronavirus' (2020). Available online at: https://www.ed.ac.uk/COVID-19-response/expert-insights/compassion-in-the-time-of-coronavirus

Vaccaro, Annemarie, 'What Lies Beneath Seemingly Positive Campus Climate Results: Institutional Sexism, Racism, and Male Hostility Toward Equity Initiatives and Liberal Bias' *Equity and Excellence in Education* 42 (2010), 202–215. Available online at: https://www.tandfonline.com/doi/full/10.1080/10665680903520231.

Vazquez, Evelyn Morales and Levin, John S., 'The Tyranny of Neoliberalism in the American Academic Profession' (2020). Available online at: https://www.aaup.org/article/tyranny-neoliberalism-american-academic-profession#.Xte1U25FxPY.

Veale, David, Gilbert, Paul, Wheatley, Jon, Naismith, Iona, 'A New Therapeutic Community: Development of a Compassion-Focused and Contextual Behavioural Environment' *Clinical Psychology and Psychotherapy* 22 (4) (2015), 285–303.

Waddington, Kathryn, 'The Compassion Gap in UK Universities' *International Practice Development Journal.* 6 (1) (2016). Available online at: https://doi.org/10.19043/ipdj.61.010.

Waddington, Kathryn, 'Creating Conditions for Compassion in Higher Education' in Paul Gibbs (ed), *The Pedagogy of Compassion at the Heart of Higher Education* (Switzerland: Springer International Publishing, 2017), 49–70.

Waddington, Kathryn, 'Developing Compassionate Academic Leadership: The Practice of Kindness' *Journal of Perspectives in Applied Academic Practice.* 6 (3), (2018), 87–89.

Waddington, Kathryn 'Understanding and Creating Compassionate Institutional Cultures and Practices' in P. Gibbs, P., Jameson, J. and A. Elwick (eds.) *Values of the University in a Time of Uncertainty* (Cham, Switzerland Springer, 2019), 241–260.

Waghid, Yusef, 'Compassionate citizenship and education research article' *Perspectives in Education* 22 (2004), 41–50.

Waghid, Yusef, 'Education for responsible citizenship: Conversation' *Perspectives in Education* 27 (2009a), 85–90.

Waghid, Yusef, 'Universities and Public Goods: In Defence of Democratic Deliberation, Compassionate Imagining and Cosmopolitan Justice' in E. Bitzer (ed), *Higher Education in South Africa: A Scholarly Look Behind the Scenes* (Stellenbosch: Sun Media, 2009b), 71–83.

Walker, Caroline and Gleaves, Alan, 'Constructing the Caring Higher Education Teacher: A Theoretical Framework' *Teaching and Teacher Education* 54 (2016), 65–76.

Watkins, Peter N., *Mental Health Practice: A Guide to Compassionate Care* (Oxford: Butterworth-Heinemann, 2008).

Webster, David and Rivers, Nicola, 'Resisting resilience: disrupting discourses of self-efficacy' *Pedagogy, Culture & Society* 27:4, (2019) 523–535. Available online at: doi: 10.1080/14681366.2018.1534261.

Wehler, Melissa, 'Five Ways to Build Community in Online Classrooms' Faculty Focus Higher Ed Teaching Strategies: https://www.facultyfocus.com/articles/online-education/five-ways-to-build-community-in-online-classrooms/'Blended'; 'Blended Learning Design Planner' Available online: *Stanford Teaching Commons*: https://teachingcommons.stanford.edu/gallery/blended.

Wells, Samuel, *A Nazareth Manifesto: Being with God* (New Jersey: Wiley and Sons, 2015).

Wessel, Susan, *Passion and Compassion in Early Christianity* (Cambridge: Cambridge University Press, 2016).

Wheater, Kitty, 'What is Compassion in the Time of COVID-19?' *Edinburgh University Chaplaincy* (2020). Available online at: https://www.ed.ac.uk/chaplaincy/compassion-for-our-times/what-is-compassion-in-the-time-of-covid-19.

Wilde, Sandra, *Care in Education: Teaching with Understanding and Compassion* (London: Routledge, 2013).

Wilson, Alexander C., Mackintosh, Kate, Power, Kevin and Chan, Stella W. Y., 'Effectiveness of Self-Compassion Related Therapies: a Systematic Review and Meta-analysis' *Mindfulness* 10 (2019), 979–995.

Winslow, Luke, 'Rich, Blessed, and Tenured: A Homological Exploration of Grant Writing, Prosperity Theology, and Neoliberalism', *Western Journal of Communication* 79 (2015), 257–282. Available online at: https://www.tandfonline.com/doi/abs/10.1080/10570314.2015.1035748.

Wolframe, P., 'The Madwomen in the Academy, or, Revealing the Invisible Straitjacket: Theorizing and Teaching Sanism and Sane Privilege' *Disability Studies Quarterly* Vol 33 (2013). Available online at: http://dsq-sds.org/article/view/3425/3200.

Wong, C. C. and Mak, W., 'Writing can heal: Effects of self-compassion writing among Hong Kong Chinese college students' *Asian American Journal of Psychology*, 7(1) (2016), 74–82. Available online at: doi:https://doi.org/10.1037/aap0000041.

Yoder, John Howard, *The Politics of Jesus* (Grand Rapids: William B. Eerdmans Publishing Company, 1972).

Young, Stephen, 'Love the Scholarship but Hate the Scholar's Sin: 'Himpathy' for an Academic Paedophile Enables a Culture of Abuse' *Religion Dispatches* (24th June 2020), Religion Dispatches Available online at: https://religiondispatches.org/love-the-scholarship-but-hate-the-scholars-sin-himpathy-for-an-academic-pedophile-enables-a-culture-of-abuse/.

Zaki, Jamil, 'Catastrophe Compassion: Understanding and Extending Prosociality Under Crisis' *Trends in Cognitive Sciences* (2020). Available online at: doi:https://doi.org/10.1016/j.tics.2020.05.006.

Zembylas, Michalinos, 'The "Crisis of Pity" and the Radicalization of Solidarity: Toward Critical Pedagogies of Compassion', *Educational Studies* 49:6 (2013), 504–521. Available online at: doi:https://doi.org/10.1080/0013194 6.2013.844148.

Zulueta, Paquita C de, 'Developing compassionate leadership in health care: an integrative review' *Journal of Healthcare Leadership* 8 (2016), 1–1

Index[1]

[1] Note: Page numbers followed by 'n' refer to notes.

© The Author(s), under exclusive license to Springer Nature Switzerland AG 2021
L. J. Lawrence, *Refiguring Universities in an Age of Neoliberalism*, Palgrave Critical University Studies,
https://doi.org/10.1007/978-3-030-73371-1

Printed by Printforce, the Netherlands